CULTS

A Reference Handbook, Second Edition

Other Titles in ABC-CLIO's
**CONTEMPORARY
WORLD ISSUES**
Series

Books in the Contemporary World Issues series address vital issues in today's society such as genetic engineering, pollution, and biodiversity. Written by professional writers, scholars, and nonacademic experts, these books are authoritative, clearly written, up-to-date, and objective. They provide a good starting point for research by high school and college students, scholars, and general readers as well as by legislators, businesspeople, activists, and others.

Each book, carefully organized and easy to use, contains an overview of the subject, a detailed chronology, biographical sketches, facts and data and/or documents and other primary-source material, a directory of organizations and agencies, annotated lists of print and nonprint resources, and an index.

Readers of books in the Contemporary World Issues series will find the information they need in order to have a better understanding of the social, political, environmental, and economic issues facing the world today.

CULTS

A Reference Handbook, Second Edition

James R. Lewis

CONTEMPORARY WORLD ISSUES

A B C - C L I O

Santa Barbara, California
Denver, Colorado
Oxford, England

Library of Congress Cataloging-in-Publication Data
Lewis, James R.
    Cults : a reference handbook / James R. Lewis.— 2nd ed.
        p. cm. — (Contemporary world issues)
    Rev. ed. of: Cults in America. c1998.
    Includes bibliographical references and index.
    ISBN 1-85109-618-3 (hardcover : alk. paper) — ISBN 1-85109-623-X
(ebook)   1. Cults—United States.   2. Sects—United States.
3. United States—Religion.   I. Lewis, James R. Cults in America.
II. Title.   III. Series.

    BL2525.L486 2005
    200—dc22

                                        2005004574

07   06   05   10 9 8 7 6 5 4 3 2 1

This book is also available on the World Wide Web as an e-book. Visit
http://www.abc-clio.com for details.

ABC-CLIO, Inc.
130 Cremona Drive, P.O. Box 1911
Santa Barbara, California 93116-1911

This book is printed on acid-free paper ∞ .
Manufactured in the United States of America

Contents

1

Introduction

New Religions East and West

The controversy over new religions is a complex social issue that has engendered an emotional and often mean-spirited debate. At the center of this debate is a wide variety of diverse groups that often have little in common. Most embrace belief systems at odds with mainstream religion, though some are quite orthodox. Also, though they are usually relatively small, new organizations almost always have roots in older, larger traditions. The one trait these groups share is that they have been controversial at one point or another in their existence. Decades of social conflict have left their impression on the term *cult*, which, to the general public, indicates a religious group that is false, dangerous, or otherwise *bad*.

The sharpness of this controversy has tended to polarize participants into extreme positions, making it difficult to find a middle ground from which to approach the issue. Hence, rather than tackling the problem directly, it might well repay our efforts to work our way into the debate indirectly, through the stories of two contrasting religious groups that will serve to highlight some of the dilemmas associated with the cult controversy.

In the following sections, the story of the Solar Temple, the group involved in a series of murder-suicides in 1994, 1995, and 1997, will be used to exemplify the concerns that "anticultists" bring to the controversy. Falun Gong, the physical culture group that has been heavily persecuted in China since 1999, will, on the other hand, be used to exemplify the concerns of religious libertarians.

1

The Solar Temple

In October 1994, fifty-three members of the Solar Temple in Switzerland and in Quebec were murdered or committed suicide. On October 4, a fire in Morin Heights, Canada, destroyed the villa of Joseph Di Mambro, the group's primary leader. Police found five charred bodies in the ruins. Three had been stabbed to death before the fire. At one o'clock on the morning of October 5, a fire started in Ferme des Rochettes, near Cheiry, in the Canton of Fribourg, one of the centers of the Solar Temple in Switzerland. Police found twenty-three bodies in a room that had been converted into a temple. Some had been shot; many others were found with their heads inside plastic bags. Two hours later, three chalets inhabited by members of the Solar Temple caught fire almost simultaneously at Les Granges sur Salvan, in the Valais Canton. Police found twenty-five bodies, along with the remains of the devices that had initiated the fires and the pistol used to shoot the people near Cheiry.

For many months prior to the initial spate of murder-suicides, rumors of financial mismanagement had been circulating among Solar Temple members. A few days before their dramatic final "transit," a three-month-old infant had been killed at their Canadian site by driving a wooden stake through its heart. Surviving members explained that Di Mambro had ordered the killing because the baby was the Anti-Christ. Several days later, Di Mambro and twelve followers convened a ritual Last Supper together. The suicide-murders took place a few days following this meeting. Fifteen members of the inner circle—referred to as the "awakened"—took poison. Thirty others—the "immortals"—were shot or smothered to death. Eight others—termed "traitors"—were also murdered.

Subsequently, sixteen members of the Solar Temple died in France in December 1995 and five more in Quebec in March 1997. On December 16, 1995, sixteen of the remaining European members disappeared from their homes in France and Switzerland. Four left notes hinting at a second mass suicide. Thirteen adults and three children were later found dead in a remote forest in southeastern France. Investigators concluded that at least four of the sixteen did not die willingly. Most had been drugged. Two of the sixteen shot the others, poured gasoline over their bodies, set them on fire, and then shot themselves so that they would also fall into the flames.

Finally, five additional adult members and three teenage children apparently tried to commit suicide on the spring equinox of March 20, 1997, in Quebec. The attempt failed due to faulty equipment. The teenage sons and daughter of one of the couples convinced their parents that they wanted to live. They were allowed to leave, and the adults subsequently succeeded in burning down their house with themselves in it. Four of the bodies were arranged to form a cross. The teens were found drugged and disoriented, but otherwise safe, in a nearby building. A note was found that described the group belief that death on earth leads to a transit to a new planet where their lives would continue.

Di Mambro had been fascinated with esotericism from a young age. He joined the Ancient and Mystical Order Rosae Crucis in 1956 and was a member until at least 1968. In the 1960s, he came into contact with several persons who would later play a role in Solar Temple history, including Jacques Breyer, who had initiated a "Templar resurgence" in France in 1952. Several groups, including Di Mambro's, trace part of their roots to Breyer's work. *Templar* in this context refers to the Knights Templars, the medieval order to which groups in the neo-Templar tradition ultimately trace their lineage. (This claimed lineage is almost certainly spurious; instead, neo-Templar groups are esoteric organizations loosely in the larger Theosophical tradition.) Several major points of doctrine, as well as an initial group of followers, began to come together in the 1960s. In 1971, after dealing with some legal problems in Nîmes, France, connected with a number of petty crimes such as writing bad checks, Di Mambro established himself in Annemasse, near the Swiss border. In 1978, he founded the Golden Way Foundation in Geneva, the predecessor of the Solar Temple.

Recognizing Luc Jouret as a man of intelligence and charisma, Di Mambro brought him in to become the public face of his organization. Jouret was trained as a medical doctor and was an accomplished practitioner of homeopathy. He also lectured on naturopathy and ecological topics and was active in the wider circuit of the French-speaking New Age movement. He spoke in New Age bookstores and to eclectic esoteric groups in France, Switzerland, Belgium, and Canada.

The International Chivalric Order Solar Tradition (Solar Temple) was founded in 1984. It absorbed the Golden Way Foundation. Jouret claimed that he had been a member of the fourteenth-century Christian Order of the Knights Templar during a previous incarnation, that his daughter Emmanuelle was "the cosmic child," and that after death he would lead the group to a planet that revolves around the star Sirius. Jouret also believed himself to be Christ. Solar Temple groups were organized in Quebec, as well as in Australia, Switzerland, France, and other countries. The leadership saw themselves as playing a pivotal role on the world stage. Partially as a consequence of this view, they believed that the Solar Temple was being persecuted by the various governments with which they had problems.

Temple teachings emphasized apocalyptic themes drawn from certain elements of extremist survivalist thinking, from the New Age notion of an imminent end of the world due to an environmental catastrophe and other sources. The group believed that they were to play a major role in this collapse. It seems that in the years 1986 to 1993, Jouret received a series of revelations until it was revealed to him that between the end of 1993 and the beginning of 1994 the earth would be forsaken by its last "guardians."

On March 8, 1993, two Canadian members were arrested while attempting to buy three semiautomatic guns with silencers (illegal in Canada). Although committed to trial, they were freed on bail the next day. Because Jouret had prompted them to buy the weapons, he was also committed to trial (he was in Europe at the time), and a warrant was issued for his arrest. This seems to have been the critical event precipitating the leadership's decision to make their final dramatic "transit."

The Anticult Movement: A Response to the Antisocial Actions of Extreme Groups

The deaths of Solar Temple members were part of a series of dramatic incidents involving members of nontraditional religions. Other incidents include the Jonestown murder-suicides (1978), the Bureau of Alcohol, Tobacco, and Firearms (ATF) and Federal Bureau of Investigation (FBI) raid on the Branch Davidian community (1993), the Tokyo subway poison-gas attack (1995), the Heaven's Gate suicides (1997), and the deaths of members of the Movement for the Restoration of the Ten Commandments of God (2000). In the wake of these events, the mass media sought a variety of "cult experts" in an effort to make sense of seemingly irrational behavior. Most of these experts offered the public an explanation in terms of the notion of cultic mind control, colloquially known as "brainwashing." The seemingly crazy actions of "cult" members were not difficult to explain, this group of experts claimed, as long as one understands that megalomaniacal cult leaders are able to control the thought processes of their followers: under the influence of mind control, members of such groups are capable of anything because they have given up their will to the leader.

According to spokespeople for "cult watchdog" groups, our society is populated by hundreds—perhaps even thousands—of cult groups, many of which are capable of extreme actions. Beyond mind control and the imputation of sinister motives to the leader, standard accusations leveled against minority religions unfortunate enough to be labeled cults include: deceptive recruiting practices, financial and sexual exploitation, food and sleep deprivation of members, various forms of illegal activities, child abuse, ritual abuse, and so forth. Because of the interest the mass media have taken in this issue, this stereotype has become widely accepted in contemporary society.

Putting aside the problematic notion of "cultic brainwashing" for the moment, there are or have been groups for which some of these accusations are or were appropriate. In particular, children have been abused within a few religious communities. Members of certain organizations have been financially or sexually exploited or both by the leadership. A handful of minority religions have taken the law into their own hands. And at least one group consciously deceived potential recruits by systematically hiding their identity until after workshop attendees had become de facto members.

There are, however, obvious dangers in unreflectively applying the cult stereotype to every religious group that strikes one as strange or different. The situation is not unlike that of viewing a race or an ethnicity in terms of a generalization derived from the minority group's least-reputable members. The types of problems that can be generated by jumping to the conclusion that all unusual religious communities must be guilty of misdeeds simply because extreme accusations are leveled against them are well exemplified in the campaign against Falun Gong that is being carried out by the People's Republic of China.

Falun Gong

In 1999, the Chinese regime launched a new campaign against spiritual and religious groups. Falun Gong was one of the groups targeted as superstitious and reactionary by a press campaign. Unlike other targets of this campaign, 10,000 members of Falun Gong, which is a Qi Gong physical-culture movement, reacted by staging a peaceful demonstration on April 25, 1999, outside Beijing's Zhongnanhai, the residence of China's top leaders. This was the largest such demonstration in recent Chinese history. The regime seemed to be especially frightened by the failure of its intelligence service to prevent the demonstration and by membership in Falun Gong of some midlevel political and military leaders.

In subsequent months, practitioners were harassed in various areas of the country. Some were told that their phones were being monitored and that, if they continued participation in the group, their retirement pensions would be terminated. Police and other officials began breaking into practitioners' homes and confiscating Falun Gong material. Some followers were arrested and disappeared. Thousands of members demonstrated peacefully in about thirty Chinese cities to protest these actions.

Qi Gong is the generic name of a complex of techniques aimed at attaining physical and spiritual well-being, with a tradition in China predating the Christian era. It is often referred to as Chinese yoga. Although spiritual and religious activities in general are viewed with suspicion in Communist China, Qi Gong has been tolerated as a traditional set of physical exercises. The semiofficial National Qi Gong Federation has never been seriously disturbed by the regime. The situation is different, however, with respect to Qi Gong groups that strongly claim the primacy of the spiritual element and recognize a charismatic living leader.

The largest (but by no means the only) such Qi Gong group is Falun Gong. Its founder, Li Hongzi, established his peculiar brand of Qi Gong in 1992, after having left the semiofficial federation. In 1998, Li moved permanently to New York City, from which he oversees the expansion of Falun Gong internationally. Small groups exist in the main metropolitan areas of the United States, Canada, and some thirty other countries.

Although the persecution has scared many followers and driven them underground, millions remain in China and several thousand abroad. Exactly how many members Falun Gong has is a matter of dispute (the government uses a figure of 2 million; Li claims 100 million), and "membership" may not be an entirely applicable concept. In fact, although the movement recommends a nine-day introduction course and frequent contact with local centers, it also states that everybody can simply start practicing Falun Gong by following the instructions from one of the many books, cassettes, and Web sites (the principal of the latter being http://www.falundafa.org) readily available in a variety of languages. The possibility of such a self-initiation, without a master and lengthy discipline, is at the core of the criticism by other Qi Gong groups against Li and his movement.

The group was officially outlawed on July 22, 1999. The Chinese government accused it of "spreading fallacies, hoodwinking people, inciting and creating disturbances, and jeopardizing social stability" (Associated Press 1999). On July 29, Chinese authorities issued an arrest warrant for Master Li. The government arrested hundreds of Falun Gong practitioners and proceeded with show trials. Some were sent directly to labor camps without trials. A spokesperson for Falun Gong Practitioners in North America asserted: "Lawyers in China have already been told not to defend these innocent civilians unless they agree with the government propaganda. Also, no legal representation on behalf of them from the concerned international community is allowed to be present at the trial" (Robinson 1999).

The U.S. House and Senate unanimously passed resolutions on November 18–19, 1999, that criticized the Chinese government for its crackdown on Falun Gong. Chinese foreign ministry spokesman Sun Yuxi responded by asserting that Falun Gong is not a religious organization, nor is it simply a Qi Gong group. Rather, it is a destructive cult that harms Chinese society and its people. In describing Falun Gong as a dangerous "cult," the Chinese government drew heavily on the cult stereotype that had been circulating in Western countries for the prior three decades. For example, authorities accused the group of:

- Brainwashing its members
- Worshiping Li
- Turning Communist officials into cult members in order to learn state secrets
- Suggesting that its followers not take any medication
- Suffering from paranoia and hallucinations

Ignoring international pressure, authorities responded with an unprecedented public campaign against the movement, propagating anti–Falun Gong propaganda via the media of tracts and comics. China also asked the United States to arrest and extradite Li, a request the United States quickly turned down, inviting the Chinese instead to stop what the outside world perceived as an obvious instance of religious persecution.

The Chinese government's campaign against the group is the most serious government crackdown since the demonstrations at Tiananmen Square, which took place more than a decade prior. Falun Gong has received global political attention as other nations specify this incident of China's religious intolerance as grounds for limiting trade and normal relations. The proliferation of Falun Gong Web sites and information on the Internet quickly expanded international awareness. Also, the free access to Li Hongzi's teachings via the Internet have aided the spread of the practice, promoting a global movement.

Several scholars have advanced hypotheses to explain China and Falun Gong's turbulent interactions. In *The Mystery of China's Falun Gong: Its Rise and Its Sociological Implications,* National University of Singapore sociologists John Wong and William T. Liu hypothesize that China's fear of Falun Gong reflects its anxieties over the power of the Internet. The authors forecast the group's survival in- and outside of China, concluding that the Chinese government's crackdown has been ineffective. Wong and Liu investigated the movement's tremendous popularity, identifying China's growing elderly and retired population seeking cheaper health-care alternatives to the state system as a factor in its growth.

Authorities may perceive the Falun Gong as a political threat for several reasons. The Chinese government had become concerned about the size of the movement. Though the exact number of practitioners is unknown, the movement probably did outnumber members of the Communist Party. Furthermore, a not inconsiderable number of Communist Party members and military officials were also practitioners. Another concern was undoubtedly Falun Gong's large international membership, a cause for concern for the historically isolationist Chinese government.

Authorities were almost certainly reacting to the sheer numbers of the initial mass demonstrations. Some observers have pointed to China's long history of religious rebellion as a factor in the government's concern (see Robinson 1999). For example, the Taiping rebellion during the Ming dynasty began a major religious rebellion. Another scholar, Michael Lestz, argues that rather than feeling the historical pressures of regime-toppling religious rebellion, the Chinese government is acting out its standard knee-jerk response to any perceived target, threat, or antagonism (1999). Lestz also points to the international makeup of the Falun Gong as a point of concern for the government. He concludes that instead of religious intolerance, the government's crackdown is motivated by a need to save face, preserve predictability, and reestablish state control and order.

Religious Libertarianism: A Response to the Persecution of Minority Religions

It is the concern generated by such activities as the persecution of Falun Gong on the flimsy pretext of its imputed status as a dangerous cult that has led to the emergence of an alternative school of opinion opposed to the "anticult" perspective. This opposing group comprises a diverse assortment of religions, religious liberty organizations, and scholars of minority religions. Although not seeking to defend organizations like the Solar Temple, this school of thought asserts that the extreme actions of a few groups should not be taken as representative of all minority religions, any more than that the criminal tendencies of a handful of members of certain racial minorities should be imputed to the race as a whole. Individuals associated with this opposition group see themselves as defending religious liberty.

Because the word *cult* has acquired negative connotations, the people and organizations who defend minority religions do not call themselves the "procult movement" and, further, would not accept the label "cult apologists" with which anticultists seek to stigmatize them. In fact, this opposition group would reject the use of the term *cult* altogether, instead referring to such organizations as new religious movements (the preferred term among academics), alternative religions, nontraditional religions, or minority religions. Recognizing the term's problematic status, *cult* will be avoided when referring to a specific religion throughout this book. It is, nevertheless, still useful to talk about the *cult controversy,* and, where appropriate, *cult* will be utilized when discussing the stereotype associated with minority religions more generally.

At the broadest level, the anticult movement can be subdivided into two wings, consisting of secular anticultists and conservative Christian anticultists. Although these two wings share certain traits and in the past have occasionally cooperated with each other, the target of much Christian anticultism is a minority religion's deviation from traditional doctrine—a concern most secular anticultists do not share. Also, Christian anticultists tend not to be involved in the controversial practice of deprogramming— one of the hallmarks of the secular anticult movement. When discussing the anticult movement, the present book will be referring to the secular wing of this movement, unless otherwise noted.

As with other social conflicts, opponents in the cult controversy have become polarized into extreme positions. Many anticultists have come to adopt an attitude of suspicion toward a broad spectrum of religions, ready to portray almost any unusual group as a potential Heaven's Gate and almost any charismatic religious leader as a potential David Koresh. Defenders of the rights of minority religions, on the other hand, have tended to downplay all issues except the theme of religious liberty. The result of this polarization is an ongoing and frequently bitter debate that periodically finds expression in books, articles, court cases, and, in recent years, official reports issued by European governments.

Though the contemporary controversy has certain unique aspects, it is, in many ways, an extension of historically earlier religious conflicts. As a way of providing a background for our discussion of the cult controversy, we will look briefly at the anti-Catholic and anti-Mormon movements of the nineteenth century and at the quaint nineteenth-century notion of "religious insanity."

Religious Persecution in the Nineteenth Century

A phenomenon that can often be observed in the wake of a dynamic social movement is the emergence of a countermovement that comes into being for the sole purpose of opposing the original movement. Of particular interest for students of the contemporary cult controversy who would like to set this phenomenon in historical perspective are the anti-Catholic and anti-Mormon movements that emerged during the nineteenth century. Both of these movements produced extensive bodies of literature that show distinct parallels with anticult literature, particularly if one focuses on the genre of apostate stories.

Contemporary themes of the "psychological kidnapping" and exploitation of young people by sinister cults are paralleled in anti-Catholic literature by the themes of the "captivity" (Slotkin 1973, 444) and abuse of young females in nunneries. This Protestant fantasy led to the production of numerous apostate tales authored by "escaped" nuns. These women were sometimes genuine ex-nuns who presented highly embellished accounts of their experiences (for example, Reed 1835) or fake ex-nuns who fabricated their stories from whole cloth (for example, Monk 1836 [1977]).

For nuns to escape, however, they first had to be in a state of bondage, and this condition required a certain amount of explanation because Catholics did not bodily carry off their "prisoners." The initial "capture" was explained in terms of flattery and in terms of devious indoctrination designed to influence impressionable young ladies to take the veil. Once inside the convent, the means of retaining captives varied from one author to another. In cruder narratives, "inmates" were physically imprisoned in the institution and controlled by threat of corporal punishment, and especially reluctant nuns were locked up in subterranean dungeons. In more nuanced accounts, inmates were controlled by subtler psychological means, such as fear of hell and the belief that any doubts were inspired by Satan. "[The Bishop] said the Devil would assail me, as he did Saint Teresa, and make me think I ought to go back to the world; and make me offers of worldly pleasures, and promise me happiness. In order to prevent this, I must watch and pray all the time, and banish entirely worldly thoughts from my mind" (Reed 1835, 89).

These tales typically consisted of the recounting of one atrocity after another, held together by a thin strand of narrative. In the more extreme stories, these atrocities ranged from sexual abuse to murder. Maria Monk, for example, claimed that infants born to nuns (a supposedly frequent event because of regular sexual intercourse with priests) were murdered. Monk recounted observing two infants who, after being baptized, "were then taken, one after another, by one of the old nuns, in the presence of us all. She pressed her hand upon the mouth and nose of the first so tight that it could not breathe, and in a few minutes, when the hand was removed, it was dead. She then took the other and treated it in the same way. No sound was heard, and both children were corpses. The greatest indifference was shown by all present during this operation; for all, as I well knew, were long accustomed to such scenes" (1977, 155–156).

Apostate tales were designed to evoke and to legitimate public reaction, and they often succeeded in this purpose. For example, very soon after ex-nun Rebecca Reed began to tell her story, a Protestant mob burned her former convent to the ground. These narratives usually also contained calls for governmental action. At the conclusion of one ex-nun's story, for example, she pleaded that "the Legislature . . . enact laws for the inspection of Convents . . . Let the prison doors of monasteries and Convents be thrown open to their deluded inmates" (O'Gorman ca. 1881, 131).

In anti-Mormon literature, polygamous wives played essentially the same role that nuns played in anti-Catholic literature, and apostate (and pseudoapostate) Mormon females composed similar captivity narratives. However, a conceptual problem emerged in Mormon apostate stories: How could one make the case for a state of bondage in a situation where the alleged captive was apparently free to walk out at any time? Nunneries could be portrayed as prisons, but Mormon women were obviously not so confined. Thus, in addition to the deluded follower theme used to characterize Catholic bondage, one finds the first theory of "hypnotic mind control" in anti-Mormon literature. For example, in the totally fabricated apostate tale *Female Life among the Mormons,* Maria Ward describes her entrapment in terms of *mesmerism* (the original term for hypnosis):

> At the time I was wholly unacquainted with the doctrine of magnetic influence; but I soon became aware of some unaccountable power exercised over me by my fellow traveler. His presence seemed an irresistible fascination. His glittering eyes were fixed on mine; his breath fanned my cheek; I felt bewildered and intoxicated, and partially lost the sense of consciousness, and the power of motion. . . . I became immediately sensible of some unaccountable influence drawing my sympathies toward him. In vain I struggled to break the spell. I was like a fluttering bird before the gaze of a serpent-charmer. (1855, 12)

Via such pseudoscientific notions—precursors to more recent theories of cult "mind control"—the captivity motif could be extended to situations where it would normally have been inappropriate except as a metaphor.

The Mormon apostate tales, like the Catholic apostate stories, were loosely connected accounts of one sensationalistic atrocity after another, containing many crudely crafted descriptions of violence and the same kinds of sexual allusions found in convent tales. The violence in anti-Mormon tales was often quite vivid. For example, in the totally fictional apostate tale *Boadicea: The Mormon Wife*, Alfreda Eva Bell describes the following cold-hearted murder: "'Will you go with me?' asked he. 'No,' answered the dying woman. 'Then you are done for,' said Yale; and deliberately, before my very eyes, in spite of my wild screams for his mercy, he fired at her and scattered her brains over the floor" (1855, 55).

Lurid descriptions of violence against women can also be used to suggest sexual assault. In Ward's account, for instance, a female who dared raise her voice in dissent against the Mormon hierarchy was "gagged, carried a mile into the woods, stripped nude, tied to a tree, and scourged till the blood ran from her wounds to the ground" (1855, 429).

As already noted with respect to Catholic captivities, this kind of sensationalism was mixed with propagandistic themes calling for the repression of Mormonism. Even in some of the fictional tales, this theme was overtly set forth, as, for instance, toward the end of Bell's story: "I prayed that I might be permitted to reach the States, and, by my pen, put forth the horrors I had witnessed, in order to swell the outcry for the speedy destruction of such a hell of vice as the Mormon colony, and do my 'little all' towards arresting further horrors" (1855, 69).

The portrayal of mesmeric captures was supplemented by the accusation that Mormons bodily carried off Gentile women to fill their "harems," and this particular accusation was one of the more scandalous themes in anti-Mormon propaganda. The kidnapping accusation seemed, to the minds of some of the authors of anti-Mormon tales, to legitimate the physical extermination of all Mormons. For example, one of the heroes of *The Prophets; or, Mormonism Unveiled*, after rescuing his wife from the clutches of Joseph Smith, vows to kill every Mormon in Nauvoo, Illinois: "I swear by the heaven above me, I will shoulder my rifle, and never lay it down until Nauvoo is razed to the ground. It makes me feel like a demon to think they should dare raise their polluted thoughts to my wife; but they shall rue the deed, for devastation shall follow them until there shall not be one left in a week's travel from Nauvoo" (Belisle 1855, 312).

Like sensationalistic anti-Catholic stories, anti-Mormon tales were capable of evoking violent, vigilante-style activity, as is evident in such events as the murder of Joseph Smith, and governmental intervention, as witnessed by such actions as the 1857 invasion of Utah by federal troops.

Contemporary anticult literature replicates this same structure, but here the metaphor of captivity is even more strained: nuns were behind walls and Mormons were at least geographically isolated, but the stereotypical cult member is out on the streets every day hustling strangers and is thereby fully immersed in the noncult world. Contemporary anticult proponents are thus forced to rely on pseudoscientific theories of "brainwashing" and "cultic mind control"—notions of mental enslavement that we saw in embryo in anti-Catholic and anti-Mormon literature. The link with notions from earlier eras is quite evident, especially in more popular tales. For example, compare the following passage from Chris Edwards's *Crazy for God* with the description of Mormon mesmerism cited earlier: "She took my hand and looked me straight in the eyes. As her wide eyes gazed into mine, I felt myself rapidly losing control, being drawn to her by a strange and frightening force. I had never felt such mysterious power radiate from a human being before . . . touching something within me that undermined thought itself" (1979, 60).

Although the stage settings are different, the plot has not changed. Former "cult" members recount the same stories of deception and exploitation, which in turn evoke vigilante-style violence in the form of kidnappings of current members of controversial religions (Patrick with Dulack 1976) and, in some instances, attacks upon "cult" facilities (Terry and Manegold 1984). Success in stimulating governmental intervention eluded the anticult movement during the height of the cult scare, with the exception of a few isolated incidents such as the Branch Davidian fiasco.

Religious Insanity

By the mid-1840s, the asylum movement had expanded to the point where specialists in the field of mental disorders could begin to publish their own journal, the *American Journal of Insan-*

ity. The very first volume of this new publication, in an article called "The Importance of Early Treatment in Preventing Suicide" (1845), contained six brief case studies, three of which documented cases of individuals afflicted with "religious insanity." The first case, a woman driven "insane from continued religious excitement, in connection with the doctrine of Miller" (referring to the Millerite movement, which later developed into the Adventist tradition), had become quite melancholy. Although otherwise not disordered (as indicated by such remarks as "she conversed intelligently on many subjects"), her husband, "becoming alarmed at her condition, brought her to the Asylum." After a short course of treatment, consisting primarily of morphine "in sufficient doses to procure sleep," she was pronounced "cured" and allowed to return home.

The second case was that of a middle-aged man who had become "much disturbed in mind while attending a protracted religious meeting." Although the only symptom of his "disturbed mind" was melancholia—the usual state of mind one experiences immediately prior to being "born again"—his friends became fearful that he might commit suicide and had him committed. After three months of medicines, laxatives, and warm baths, he "left the Asylum in perfect health."

The final case was a young woman who, from "much attention to religion during a revival, became nervous and sleepless." As in the other cases mentioned, her friends "became apprehensive" and "brought her to the Asylum." Following a physiological course of treatment similar to the ones that were administered to the above individuals, she "regained her health" and was able to leave in about two months.

The article used these cases to illustrate the more general point that when a person becomes melancholy and loses interest in family and business affairs, "immediate action in his behalf may be necessary." The unnamed author of this piece was bold enough to assert further that people who exhibit such symptoms "are insane" and "need restraint" and went on to observe that, "in all, there was but little mental derangement, but sufficient to alarm their friends, who by adopting the course they did, prevented, we apprehend, dangerous results."

The conceptualization of mental illness had gone through certain changes over the course of the nineteenth century, but the generally accepted theory was firmly physiological, hence the basically physiological treatments administered to victims of religious insanity. Although acknowledging certain predisposing factors such as heredity, the actual initiating cause was portrayed as some kind of "shock" to the system, either directly physical, as in the case of a blow to the head, or through what nineteenth-century *alienists* (the older term for psychiatrists) referred to as "moral" causes—bereavement, loss of employment, and so forth (Cardno 1968). Within this schema, religious enthusiasm was viewed as a moral factor that, when taken to extremes, could result in physiological damage; in the words of Amariah Brigham, one early-nineteenth-century theorist of religious insanity: "All long continued or violent excitement of the mind is dangerous, because it is likely to injure the brain and nervous system. Religious excitement, therefore, like all mental excitement, by affecting the brain, may cause insanity or other diseases" (1835, 284–285).

Revivals were the paradigmatic context in which this "violent excitement of mind" was experienced. For instance, William Sweetser, another nineteenth-century psychiatrist, observes:

> At the field-meetings that are annually held among us I have been witness to the most frightful nervous affections, as convulsions, epilepsy, hysteria, distressing spasms, violent contortions of the body, not only in females in whom, from their more sensitive and sympathetic temperament, such affections are most readily excited, but also in the more hardy and robust of our own sex. Even spectators, such as attend for the purpose of amusement or merriment, will oftentimes be overtaken by the same nervous disorders. (1850, 196)

To clinical observers, it was clear that disordered environments, such as could be found at revivals, produced disordered minds.

This etiology was, however, only superficially physiological; de facto, the criterion for determining mental illness was verbal and behavioral expression. The obvious problem with such a criterion was that any unusual expression of belief or behavior that appeared to "exceed the common deviations of human belief and conduct" could be labeled crazy and result in the incarceration of a nonconforming individual (Arnold 1806, 219). This seems to have particularly been the case with the majority of religious enthusiasts committed to asylums; the "high reported cure rate for religious insanity" as contrasted with other forms of insanity indicates that in most cases, incarceration was probably being "used by families to punish deviant members" and bring them back into line with accepted norms (Bainbridge 1984, 235). This is not to say that either families or physicians cynically deployed medical labels that they knew were spurious, but rather to say that a medical explanation was seized upon because it "made sense," that is, it seemed to substantiate popular prejudice as well as to legitimate a vigorous response. This kind of "medicalization of deviance" (Conrad and Schneider 1980) perspective seems especially likely when we consider some of the more unusual "causes of insanity" mentioned in the psychiatric literature of the nineteenth century: masturbation, intemperance, novel reading, "effeminate education," tobacco use, the onset of puberty, and dealing in lottery tickets.

From the standpoint of the early twenty-first century, it is easy to be amused by the perceptions and formulations of our predecessors. Our amusement should be tempered, however, by the realization that the notion of religious insanity was devised and promulgated by some of the more thoughtful and liberal minds of the age. We moderns are certainly not immune to the propensity to label ideas with which we disagree, or behaviors of which we disapprove, as sick or crazy. This seems to be particularly true of the attitude of certain members of the mental health profession toward "cults." When, for example, one prominent anticult psychiatrist can seriously assert that the question motivating his work is "What kind of nutty people get into these crazy groups?" (cited in Bromley and Richardson 1983, 5) and commit patients he has never examined to medical institutions on the basis of their membership in alternative religions, we should suspect that contemporary "cultic mind control" is a close relative of nineteenth-century "religious insanity."

Emergence of the Contemporary Cult Controversy and the "Brainwashing" Debate

Cultic Mind Control

Shifting our attention back to the present period, the origins of the contemporary cult controversy can be traced to the early 1970s. In that period, many new religions were arising out of the ashes of the counterculture to become successor movements to the youth movement of the 1960s. Unable to comprehend the appeal of these religions, observers concluded that the founders or leaders of such groups had discovered a special form of social control that enabled them to recruit their followers in nonordinary ways and, more particularly, to short-circuit their rational, questioning minds by keeping them locked in special trance states. A handful of professionals, mostly psychologists and psychiatrists associated with the anticult movement, attempted to provide scientific grounding for this notion of cultic brainwashing, or mind control.

No serious observer would disagree that there are genuine issues of abuse, exploitation, and undue influence associated with at least some minority religions. Serious discussions and analyses of such abuses were, however, overshadowed almost from the very beginning when the debate over new religions came to focus on the notion of cultic mind control. Rather than viewing the social pressures found in minority religions as extensions of garden-variety forms of social influence, anticult professionals argued for the existence of a unique form of influence confined to "cult" subcultures. Viewing this argument as a form of special pleading with potentially grave implications for religious liberty, other professionals—particularly sociologists of religion—focused their scholarly responses to the cult controversy on a critique of cultic mind control. By the mid-seventies, battle lines had been drawn, and the debate would rage back and forth over the same ground for the next several decades and beyond.

Since the beginning of the debate, mainstream scholars have been steadily churning out studies directly relevant to the cult controversy. Because of the nature of this conflict, mainstream academic researchers have been forced to work in a highly politicized atmosphere. Articles on controversial religious groups published in specialized academic journals can directly impact people's lives, particularly when cited in legal briefs and judicial decisions. Thus, in contrast to academics, who study things like the mating habits of field mice or the impact of black holes on space and time, new religion specialists regularly find themselves the subjects of scrutiny and criticism.

Because mainstream scholars of nontraditional religions have generally been critical of the cult stereotype—particularly the notion of cultic mind control—they have, in turn, been criticized by those interested in perpetuating this stereotype. One counterstrategy commonly utilized by such interest groups is to refer to academicians whose research tends to undermine anticult ideology as "cult apologists," implying that they are in a conspiracy with—perhaps even covertly accepting money from—malevolent religious groups. The cult-apologist accusation is a handy ideological tool because, in the hands of most anticultists, it is wielded as a tautology, immune to empirical disconfirmation. In other words, if a cult apologist is defined as any researcher producing scholarship critical of the cult stereotype, then anyone whose scholarship is critical of the cult stereotype is ipso facto a cult apologist. Anticultists adhering to this rhetorical strategy sometimes make it appear that sinister pseudoreligious organizations regularly seek out scholars to legitimate their groups and to attack their critics. This strategy allows anticultists to reject any scholarship with which they disagree a priori, saving them from the awkward necessity of taking it seriously.

The following discussion of mainstream scholarship on the cultic mind control notion will draw heavily on the analysis found in Dick Anthony and Thomas Robbins's survey of research on this issue (2003). This research and related theorizing have disproportionately focused on the claim that joining a "cult" is essentially involuntary because powerful techniques of "brainwashing" or "mind control" have psychologically coerced the convert's conversion and subsequent commitment (Clark 1976, 1979; Ofshe and Singer 1986; Singer and Lalich 1995; Verdier, 1980). Although the existence of such an exotic psychotechnology has been advocated by a variety of different "cult experts," most scholars who have actually researched this topic disagree with the brainwashing thesis (Anthony and Robbins 1994; Barker 1984; Lewis 1989; Richardson 1993).

In a survey article on conversion, sociologists David Snow and Robert Machalek note: "The 'brainwashing' or 'coercive persuasion' model is the most popular explanation of conversion outside of sociological circles. The basic thesis is that conversion is the product of devious and specifiable forces acting upon unsuspecting and therefore vulnerable individuals" (1984, 178–179). The brainwashing model for joining nontraditional religions "has gained considerable currency among the public," in part because "it provides a convenient and 'sensible' account for those who are otherwise at a loss to explain why individuals are attracted to 'deviant' and 'menacing' groups" (179). One prominent anticultist psychologist asserts: "Today's [cultic] thought reform programs are sophisticated, subtle and insidious, creating a psychological bond that in many ways is far more powerful than gun-at-the-head methods of influence" (Singer 1994, 3–4).

Brainwashing notions of recruitment and commitment entail an overwhelming preponderance of extrinsic alien forces—in contrast to intrinsic self-related forces—that compel religious choices. Such religious "choices" are irrational, in the sense of being based on emotion and debilitation rather than on reason and conscious deliberation. Anticult theorists frequently invoke the notion of a *false self* that emerges as a result of cultic mind control and that mind control techniques supposedly superimpose on the "real" selves of recruits. One psychiatrist, for instance, draws a distinction between the "original" behavioral and cognitive patterns of converts and the "imposed" patterns artificially induced by intensive cult regimens (Clark 1976, 2–3).

From the viewpoint of anticultists, true autonomy and individuality cannot be grounded in transcendental experiences, ecstatic or mystical states of consciousness, or intense religious emotions. In anticult literature, such experiences are portrayed as hypnotic trances, dangerous dissociative states, pathological regression, and manipulated emotions said to undermine individual autonomy and superimpose an artificial identity on the convert. To the extent that the mind control hypothesis can be tested, it has tended to be disconfirmed by empirical research (for example, Barker 1984, 1986; Lewis 1986, 1989; and Richardson 1993). And in the absence of such empirical support, what is left is a pseudoscientific ideology legitimating society's bias against minority religions. Furthermore, if the anticult portrayal of conversion and commitment to minority religions is unable to stand up to critical and empirical examination, then it is clear that the conflict between alternative religions and anticultists is more of a value dispute, outside the power of the courts or the state to regulate.

To conceal the pseudoscientific status of the brainwashing notion, anticultists have deployed two interrelated rhetorical strategies. As Robert Shapiro (1983) notes, advocates of deprogramming tend to imply that cult members—not infrequently characterized as "zombies" or "robots"—do not really possess a self. Instead, they are "depersonalized," "dissociated," "regressed to psychological infancy," and the like (Clark 1976). This portrayal is often more implicit than explicit. At present, it has become rather outmoded, having been associated with the kind of violent deprogramming from which most anticultists have distanced themselves. The more modest—and, in the long run, more significant and influential—model of brainwashing proposes that recruits' new spiritual selves were coercively imposed through insidious mind control techniques that obviated their capacity to exercise free will.

The second strategy has been to assert that cultic mind control theory is firmly grounded in early research on Maoist thought reform. During the cold war, the original idea of communist brainwashing was developed and popularized by Edward Hunter, a journalist and Central Intelligence Agency (CIA) publicist (1951, 1960). Hunter portrayed brainwashing as a potent manipulative technology that could mold people into zombies: "The intent is to change a mind radically so that its owner becomes a living puppet—a human robot—without the atrocity being visible . . . with new beliefs and new thought processes inserted into a captive body" (1960, 309). This insidious psychotechnology utilizes "hypnotism, drugs and cunning pressures that plague the body and do not necessarily require marked violence" (1951, 11). Physical intimidation is sometimes part of the process but is not essential to Hunter's notion of brainwashing. The "brain-changers" have the power to plant false beliefs and memories (1951, 10–11). Other theorists have portrayed communist brainwashing as inducing suggestible trance states in which the victim can literally be "programmed" via scientific conditioning methods (Farber, Harlow, and West 1957).

Although this model of brainwashing has been criticized as inapplicable to alternative religious groups, it has often been assumed that it paints an accurate picture of the process applied to Korean War prisoners of war (POWs). However, an important 1956 article that examined the data from POWs came to the conclusion that the prisoners who adopted the views of their overseers had already been inclined toward those views (Hinkle and Wolff 1956).

In many 1980s "cult" cases, anticult experts testifying against minority religious groups referred to such researchers as Robert Lifton (1961) and Edgar Schein (1961) as the authoritative bases for their testimony. A important opinion delivered by the California Supreme Court in 1988 even noted that "brainwashing exists and is remarkably effective" (Mosk, Stanley, et al. 1988, 52), although a federal court in 1990 cast doubt on the authority of Lifton's and

Schein's works. In the review essay on conversion referred to ear-lier, Snow and Machalek (1984) indicate Schein and Lifton as sources of the brainwashing model.

Schein's and Lifton's formulations were, however, signifi-cantly more nuanced and sophisticated than the ideologically motivated model of brainwashing presented by popular writers like Edward Hunter. Although the process they describe is highly manipulative, they actually do not portray brainwashing as so powerfully effective that it is able to override an individual's per-sonality patterns and predispositions so as to obliterate her or his free will.

In terms of the resources allocated, Schein judges the Com-munist Chinese thought-reform program directed at prisoners to be largely ineffective (1961; Anthony 1990). Furthermore, in con-trast to anticult theorists, Schein sees imprisonment as so central to the process that he makes it part of the very definition of "co-ercive persuasion." Although debilitated, prisoners subjected to communist indoctrination were otherwise alert and rational and did not exhibit defective thought patterns (1961, 202–203, 238–239). Furthermore, he notes that the popular notion of "brain-washing" as involving "extensive self-delusion and excessive dis-tortion is a false one" (239; Anthony 1990, 312). Schein downplays the role of dissociative states and hypnotic trances because coer-cive persuasion is intended "to produce ideological and behav-ioral changes in a fully conscious, intact individual" (1959; An-thony 1990, 316). It should finally be noted that Schein rejects the term *brainwashing* (1961, 18).

In his book *Chinese Thought Reform and the Psychology of Total-ism*, Robert Lifton elaborates a "complex set of psychological themes" that include "Milieu Control," "Mystical Manipulation," "Demand for Purity," "Sacred Science," "Loading the Language," "Doctrine Over Person," and "The Dispensing of Existence" (1961, 419–437). In Lifton's formulation, an individual's conversion and commitment to what he refers to as "totalism" involve an interac-tive process between personal inclinations and ideology. His cen-tral term, *ideological totalism,* is intended "to suggest the coming together of an immoderate ideology with equally immoderate character traits—an extremist meeting ground of people and ideas" (419). The various psychoideological components of total-ism "mobilize certain individual emotional tendencies, mostly of a polarizing nature." Additionally, "psychological theme, philo-sophical rationale and polarized individual tendencies are interdependent; they require, rather than directly cause, each other" (422). Furthermore, Lifton states:

> The degree of totalism depends greatly upon factors in our personal history: early lack of trust, extreme environmental chaos, total domination by a parent or parent-representative, intolerable burdens of guilt and severe crises of identity . . . an early sense of confusion and dislocation, or an early experience of extremely intense family milieu control can produce later a complete intolerance for dislocation and confusion, and a longing for the reinstatement of milieu control. (436)

In contrast to anticult literature in which converts are pictured as being disoriented, dissociated, and deluded before they are willing to participate in a totalistic "cult," Lifton observes that "ideological totalism itself may offer a man an intense peak experience: a sense of transcending all that is ordinary and prosaic, of freeing himself from the encumbrances of human ambivalence, of entering a sphere of truth, reality, trust and sincerity beyond any he had ever known or imagined" (435).

The overwhelming majority of Westerners who went through communist thought reform did no more than respond with *behavioral compliance* as a direct result of physical harassment and threats. In Lifton's words, Chinese thought reform resulted in "the extraction of an incriminating personal confession because it made this confession a requirement for survival" (150). Only a very small minority actually changed their ideas in the direction of their captors' ideology. Lifton's extensive analysis of the conversion of these individuals examines their personalities, past histories, emotional strains, and identity problems, which are viewed as indispensable to understanding their response.

In addition to appealing to the apparent authority of cold war brainwashing notions, anticultists also legitimated the cultic mind control notion via a rhetoric of hypnosis, trances, and dissociative states, particularly during the first several decades of the cult controversy (see Singer and Ofshe 1990). In the words of one psychiatrist, "A naïve or deceived subject who is passing through or has been caused to enter a susceptible state of mind" is exposed to "highly programmed behavioral control techniques, in a controlled environment" until "the subject's attention is narrowed and focused to the point of becoming a trance." This trance "is maintained during several sleep periods until it becomes an independent structure." As a result, a "continued state of dissociation" is maintained in which her or his personality is dramatically altered (Clark 1976, 280).

Similarly, a prominent anticult sociologist maintains in a court document that "at the heart" of the Church of Scientology's "auditing procedure is the use of hypnosis," which "is important because it is used within Scientology to deceive clients and cause them to believe that they are able to accomplish para-normal feats and regain memories of past life experiences. . . . The fantasies that are induced through hypnosis have the quality of seeming more real than most memories" (Ofshe 1989, 7). A notion drawn from the *Manchurian Candidate* emerges in the remarks of another clinician who asserts that in alternative religions, "Many individuals are hypnotized. Many individuals are objects of hypnosis and autohypnosis where certain phrases and words will trigger a certain kind of thought pattern within the individual" (Benson 1977, 234). Cult recruiters have also been portrayed as actively utilizing techniques of formal hypnotism (Miller 1986).

The idea of "hypnotic rituals" as a key component of cultic brainwashing is ubiquitous in anticult theorizing (Abgrall 1990; see also Anthony 1990, 1999; Martin 1993; Singer 1983; and Singer and Lalich 1995). However, as Dick Anthony has pointed out, the scientific consensus is that "hypnosis is not an effective technique for causing people to engage involuntarily in behavior that is immoral, illegal, or against their own self-interest" (1999, 444; see also Barber 1961; Conn 1982; Fromm and Shor 1979, 6–12; Orne 1961, 1962; and Spanos 1996). Anthony continues:

> This is one of the most well-researched questions in the history of hypnosis research, and it is the consensus of informed scientific opinion that hypnosis cannot be used effectively for overwhelming free will or for substituting the will of the hypnotist for the will of the hypnotized. . . . [T]he idea that hypnosis could be used to impose a false personality on another and establish long-lasting control over their whole lifestyle is so far fetched that it [is] found only in popular science fiction on the topic of brainwashing such as the book The Manchurian Candidate (Condon, 1958). Indeed the idea that participating in a new religion changes one's basic personality is itself unsupported by empirical research. (1999, 444; Paloutzian, Richardson, and Rambo 1999)

Additionally, one significant line of research on hypnosis suggests that it is not possible to determine in a definitive manner whether an individual is "hypnotized" (Anthony 1999; Barber 1969; Gauld 1992; Kirsch 1995). In this view, a "hypnotic trance" is actually a myth, and there are no empirical criteria for distinguishing a hypnotic state of consciousness from normal consciousness. Thus, the claim that certain psychotechnologies of social influence are based on the technique of hypnosis is unprovable.

Given the bankruptcy of appeals to earlier formulations of communist brainwashing and to notions of hypnotic trances, cultic mind control appears to be little more than garden-variety social influence. Shorn of its pseudoscientific patina, how does one distinguish cultic brainwashing from other forms of social influence, such as advertising, military training, or even the normal socialization routines of the public schools? Anticult mind control theories explicitly or implicitly assert that the ability of cult members to process certain kinds of information has "snapped."

The problem with these and similar theories is that if cultic influences actually overrode the brain's ability to logically process information, then individuals suffering from cultic influences should perform poorly on IQ tests or, at the very least, manifest pathological symptoms when they take standardized tests of mental health—and when tested, they do not. If anything, such empirical studies indicate that members of new religious movements are actually smarter and healthier than the average member of mainstream society (for example, Sowards, Walser, and Hoyle 1994).

Other kinds of studies also fail to support the view that new religions rely on nonordinary forms of social influence to gain and retain members. For example, if new religions possessed powerful techniques of mind control that effectively overrode a potential convert's free will, then everyone—or at least a large percentage—of attendees at recruiting seminars should be unable to avoid conversion. However, sociologist Eileen Barker, in her important study *The Making of a Moonie: Brainwashing or Choice?* (1984), found that only a small percentage of the people attending seminars sponsored by the Unification Church (UC)—an organization that many people regard as the evil cult par excellence—eventually joined. Furthermore, of those who joined, more than half dropped out within the first year of their membership. In another important study, Canadian psychiatrist Saul Levine (1984) found that, out of a sample of more than 800 people who had joined controversial religious groups, more than 80 percent dropped out within two years of membership. These are not the kind of statistics one would anticipate in groups wielding powerful techniques of mind control.

In the face of these and other empirical studies, social scientists have asked these further questions: Given the lack of empirical support, where does the brainwashing notion originate? What is the real nature of the conflict that the "cult" stereotype obfuscates? The general conclusion of sociologists (as analyzed, for example, in David Bromley and Anson D. Shupe Jr.'s book-length study *Strange Gods: The Great American Cult Scare* [1981]) is that the principal source of the controversy is a parent-child conflict in which parents fail to understand the choices of their adult children and attempt to reassert parental control by marshaling the forces of public opinion against the religious bodies to which their offspring have converted.

This core conflict is then exacerbated by mass media that are less interested in truth than in printing exciting stories about weird cults that trap their members and keep them in psychological bondage with exotic techniques of "mind control." Also, once an industry is established that generates enormous profits through the "rescue" of entrapped "cult" members (that is, deprogramming), special-interest groups are created that have a vested interest in promoting the most negative stereotypes of alternative religions. These special-interest groups add further fuel to the parent-child conflict by scaring parents with horrific stories of what will happen to their adult child if they fail to have her or him deprogrammed. In this manner, many otherwise reasonable and well-meaning parents are recruited into the controversy.

In civil suits brought against minority religions, "cult experts" have appealed to the notion of cultic mind control as the basis for their claim that former "cult" members (in other words, the plaintiffs) had been recruited to a religion against their will. As a consequence, they were owed damages because of alleged psychological damages resulting from the period of their involuntary membership. From the mid-seventies to the mid-nineties, these kinds of lawsuits frequently succeeded. The affected new religions had to pay large compensatory and punitive damages, sometimes forcing a particular religion into bankruptcy and even dissolution. Perhaps ironically, however, the concern raised by such cases eventually brought about the decisive demise of the cultic mind control notion:

> Largely because of concern over the effects upon the civil liberties of new religions caused by testimony based upon the cultic brainwashing concept, substantial research that evaluated the coercive conversion idea was conducted by scholars of new religions. Most of this research tended to disconfirm the cultic brainwashing idea. Professional associations (the American Psychology Association, the American Sociological Association and the Society for the Scientific Study of Religion) submitted a series of Amicus Curiae briefs in the appeals of legal decisions based upon cultic brainwashing testimony, which argued that such testimony should not have been admitted because of the body of disconfirming research and because of the conflicts with constitutional and scientific standards of admissibility. At present, cultic brainwashing theory and the legal cases built upon it have been generally discredited and marginalized in the American context in which it originated. (Anthony and Robbins 2003)

Apocalypticism

Charges of cultic mind control have served to make individual involvement in controversial religions a matter of public concern. Typically, these religions are otherwise harmless. In contrast, the violence associated with a tiny handful of alternative religious groups has aroused a very different kind of concern. Even though brainwashing seems to explain how individual "cult" members could be prompted to commit acts of murder and suicide, it fails to explain why certain religions but not others become violent. One characteristic shared by most of the latter subset of religious groups—and, furthermore, embodies violent imagery—is apocalypticism.

The Solar Temple, the group examined at the beginning of the chapter, was strongly apocalyptic. Most of the other groups that have been either responsible for or else engulfed in violence—Heaven's Gate, the Branch Davidians, AUM Shinrikyo, and the Movement for the Restoration of the Ten Commandments of

God—were also apocalyptic. The People's Temple, the group that committed mass suicide in Guyana in 1978, is a notable exception to this apparent pattern.

In Western religions, the apocalypse notion originated in Zoroastrianism. The religion of Zoroaster is best known for its dualism. The god of light and his angels are locked in a cosmic struggle with the god of darkness and his demons. At the end of time, after a great final battle between good and evil—referred to as Armageddon—there will be a Final Judgment in which everyone will be put through an ordeal of fire and good individuals will have their dross burned away and evil people will be consumed. The souls of the blessed will be resurrected in physical bodies, which Ahura Mazda will make both immortal and eternally youthful.

Many of the components of this vision of the end times—a final battle between good and evil, judgment of the wicked, resurrection of the dead, and so on—were adopted by Jewish apocalyptic thinkers. From texts composed by these apocalypticists, such notions were adopted in Christianity and Islam. Although seemingly a dreadful day, many believers throughout the centuries have looked forward to the Final Judgment as the day on which their suffering for the faith will be vindicated and their persecutors and ridiculers punished.

Early Jewish apocalypses can be roughly divided into two principal groups. The first subgenre is what might be called historical apocalypses. These compositions, the most familiar of which is the book of Daniel (the only apocalypse to be incorporated into the canonical scriptures of Judaism), were extended prophecies presented in the form of allegorical visions (the book of Revelation is clearly in this tradition). The other subgenre is constituted by narratives of otherworldly journeys, focused especially on ascent through a series of heavens, culminating in a vision of the throne of God.

The contemporary period has seen a heightened interest in popular belief about the possible end of the world, and most portrayals of the end time picture an apocalyptic scenario. Although there has been a steady production of predictions that the world is coming to an end over the past several centuries, their number has slowly increased in recent decades.

Apocalypticism, which may initially strike one as a completely negative concept, is attractive because of the millenarianism that often accompanies it. Millenarianism is derived from

Christian theology and refers to the paradisiacal thousand-year period—the millennium—in which, according to the book of Revelation, history and the world as we know it will terminate. During the millennium, Satan would be chained and not allowed to pursue his evil work on earth. The expression "millenarian movement" is applied to groups that expect the imminent emergence of the millennium and whose religious life is saturated by this expectation. The arrival of the millennium has been a major theme in Christian thought, though the notions of a millennium and its accompanying apocalypticism are not confined to the Judeo-Christian-Islamic religious complex. By extension, other non-Christian religious movements that are characterized by such an expectation can be referred to as millenarian. Other terms for these types of groups are *crisis cult* and *messianic movement*. Some researchers have argued that all religions with historically specifiable origins began as millenarian movements— movements that, after they became established, lost much or all of their millennial enthusiasm.

Millenarian movements in the so-called Third World often, though certainly not invariably, arise in situations of contact between very different kinds of cultures, as when a Western nation intrudes into a geographical area in which traditional peoples reside and disrupts the patterns of life to which such peoples are accustomed. The response to this crisis is frequently a religious one in which the disrupted culture attempts to apply traditional understandings to a radically new contact situation. More often than not, this creative response will be articulated by a single individual (a prophet or a messiah) who receives a millenarian vision. In some cases, the vision will be a hostile one in which the community is counseled to resist the intruders and to adhere to the tradition of earlier generations (this subcategory is usually termed a *nativistic movement*). In other cases, the vision is a syncretistic response in which elements of both cultures are wedded into a new spiritual synthesis. Also, in some visions millenarians are advised to wait patiently for redemptive, supernatural intervention, while in others the community or group is encouraged to help bring about the millennium by some type of religious practice.

A useful example of a millennial movement outside the Judeo-Christian-Islamic complex of religions is the Ghost Dance, which arose out of the activities of the Paiute prophet Wovoka. Wovoka received a revelation of a millennium in which the earth would be renewed and the spirits of the dead return. This millennium would be preceded by a general catastrophe that would destroy Euramericans and their material culture. This event would be a cosmic rather than a military-political catastrophe. Specifically, righteous Native Americans would be lifted off the planet and a new earth rolled down across the surface, burying Euramericans and unrighteous Indians. Consequently, Native Americans were instructed to keep the peace and wait.

Beyond remaining at peace and following Wovoka's ethical injunctions, American Indians were periodically to perform what Euramericans came to call the Ghost Dance. Participants would dance in a circle until some fell down in a trance during which they received revelations, usually from departed relatives. Performing the dance would hasten the advent of the new age.

Wovoka's revelation spoke powerfully to his contemporaries, and the dance was taken up by a wide variety of different tribes, such as the Shoshone, Arapaho, Crow, Cheyenne, Pawnee, Kiowa, Comanche, and Sioux. Relatively stable tribal groups that had adjusted successfully to changed conditions were least inclined to accept the new teaching. The widespread excitement generated by Wovoka's vision declined rapidly after the U.S. Army massacred a group of peaceful Ghost Dancers at Wounded Knee, South Dakota, on December 29, 1890.

Despite the seeming connection between violent religious groups and apocalyptic theologies, there is a significant problem with using this trait as a criterion for distinguishing dangerous from nondangerous groups. The problem is that almost every religion in the larger Judeo-Christian-Islamic tradition has an apocalyptic theology, even the traditional peaceful churches that forbid members from participating in the military. Thus, contrary to the assertions of some contemporary critics of religion, having an apocalyptic theology does not, in itself, raise a red flag. This is because in most apocalyptic scenarios it is God and his angels who fight the final battle, not flesh-and-blood human beings. The human role is spiritual, and the "saved" fight a spiritual war, not a literal, physical war.

An apocalyptic theology is dangerous only when individual followers believe they are going to be called upon to be foot soldiers in God's army and prepare themselves by stocking up on weapons and ammunition. Groups that come to mind here are some of the Identity Christian churches who see themselves as preparing to fight a literal war against God's enemies. On the other hand, a community's possession of firearms—in the absence of such a theology of physical confrontation—is probably not dangerous, if no other danger signs are present. If the simple possession of firearms by members was a significant danger sign, then the Southern Baptist Convention would be the most dangerous "cult" in the United States.

Deprogramming and the Anticult Movement

The contemporary anticult movement emerged, as noted earlier, in the early 1970s, shortly after the rash of new religions that arose in the wake of the collapse of the counterculture of the 1960s. Opposition to minority religions was initially organized around deprogrammers—individuals who forcibly abducted individuals from nontraditional religions. In the heyday of deprogramming, "cult" members were snatched off the street and locked up in houses or motel rooms. Relatives and deprogrammers then attempted to demonstrate the falseness of the individual's newfound religion in an effort to convince her or him to defect.

Deprogramming began more or less accidentally when a son and a nephew of Theodore (Ted) Patrick Jr. considered joining the Children of God (COG), a "Jesus freak" organization. In 1971, Patrick was then governor Ronald Reagan's special representative for community relations in southern California, working as a kind of ombudsman. On the Fourth of July, he and his family were staying at a hotel on Mission Beach in San Diego. When his son Michael and a nephew failed to return from a fireworks display, he decided to call the police. They showed up as he was dialing, but he was struck by what seemed to be a strange look on Michael's face. The boys then related an encounter with the Children of God. Alarmed at first, Patrick and his family gradually forgot about the incident.

In his job as ombudsman, however, he began to hear other complaints about the Children of God. One person of particular importance at this early stage of development was William Rambur of Chula Vista, California. His daughter dropped out of school in order to move to a COG ranch in Thurber, Texas. Unable to persuade her to leave the group, he began a personal crusade to warn other parents about the danger of COG. Eventually, he linked up with Ted Patrick, and together they formed the first anticult organization. The name of this group, the Parent's Committee to Free Our Children from the Children of God, was later shortened to Free the Children of God and popularly referred to as FREECOG.

Increasingly frustrated by the authorities' refusal to do anything about COG, Patrick began to consider more desperate approaches. As he studied the matter, he found that kidnapping charges would be difficult if not impossible to make stick if parents were involved at every stage of such an operation. In cooperation with distraught parents, he then commenced to experiment with the tactic of abducting "cult" members bodily, locking them up, questioning their religious choices, and trying to convince them that they had been brainwashed and manipulated by their "cult." In 50 percent or more of the cases, they abandoned their new faith. Thus, the practice of "deprogramming" was born.

Initially, Patrick did not pursue deprogramming for personal enrichment. Gradually, however, he found the demand high enough that he turned his attention to kidnapping "cult" members on a full-time basis. The father of a new profession, he began to require compensation for his time. In response to critics, Patrick has soft-pedaled deprogramming by asserting that "all he does is talk to people." But in his popular book *Let Our Children Go!* it is described as follows: "Deprogramming is the term, and it may be said to involve kidnapping at the very least, quite often assault and battery, almost invariably conspiracy to commit a crime, and illegal restraint" (Patrick 1976, 63). Even though Patrick has often denied or downplayed the brutality of his work, in the same book he provides an interesting statement that contradicts his benign picture of deprogramming: "I believe firmly that the Lord helps those who help themselves—and a few little things like karate, Mace, and handcuffs can come in handy from time to time" (Patrick 1976, 70).

Other anticult organizations began springing up, with the Citizen's Freedom Foundation (CFF, later renamed the Cult Awareness Network [CAN]) becoming the national umbrella group. The support of deprogramming by anticult organizations evoked some of the most severe criticisms. As early as 1974, for example, the National Council of Churches passed a strong resolution against the practice. Deprogrammers also made the mistake of diversifying their kidnapping activities to include Evangelical Christians. This move provoked the wrath of Christian anticultists who, by the late seventies and early eighties, were withdrawing from their alliance with secular anticultists. For example, Walter Martin, the most prominent Christian anticultist, writing in 1980, asserted: "I cannot stand behind such practices. It is true that cultists have been blinded by the 'god of this age,' but it is also true that they have the right to make up their own minds, and we should not stoop to unChristian tactics to accomplish God's ends" (cited in Melton 1992, 349).

These and other criticisms influenced the secular anticult movement to rethink their stance on deprogramming. In 1981, for example, the Citizen's Freedom Foundation issued a statement that read, in part: "CFF does not support, condone, or recommend kidnapping or holding a person against his will." CFF did, however, continue to voice support for voluntary deprogramming (that is, counseling situations in which "cult" members were free to break off the conversation and leave at any time, usually referred to as "exit counseling").

The vast majority of deprogrammers have little or no background in psychological counseling. Often their only qualification is that they are themselves deprogrammed former cult members. Although advocates claim that deprogramming does nothing more than reawaken cult members' capacity for rational thought, an examination of the actual process reveals that the core technique of deprogramming involves directly assaulting a person's belief system. The deprogramming process consists of the following:

1. A breakdown in insulation from the outside world, accomplished by physically removing the member from her or his group.
2. A highlighting of the inconsistencies between group ideals and the actions of leaders, as well as internal inconsistencies *within* the group's belief system.
3. The pull of family ties. Deprogrammings are almost invariably paid for by other family members who then participate in the faith-breaking sessions.
4. The presentation of an alternative belief system. Deprogrammers often attempt to convert deprogrammees to conventional religion or, more often, to some variety of secular humanism.
5. Offering an alternative explanation for the individual's recruitment and membership—the familiar deception and mind-control ideology.

These five factors effectively disrupt the plausibility of the deprogrammee's religious beliefs. Success is not, however, guaranteed, as the high failure rate of deprogramming—between one-third to one-half return to their respective movements—demonstrates.

Deprogrammed former members of minority religions provide one of the keys to understanding the contemporary cult controversy. Groups opposed to such religions base much if not all of their attack on the testimony of former members who relate tale after tale of manipulation and abuse. Ex-members who have "actually been there," and who have supposedly witnessed all of the horrors about which outsiders can only fantasize, provide the cult stereotype with its most important source of empirical evidence. These narratives, anticultists would have the public believe, give us insights into the real nature and purpose of "cults," belying the beneficent image minority religions project to the world.

However, empirical studies contrasting the attitudes of former members who left their movements voluntarily with former members who had been deprogrammed reveal a systematic difference that calls the objectivity of such testimony into question. It was found that most voluntary defectors were ambivalent or even positive about their former religion, often characterizing their membership period as a beneficial learning experience. In sharp contrast, people who had been involuntarily removed described their membership and their former religion in terms of the popular negative stereotype of "cults." The conclusion to be drawn from these findings is that deprogramming is not the therapeutic intervention it has been portrayed, but is, rather, an intensive indoctrination process in which the abductee's religious faith is systematically destroyed and replaced with anticult ideology. Although this does not mean that there is nothing to be criticized in certain minority religions, a careful consideration of this finding should cause any thinking person to hesitate before accepting the more extreme accusations proffered by anticultists.

Thus, the ex-members who tell their tales of woe before the public have been carefully selected by the anticult movement. Even though few if any apostates are ever completely objective about their former religion, ex-members who have been intensively "counseled" by anticultists—especially those who have been kidnapped out of their religion—should be especially suspect as being less than neutral witnesses. By relying upon this subset of ex-members, the anticult movement involves itself in a hermeneutic circle. In other words, rather than forming generalizations based on a broad range of data, the anticult movement generates its own data by imposing its brainwashing ideology on a select number of individual cases (the deprogrammees) and then "discovers" evidence for its ideology in the testimony of these same individuals. Anticultists depend upon this subset of former members for the ultimate proof of their accusations.

In addition to shaping public opinion by recounting stereotypical atrocity tales, deprogrammees feed into the cult controversy in a number of other ways: In a variety of different court battles, ex-members recruited by anticultists provided negative testimony against their former movements, such as in child custody cases in which one of the parents is a "cult" member and in cases where governmental agencies need evidence for "cult" violations of various governmental regulations. The testimony of a deprogrammed Branch Davidian was, for example, part of the evidence used to obtain a search warrant before the assault on the Davidian community. And finally, at the level of basic research, these former members are interviewed in pseudoscientific surveys designed to substantiate claims such as that brainwashing techniques induce mental illness in their members and that child abuse is widespread in alternative religious groups.

Stereotypes and Public Perceptions of the Cult Issue

Stereotyping Cults

Several decades ago, sociologist Tom Robbins observed that if someone at a previously unknown vegetarian community died from being squashed by a giant cabbage, tomorrow's headline news story—splashed sensationally across the front page—would be a report on an act of "cult" violence. The incident would also immediately become fodder for the propaganda mill of anticult organizations and be used as an example of "what these awful groups are capable of." This hypothetical community, which, prior to the death, had never been considered "cultic," would then be mentioned in all future discussions of *evil cults*.

Robbins's observation seemed particularly appropriate in the wake of the Mount Carmel fiasco. Prior to the ATF attack, the Branch Davidians had been a little-noticed group on the outskirts of Waco. Although some of the people familiar with the community had found it somewhat eccentric, it was rarely mentioned in the same breath as Moonies, Hare Krishna, and so forth. In the wake of the tragedy, however, the Branch Davidians were transformed overnight into the paradigmatic *evil cult*.

The "reasoning" at work here is the same illogic of stereotyping from which many minorities have suffered:

- A black man raped a woman? Therefore, all black men are rapists.
- A Jew cheated a neighbor? Therefore, all Jews are cheaters.
- A homosexual molested a little boy? Therefore, all homosexuals are pedophiles.
- A nontraditional religious group in the boondocks of Texas shot four lawmen? Therefore, all nontraditional religions are violent cults.

And so on and so forth. We immediately recognize these biased stereotypes for what they are when applied to racial, ethnic, and sexual lifestyle minorities but fail to recognize similarly demeaning stereotypes when applied to nontraditional religions.

What is a stereotype? Stereotypes are generalizations about other groups of people, but they are a peculiar type of generalization. Stereotypes portray certain, most often derogatory, traits as being characteristic of a whole group of people and then explain or excuse social problems in light of these traits. Stereotypes are also usually held rigidly, in that we tend to ignore or to dismiss evidence that flies in the face of our generalization. Such rigidity indicates that our stereotype in some way protects our self-esteem or shields us from facing some unpleasant fact. Thus, the stereotype of certain races as "lazy," for example, simultaneously boasts the self-esteem of society's dominant racial group as well as blinds one to the inequalities of existing social arrangements. It is relatively easy to perceive that most generalizations about "cults" are little more than negative stereotypes, but what are the social forces that make such stereotypes about nontraditional religions peculiarly attractive to contemporary society?

One of the more widely accepted dictums of sociology is that societies need enemies, particularly societies that are going through a disturbing period of change. External threats provide motivation for people to overcome internal divisiveness in order to work together as a unit. Having an enemy one can portray as evil and perverse also provides support for the normative values and institutions of one's society: "They" are communists; "we" are capitalists. "They" are totalitarian; "we" are democratic. And so on and so forth.

One of the more interesting corollaries of this general line of thinking is that in situations where external enemies no longer threaten, a society will find groups or individuals within itself that it can construe as threatening and evil. Such enemies become particularly important to communities passing through a crisis in which fundamental values are being called into question. In the words of Albert Bergesen, from his important study *The Sacred and the Subversive,* "a community will commence to ritually persecute imaginary enemies—conduct a witchhunt—to manufacture moral deviants as a means of ritually reaffirming the group's problematical values and collective purposes" (1984, vii). This notion has been effectively supported by certain sociohistorical studies. For example, in an interesting and creative study of New England witchcraft, *Entertaining Satan* (1982), John Demos demonstrates that the persecution and execution of "witches"— usually unsocial, crabby little old ladies—abated during periods of war and reappeared after peace had returned. This sheds light on our current social situation.

Unless there are groups that are consciously antisocial or criminal like the Mafia or gangs, the deviations from the norm that a community chooses to perceive as threatening are somewhat arbitrary. The people that our culture have traditionally construed as "deviants" have been racial (that is, blacks), ethnic (Jews), and sexual (homosexuals) minorities. In recent years, however, it has become socially unacceptable to persecute these traditional groups, at least in the overt manner in which they were attacked in the past. This leaves few groups of any significant size to persecute. One of the few minorities that liberals have been slow to defend is nontraditional religions. This is due to a number of different factors, including the resistance of traditionally conservative religions to liberal change.

Groups of people experienced as threatening frequently become screens onto which a society projects its anxieties. If, for example, a culture is troubled by sexual issues (as is often the case), then its enemies are perceived as perverse, sexually deviant, and so on. Racial minorities, who have often been viewed as "loose" and sexually aggressive, have suffered from this projection. This was also a dominant theme in nineteenth-century anti-Catholic and anti-Mormon literature. Contemporary "cults," of course, suffer from the same projection.

In the classic formulation of psychological projection, Freud, who was especially concerned with sex and violence, viewed projection as a defense mechanism against unacceptable inner urges. Thus, in a society with strict sexual mores, an individual constantly keeping a lid on his desires might perceive ordinary dancing, let us say, as sexually suggestive. Becoming enraged at such "loose" behavior, he might then attempt to lead a movement to have all of the dance halls in town closed down. It should be clear that this hypothetical individual's *inner* struggle is being "projected" outward to provide a script for an *outer* struggle (that is, he is internally repressing his desires while symbolically battling the same desires in the outer world). The same process is at work in the collective mind of society, perceiving marginal groups as sexually deviant. For instance, the stereotype of the sexually abusive "cult" leader, routinely forcing devotees to satisfy his or her sexual whims, perfectly captures the fantasy of many members of our society who desire to sexually control any person they wish.

The same kind of thing happens with repressed aggressive urges. We live in a society with strict sanctions against overt violence; simultaneously, violence is glorified in the entertainment media. This sets up a cultural contradiction that is projected onto enemies and deviant groups, with the result that minorities are often perceived as violent and belligerent. This accusation is also regularly projected onto nontraditional religions. In particular, the radical actions of a tiny handful of alternative religions are mistakenly taken to indicate a widespread tendency among all such groups.

We can generalize beyond Freudian psychology's emphasis on sex and aggression to see that many other cultural anxieties and contradictions are projected onto minority groups. For instance, our society gives us contradictory messages about the relative importance of money and possessions. On the one hand, we are taught that economic pursuits are supposed to be secondary to social and spiritual activities. On the other, we receive many messages from the surrounding society that the single-minded pursuit of wealth is the be-all and end-all of life. This self-contradiction is projected onto alternative religions, as represented in the stereotype of the money-hungry "cult" leader who demands that her or his followers lead lives of poverty while the leader wallows in riches.

Similarly, the child abuse accusation and contemporary society's seeming obsession with child abuse flow out of another cultural contradiction. Our cultural heritage as well as many modern psychologists hold out the ideal of a child who is constantly under the wing of a loving parent, usually the mother. Current economic conditions, however, often require both parents to work full time, which usually entails leaving young children in the care of strangers. This results in a good deal of guilt, which is easily displaced onto such "deviant" groups as nontraditional religions. Like the accusation of violence, the radical actions of a tiny handful of alternative religions that have abused children are mistakenly taken to indicate a widespread tendency among all such groups. Despite the outcry against the Branch Davidians, for example, our best current information is that, though strict, the Davidians did *not* abuse their children. However, the readiness of people to buy into the stereotype of child-abusing cultists convicted David Koresh and sentenced him to death before he was able to receive a fair hearing.

One of the more important cultural contradictions that is projected onto alternative religions is tied up in the brainwashing, or mind control, notion that is the core accusation leveled against such groups. Discourse that glorifies mainstream society usually does so in terms of a rhetoric of liberty and freedom. However, while holding liberty as an ideal, we experience a social environment that is often quite restrictive. Most citizens work as employees in highly disciplined jobs where the only real freedom is the freedom to quit. Also, we are bombarded by advertising designed to influence our decisions and even to create new needs. Our frustration with these forms of influence and control is easily displaced and projected onto the separated societies of alternative religions in which the seemingly restricted flow of information offers a distorted reflection of the situation we experience as members of the dominant society.

The components of the "cult" stereotype that have been enumerated, and others, explain certain themes in anticult discourse as well as why this stereotype is attractive to members of present-day society. Without this preexisting disposition to construe nontraditional religions negatively, the anticult movement would have little or no social influence. However, whereas the anticult movement has relatively little direct social power, the stereotype it has helped to shape has taken on a life of its own, independent of organized anticultism.

Self-Fulfilling Stereotypes

Once a stereotype is in place, a variety of different kinds of studies have shown that it becomes self-fulfilling and self-reinforcing. Thus, in a study by Mark Snyder and Seymour Uranowitz, as reported in Paula Rothenberg's book *Racism and Sexism*, students were asked to read a short biography about Betty K., a fictitious woman. Her life story was constructed so that it would fulfill certain stereotypes of both heterosexuals and lesbians. In the words of Snyder and Uranowitz: "Betty, we wrote, never had a steady boyfriend in high school, but did go out on dates. And although we gave her a steady boyfriend in college, we specified that he was more of a close friend than anything else" (Snyder and Uranowitz 1988). A week later, they told some of the students that Betty was currently living with her husband and another group of students that she was living with another woman in a lesbian relationship. When subsequently requested to answer a series of questions about Betty, they found a marked tendency on the part of students to reconstruct her biography so as to conform to stereotypes about either heterosexuality or homosexuality, depending on the information they had received. "Those who believed that Betty was a lesbian remembered that Betty had never had a steady boyfriend in high school, but tended to neglect the fact that she had gone out on many dates in college. Those who believed that Betty was now a heterosexual, tended to remember that she had formed a steady relationship with a man in college, but tended to ignore the fact that this relationship was more of a friendship than a romance" (Snyder and Uranowitz 1988).

More directly relevant to the case at hand is an important article by Jeffrey E. Pfeifer, "The Psychological Framing of Cults: Schematic Representations and Cult Evaluations," reporting the results of a similar study that compared responses to a biography in which a fictitious student, Bill, dropped out of college to enter a Catholic seminary, join the marines, or join the Moonies. The short biography incorporated elements of indoctrination often attributed to "cults": "While at the facility, Bill is not allowed very much contact with his friends or family and he notices that he is seldom left alone. He also notices that he never seems to be able to talk to the other four people who signed up for the program and that he is continually surrounded by [Moonies, marines, or priests] who make him feel guilty if he questions any of their actions or beliefs" (Pfeifer 1992).

When given a choice of describing Bill's indoctrination experience, subjects who thought Bill had joined the Catholic priesthood most often labeled his indoctrination "resocialization," those who were told that he had joined the marines most frequently labeled the process "conversion," and those who were under the impression that he had become a Moonie applied the label "brainwashing." On various other questions regarding the desirability and fairness of the indoctrination process, subjects who were told that Bill had joined the Moonies consistently evaluated his experience more negatively than subjects who were under the impression that Bill had joined either the marines or a priestly order.

The implications of this research for the cult controversy are that the minority religions lose their chance for a fair hearing as soon as the label "cult" is applied. After that, the mass media selectively seek out and present information about the group that fits the stereotype. In the Branch Davidian case, it was only a matter of time before the media had completely "demonized" Koresh and his followers.

Cults and the Media

Less than a week after the ATF attack on the Branch Davidian community, the Reverend Mike Evans, who in 1986 had published a popular book about the end of the world, publicly pronounced that David Koresh was demon-possessed. The Waco confrontation had already begun to settle into the routine of an uneventful standoff, and the media were searching around for colorful news—hence the decision to feature a story on the Texas evangelist. "Satan is alive and well on planet earth," claimed Evans in the words of a popular book title. "The spirit that is in Koresh and his followers needs to be exorcised." He offered his services to the authorities: "If it would save innocent lives, I would be willing to go in there one on one with him and cast that demon out." Although he said that he "would prefer going in there and laying hands on him and rebuking the demons in him," Brother Evans also noted that the next best thing to a personal exorcism would be to repeat a prayer through a loudspeaker, "rebuking the demon spirits in Koresh and commanding them to come out in the name of Jesus. Turn it up so loud that Koresh will not have a moment of rest 24 hours a day."

Perhaps taking their cue from Pastor Evans, it was not long afterward that the FBI initiated a harassment campaign against Mount Carmel. However, rather than attempting to exorcise Koresh, the FBI seemed intent on feeding his demon. Instead of prayers, authorities broadcast, among other sound tracks, Nancy Sinatra music, the sound of a dentist's drill, and the cries of rabbits being tortured to death. (One wonders what kind of tape library stocks rabbit murder sounds—or were the fuzzy cottontails slain at the behest of the FBI and custom-taped for the occasion?) It is difficult to understand what this audio assault and the accompanying light show could have accomplished, except to increase the level of paranoia among the Davidians.

The fact that the media saw fit to give sideshows like Evans that sprang up around the Davidian siege as much coverage as the siege itself reflects a salient characteristic of the contemporary news media, which is that—because of the intense competition among different news agencies—the media seek to *entertain* consumers of news, sometimes at the cost of *informing* them. The same drive to increase viewer or reader ratings is evident in the media portrayal of the Branch Davidians. Although Evans had recommended casting out demons, and though the FBI tried to provoke Koresh's inner devils, the media took a somewhat different approach and proceeded to demonize the Davidian leader. In addition to the usual generic accusations about evil cult leaders and ad nauseam comparisons with Jim Jones, reporters dutifully repeated every slanderous remark made about Koresh and the Davidians, whatever the source. Clearly, the intention was to appeal to readers and viewers with sensationalism rather than to produce a balanced picture of the Branch Davidians.

More generally, the journalistic penchant for sensationalism has been a decisive factor in promoting the stereotype of "evil cults" to the larger society. The mass media are not, of course, motivated primarily by the quest for truth, although some reporters have more integrity than others. Instead, the mainstream media are driven by market forces and by the necessity of competing with other newspapers, TV news shows, and so forth.

This is not to say that reporters necessarily lie or fabricate their stories. Rather, in the case of new religious movements (NRMs), newspeople tend to accentuate those facets of "cults" that seem to be strange, exploitative, dangerous, totalitarian, sensational, and the like because such portrayals titillate consumers of news. This kind of reporting contributes to the perpetuation of the cult stereotype. In the words of British sociologist James Beckford,

> Journalists need no other reason for writing about any particular NRM except that it is counted as a cult. This categorization is sufficient to justify a story, especially if the story illustrates many of the other components which conventionally make up the "cult" category. This puts pressure on journalists to find more and more evidence which conforms with the categorical image of cults and therefore confirms the idea that a NRM is newsworthy to the extent that it does match the category. It is no part of conventional journalistic practice to look for stories about NRMs which do *not* conform to the category of cult. (Beckford 1994, 146)

Another important factor is the marked tendency of the mass media to report on a phenomenon only when it results in conflicts and problems. To again cite from Beckford's important paper "The Media and New Religious Movements," "NRMs are only newsworthy when a problem occurs. Scandals, atrocities, spectacular failures, 'tug-of-love' stories, defections, exposés, outrageous conduct—these are the main criteria of NRMs' newsworthiness. . . . And, of course, the unspectacular, nonsensational NRMs are permanently invisible in journalists' accounts" (Beckford 1994, 144–145).

The different media vary somewhat in their tendency to produce imbalanced reports. "TV tabloids" such as *20/20* and *Hard Copy* that have to compete with prime-time TV programming tend to be the most imbalanced. Rather than attempting to produce programs that examine the complex ramifications of issues, news shows usually present melodramas in which guys in white hats are shown locked in conflict with other guys in black hats. On the opposite extreme are the major newspapers, such as the *Los Angeles Times* and the *Washington Post*, which tend to do the best job of attempting to present balanced articles on controversial subjects. Such "balance," however, usually only means finding the space for opposing views. The journalist appears to be objective when her or his story is two-sided rather than one-sided. The news magazines such as *Time* and *Newsweek* tend to fall somewhere in between.

One of the more unusual aspects of the Waco standoff was the decision by NBC to create a "docudrama" about the Branch Davidians and the events leading up to the original ATF assault *before* the siege ended. The title of this made-for-TV movie, *Ambush in Waco,* seemed to evoke images from the quasi-mythical past of frontier Texas, when sinister savages ambushed noble lawmen. Television, as we have already mentioned, is the least suitable medium for coming to grips with complex moral issues. In the case of *Ambush in Waco,* the ATF agents were dressed in white hats and David Koresh in a black hat. It was, as might be expected, a shallow, rambling production built around a disconnected framework of the most slanderous accusations leveled against Koresh. The ATF was completely whitewashed as a group of noble-minded public servants—not a single question was raised about the propriety of the ATF's actions. The filming of *Ambush in Waco* was still in process when the FBI attacked Mount Carmel. Appealing to the public hunger for sensationalism and violence, the docudrama was a smashing success.

The collapse of the distinction between dramatic time and real time in this and other productions represents a disturbing trend. One can well imagine the creation of a "quickie" docudrama on a sensationalistic murder in which the murderer suspect is convicted on TV—but who later turns out to be innocent. It has become increasingly clear that something like this was the case with the Davidians (that is, a TV conviction), but the "evidence"—as presented in *Ambush in Waco*—has helped to blind the public to the possibility that Koresh and company could have been innocent. Instead, *Ambush in Waco* merely reinforced the news media's demonization of the Branch Davidians and helped to make the final holocaust at Mount Carmel more acceptable.

In an important article on the docudrama trend, "From Headline to Prime Time" (published in *TV Guide*), David Shaw observes that "fact based movies are suddenly the Hula-Hoop, the skateboard, the nintendo of the '90s" (Shaw 1993). He further points out that most such movies are based on disasters and that "the instant dramatization of real tragedy has become a kind of video fast food, drama McNuggets" (Shaw 1993). Shaw's conclusion is worth citing at length:

Using the powerful and intimate medium of television to pander to the viewer's base instincts is not new, but this rush to do so is the latest step down a very dangerous road. Where will it all end? Will the next David Koresh be able to sit in his compound and watch his own dramatized death on television—and maybe figure out how to kill the cops instead? . . . Will producers decide that, rather than risk waiting until dramatic events actually take place before they begin costly bidding wars for the dramatic rights of the players, they should open negotiations with soldiers of fortune, jilted lovers, and putative terrorists *before* they do their dastardly deeds . . . perhaps even suggesting a traumatic twist or two in the ultimate execution to jack up the asking price? (Shaw 1993)

The Appeal of New Religions

Up to this point, the discussion has been focused on the cult *controversy* and on how that controversy has been misperceived and misrepresented. I now want to turn your attention to understanding the sources of spiritual innovation as well as understanding the appeal of new religions. In successive sections, I will examine the real issues—and, in some cases, the real dangers—associated with certain minority religious groups.

There have been a variety of historical periods during which religious innovation has flourished. The most general observation we can make is that periods of renewed spiritual activity occur in the wake of disruptive social and economic changes: the established vision of "how things work" no longer seems to apply, and people begin searching for new visions. In previous cycles of Western—especially U.S.—religious experimentation, innovative forms of Protestantism often formed the basis for these new visions. As revivalist fervor died down, new or reinvigorated Protestant denominations became the pillars of a new cultural hegemony.

The most recent period of religious innovation occurred in the decades following the demise of the 1960s counterculture. However, unlike previous cycles of revival, the religious explosion that occurred in the 1970s and 1980s has not provided a basis for a new spiritual and cultural synthesis. Even though there has been a growth in conservative Protestant denominations during this period (a growth parallel to the pattern of earlier awakenings), there has also been a marked growth in "metaphysical" religion. The most visible manifestation of this latter strand of spirituality has been the New Age movement, which offers a vision of the world fundamentally different from that of traditional Christianity. Thus, during this most recent cycle of religious enthusiasm, Protestantism has failed to reestablish its traditional hegemony.

Other factors inhibiting the formation of a new cultural synthesis have been the growing power of secularization and the influx of new immigrants from non-Protestant (and even non-Christian) countries. In the West's new pluralistic society, Hindus, Buddhists, Muslims, and so forth represent a growing segment of the culture—a segment for whom neither Protestantism nor the New Age exercises much appeal. Also, a trend toward secularization that was set in motion in the preceding century has shaped yet another important segment of contemporary society, one alienated from religion altogether.

Lacking the power to generate a new basis for cultural synthesis, the current proliferation of new religious movements cannot help but strike the casual observer as a negative phase of contemporary life—a factor contributing to the disintegration of modern life. However, it is the very disconnectedness of the contemporary experience that contributes to the attraction of nonmainstream religions. This "something" is that many alternative religions hold out the possibility of life-transforming experiences—experiences that, to a greater or lesser extent, help one to drop the burden of the past and be reborn into a new and more whole life.

The mainstream Protestant denominations—Methodists, Baptists, and Presbyterians—once offered the seeker life-transforming experiences in the context of revivals and camp meetings. But as these religious bodies settled down into comfortable accommodation with the surrounding (largely secular) society, they lost their intensity. One result of this accommodation was that revivals and camp meetings—and the accompanying intense religious experiences—were relegated to a quaint and mildly embarrassing chapter in denominational histories.

Those of us who are happily adjusted to the social-cultural mainstream often have a difficult time understanding intense religiosity. Academics have not been exempt from this tendency. An earlier generation of sociologists of religion, seemingly obsessed with the issue of conversion to nonmainstream "sect" groups, gave excessive attention to explaining why individuals became involved in such bizarre churches.

If, however, rather than dwelling on strange externals, we change our point of focus and attempt to really look at what might attract someone to an alternative religion, such involvement is not really difficult to understand. Is the attraction of transformational experiences, for example, really so hard to comprehend? What if we actually could let go of the burden of our past and be reborn as new people? Such transformation may or may not be attainable, but the attractiveness of the possibility is certainly understandable. Many nonmainstream religions—conservative Christian sects included—hold out the promise of such life-changing experiences.

Many people become involved in a religious group in the wake of a spiritual experience. This factor was particularly emphasized in older academic literature about religious conversion. In this body of literature, the suddenness of the experience is stressed. The implicit or explicit paradigm is the Damascus Road experience, in which the apostle Paul was knocked off his horse by a bolt out of the blue, confronted by Jesus, and converted on the spot. Contemporary studies have found, however, that it rarely works that way. Rather, in most cases, individuals just gradually "drift" into a religious group until they cross a barely perceptible line between outsider and insider, undergoing a series of "miniconversions" en route.

Religious experience is, however, only one aspect of the spiritual life and only one of the factors that attract individuals to deeper religious involvement. Among the many approaches to religious studies, one of the older, yet still useful, scholarly analyses was articulated by the influential historian of religion Joachim Wach (1944). The primary core of religion, according to Wach, is religious experience. Religious experience, in turn, is expressed in at least three ways:

- In a community (church, ashram, and so on)
- In a doctrine (theology, worldview, or ideology)
- In a "cultus" (ritual, ceremony, or gathering)

Wach's analysis should give us a basic feel for the fundamental constituents of religion. In outline form, these constituents are:

- Spiritual experience
- Community
- Doctrine or idea system
- Gatherings or rites

Each of these four components sheds light on how individuals become involved in religious groups. I have already discussed the role of spiritual experiences. Often, it is the community dimension of any religious group that is the key element in initially attracting new members. We live in a society that would have been an alien world to our ancestors. Surrounded by masses of people, we rarely know the names of our closest neighbors. In traditional societies, by way of contrast, everyone in a particular village knew everyone else and took care of everyone else. If, for instance, you saw someone have an accident, you did not call 911; instead, you ran over and helped out as best you could. Some churches and most alternative religions re-create this kind of community—a community comparable to an extended family.

The family metaphor is particularly apt. In modern society, our families are not the close emotional units they were in traditional societies. A small religious group many times re-creates the sense of belonging to a family. If one has never experienced the closeness of a traditional family, it is easy to understand how the sense of belonging to a family unit would be attractive, and even healing.

Something similar can be said about worldviews. In a traditional society, beliefs about the ultimate nature of the universe are largely taken for granted. In contemporary society, by way of contrast, nothing can be taken for granted except death and taxes. We are taught to be "nice" by our school system, but this moral teaching is not grounded in an ultimate source of value. We are also instructed in the basic skills necessary to operate in society, but public school teachers are quiet about the greater questions of death, purpose, and the meaning of life.

We may place a positive or a negative evaluation on this relativistic education, but in any case we have to acknowledge that our culture's ambiguous approach to socialization departs radically from the socialization strategies of earlier societies. Our choices are always varying shades of gray, rather than black and white or good and bad. The results of this ambiguity may be liberating to some people, but to others it is confusing. Without some kind of ultimate grounding, this is necessarily the case.

Nontraditional religions are often criticized for offering their followers the "easy" answers that come with black-and-white thinking. However, to many of the people who belong to such religions, the seeming narrowness of such thinking can be a liberating experience: once one has stable criteria for what is good and true, this clarity and stability can then free one to go about the business of working, loving, and living life without debilitating anxieties about transcendent meaning and value. This is not, of course, to advocate a rigid belief system, but rather to point out why such a system is attractive without depreciating adherents as being somehow weak or defective.

In summary, we may say that people join alternate religions for the same sorts of reasons one would join any other religion, namely, fellowship, a satisfying belief system, and so forth. When these needs are no longer being fulfilled in an acceptable manner, people leave, much as one would leave an unsatisfying marriage.

Social Influence in Genuinely Dangerous Religions

The Nature of "Cultic" Influence

Even though we can dismiss the notion of a unique form of influence exerted by minority religions over their followers, it is nevertheless still clear that the members of any group—particularly a tightly knit spiritual community—experience various forms of social influence. Social pressure, conformity, and attitude change are bread-and-butter issues for social psychology, and small-group dynamics are ideal situations in which to study such processes. However, the "garden variety" group influences examined by social psychologists rarely find their way into the "cult" debate. On the one hand, they do not serve the purposes of anticultists who are intent on making the case for "cultic mind control." On the other hand, defenders of religious liberty are so focused on demonstrating the presence of free will among members of controversial religions that they tend to gloss over the question of the other less noble social dynamics found within such groups.

In approaching these dynamics, it should initially be noted that somewhat different factors are involved in *recruitment* as opposed to the ongoing *maintenance* of commitment to a group of any type. Proponents of the brainwashing theory have tended to ignore this particular distinction. At an earlier stage of the cult controversy, anticultists, particularly deprogrammers, tended to portray recruitment as a kind of "spot hypnosis" that was able to override the will of the recruit. This perspective ignored the obvious, which was that not everyone was susceptible to prose-lytizers—indicating that factors other than an irresistible hypno-sis technique were at work in the recruiting situation. In partic-ular, more objective observers noted that the great majority of individuals who joined high-demand religions were unattached young people—people with few responsibilities and who were thus relatively free to experiment with an alternative lifestyle.

Another point infrequently emphasized in anticult literature is that comparatively few nontraditional religions are as demand-ing as the Moonies or the Hare Krishna movement. In fact, the great majority of religions stigmatized as "cults" are more like mainstream churches and synagogues in that they do not require members to leave their families or their jobs and move into an iso-lated communal facility. Recruitment to such groups thus tends to take place quite differently—through family, friend, and employ-ment networks—and more gradually than the "Pied Piper" syn-drome that is a cornerstone of the stereotype of cult recruitment.

As has already been indicated in previous sections, it does not require a great leap of the imagination to understand the ini-tial attraction of becoming a member of such communities. In-tensive religious groups provide participants with a ready-made fellowship, a stable worldview, and clear ethical guidelines that sharply contrast with the ambivalence and ambiguity of life in contemporary mass society.

Once one joins a religious group, the ordinary forces of so-cial conformity come into play to further socialize the recruit into the mores of her or his new community. In a classic study of the sociology of knowledge, *The Social Construction of Reality* (1966), Peter L. Berger make the case that the plausibility of any given idea is dependent upon the people one is in conversation with on a day-to-day basis. Thus, if all of one's acquaintances are Repub-licans, even someone who had previously been a Democrat tends to "convert" to Republicanism, and vice versa. Similarly, the no-tion that the Reverend Sun Myung Moon might be the new mes-siah seems silly to non-Moonies. But if one was to live in a com-munity in which all of one's conversation partners held this belief, it would not be long before one would begin to entertain the idea as a plausible option.

The motives in such situations are the natural human desire to be accepted and the socially learned value of not wanting to disagree with others. These motives can actually alter the manner in which we perceive the world, as demonstrated in a classic experiment designed by social psychologist Solomon Asch. In the Asch experiment, a subject was asked to judge which of three sample lines a given line was closest to in length. Unknown to the subject, however, the other seven people in the room were only pretending to be experimental subjects. Instead, they had been instructed to falsely identify a different line—one that was obviously unequal in length. When it came the subject's turn—who was always the last person to speak—he or she was thus faced with the dilemma of listening to his own senses or to the group judgment. A full 80 percent of the subjects in Asch's original experiment were influenced by the group to go against the evidence of their senses at least some of the time.

If the social forces influencing people to conform can have this high success rate with a group of strangers, imagine how such forces must be amplified within a group of friends—or, to take the case at hand, within a close-knit religious fellowship. It should not be too difficult to perceive how the desire to conform, in combination with the ongoing conversation that gives a belief system much of its plausibility, influences group members to become convinced of ideas that seem odd or nutty to outsiders. Clearly, it is unnecessary to posit a special form of social influence conforming to the popular notion of "cultic brainwashing" in order to explain such behavior.

In most cases, the results of these forces of social influence are benign. There are, however, situations in which the very same forces can be put to socially undesirable ends. In a different series of experiments, psychologist Stanley Milgram demonstrated that, in the right circumstances, ordinary individuals could be manipulated into obeying orders to torture and even kill other human beings. (No one was actually harmed; instead, experimental subjects were tricked into believing they had murdered someone.) Although the implications of these experiments are frightening, at the same time they shed light on such apparently crazy acts as the Jonestown and Heaven's Gate suicides: under the right circumstances, people can be led to undertake extreme actions—even mass suicide. Once again, it should be noted that it is unnecessary to invoke ad hoc notions of cultic mind control to explain such events.

If, however, the forms of social influence at work within minority religions are not distinctive enough to allow one to distinguish a dangerous group from a healthy group on the basis of socialization routines, then how can we distinguish the Solar Temples, Jonestowns, and Heaven's Gates from benign religious organizations? Although any simple criterion for making such a distinction is likely impossible, there are, nevertheless, a few guidelines that could function as "early warning signs" for a religion that has gone or is going "bad."

"Cults" or Bad Religion?

Although the majority of minority religions are innocuous, many have been involved in social conflicts. A handful of these conflicts have made national and even international headlines, from the siege of the Branch Davidian community to the group suicide of Heaven's Gate members. One consequence of these highly publicized incidents is that they have served to reinforce unreflective stereotypes about "cults" and "cult leaders" that are appropriate for some—but certainly not the majority of—minority religions. Unfortunately, such stereotyped information is often the only "data" readily available to the media and law enforcement at the onset of such conflicts.

Putting aside the technical discourse of sociologists, in ordinary language people talk as if there is an objective category of groups called "cults" that can be distinguished from genuine religions. In this commonly accepted view, cults are by definition socially dangerous false religions, led by cynical cult leaders who exploit followers for their own gain.

This stereotype is, however, deeply flawed, and for more than one reason. In the first place, as we have already seen, "cult" is a socially negotiated label that often means little more than a religion one dislikes for some reason. To certain conservative Christians, for example, a "cult" is any religion that departs from a certain traditional interpretation of Scripture. Alternately, ultraconservative Christians who take a strictly fundamentalist approach to Scripture often appear "cultlike" to many mainline Christians. In other words, one person's cult is another person's religion.

In the second place, the founders of new groups are—despite whatever personal flaws some might have—almost always sincerely religious. Part of the problem here is that most people unreflectively assume that religion is always something "good." If, therefore, a given religious body does something "bad," then ipso facto it must not be a "real" religion. Instead, it must be a false religion, created for no other reason than the founder or leader's personal gain. This attitude is, however, naive. The ancient Aztecs, to take an extreme example, regularly tortured and sacrificed other human beings as part of their religious rites. These practices were, in fact, a central aspect of the Aztec religion. But however much we might be able to explain and even to understand why the Aztecs engaged in such practices, no contemporary person would defend these rites as "good."

The proper question to ask, then, is not whether some particular group is a cult (in the sense of a "false religion") but, rather, whether the social-psychological dynamics within a particular religion are potentially dangerous to its members or to the larger society or both. Unfortunately, once we get beyond such actions as torturing and murdering other human beings, the criteria for what one regards as harmful can be quite subjective. It has been seriously asserted, for example, that requiring "cult" members to be celibate and to follow vegetarian diets are harmful practices. Similarly, requiring followers to engage in several hours of meditation per day plus discouraging the questioning of "cult" doctrine have often been portrayed as parts of a group's "brainwashing" regime designed to damage one's ability to reason properly.

Once again, the problem with such criteria is that they are naive. If celibacy was harmful, for example, then how does one explain the lack of more-than-ordinary pathology among monks and nuns? Also, if certain mental practices actually damaged the brain, then why do members of intensive religious groups perform so well on IQ tests and other measures of individual reasoning ability? Such critical criteria also reflect an abysmal ignorance of traditional religious practices: many traditional religions have promoted celibacy, restricted diets, prescribed lengthy prayers and meditations, discouraged the questioning of group ideology, and so forth. Clearly, if one wants to delineate serious criteria for determining "bad religion," then one must avoid focusing on traits that embody more than the observer's ethnocentric attitudes.

To begin, making a radical lifestyle change as part of joining a religious group should not, in itself, be taken to indicate that the individual has therefore become involved in something harmful. Friends and family members may feel that an individual is making a mistake to quit a job or to drop out of school—actions that, by the way, *very few* contemporary new religions would actively encourage—but a free society means nothing if one is not also free to make mistakes.

If one wishes to develop objective criteria for distinguishing harmful or potentially harmful religious organizations from harmless religions, one needs to place oneself in the position of a public policy maker. From this perspective, religions that should raise the most concern are those groups that tangibly, physically harm members or nonmembers or both or that engage in other antisocial or illegal acts. However, a public policy maker might well respond that this *post facto* criterion is too little too late and that what is needed are criteria that could act as early warning signs—criteria indicating that a previously innocuous group is potentially "going bad." In the following discussion, I will make a stab at developing such criteria, with the caveat that the presence of the less serious factors listed below in any given group does not automatically mean they are on the verge of becoming the next Heaven's Gate.

Early Warning Signs

As part of this discussion, I shall be referring to a few false criteria for distinguishing a healthy from an unhealthy religion. In the first place, the mere fact that a group is headed by a charismatic leader does not automatically raise a red flag. This is because new religions are much like new businesses: new businesses are almost always the manifestation of the vision and work of a single entrepreneur. In contrast, few if any successful businesses are the outgrowth of the work of a committee. Also, to found a religion, a leader usually makes some sort of claim to a special insight or to a special revelation that legitimates both the new religion and the leader's right to lead. The founder may even claim to be a prophet, messiah, or avatar. Although many critics of alternative religions have asserted that the assumption of such authority is in itself a danger sign, too many objectively harmless groups have come into being with the leader asserting divine authority for such claims to be meaningful danger signs.

Far more important than one's claim to authority is what one does with the authority once he or she attracts followers who choose to recognize it. A minister or guru who focuses her or his pronouncements on the interpretation of Scripture or on other matters having to do with religion proper is far less problematic than a leader who takes it upon her- or himself to make decisions in the personal lives of individual parishioners, such as dictating (as opposed to suggesting) who and when one will marry. The line between *advising* and *ordering* others with respect to their personal lives can, however, be quite thin. A useful criterion for determining whether this line has been crossed is to examine what happens when one acts against the guru's advice in such matters: if one can respectfully disagree without suffering negative consequences as a result, then the leadership dynamics within the group are healthy with respect to authority issues.

One of the clearest signs that leaders are overstepping their proper sphere of authority is when they articulate certain ethical guidelines that everyone must follow *except for* the guru or minister. This is especially the case with a differential sexual ethic that restricts the sexual activity of followers but allows leaders to initiate liaisons with whomever they choose.

Perhaps the most serious danger sign is when a religious group places itself above the law, although there are some nuances that make this point trickier than it might first appear. All of us, in some sphere of life, place ourselves above the law, if only when we go a few miles per hour over the speed limit or fudge a few figures on our income tax returns. Also, when push comes to shove, almost every religion in the world would be willing to assert that divine law takes precedence over human law—should they ever come into conflict. Hence, a group that, for example, solicits donations in an area where soliciting is forbidden should not, on that basis alone, be viewed as a danger to society. Exceptions should also be made for groups or individuals who make a very public protest against certain laws judged as immoral, as when a conscientious objector goes to jail rather than be drafted into the military.

On the other hand, it should be clear that a group leader who consistently violates serious laws has developed a rationale that could easily be used to legitimate more serious antisocial acts. Examples that come readily to mind are Marshall Applewhite, the founder and leader of Heaven's Gate, who regularly ducked out on motel bills and was once even arrested for stealing a rental car, and Swami Kirtananda, founder of the New Vrindavan community, who was caught authorizing the stealing of computer software before being arrested for ordering the murder of a community critic. Documentable child abuse and other illegalities committed within the organization are also covered by this criterion.

Another misconceived criterion is perceiving groups as dangerous because of apocalyptic theologies. As discussed earlier, almost every religion in the larger Judeo-Christian-Islamic tradition has an apocalyptic theology. The fact that a given group has an apocalyptic theology is not, in itself, dangerous because in most apocalyptic scenarios it is God and his angels who fight the final battle. The human role is spiritual, and the "saved" fight a spiritual war, not a literal, physical war. An apocalyptic theology is dangerous only when individual followers believe they are going to be called upon to be foot soldiers in God's army and prepare themselves by stocking up on weapons and ammunition. However, a community's possession of firearms—in the absence of such a theology of physical confrontation—is probably not dangerous, if no other danger signs are present.

Another false, yet frequently voiced, criterion is that religious groups are dangerous when they see only themselves as saved and the rest of the world as damned. Like apocalypticism, this trait is far too widespread among traditional religions to constitute an authentic danger sign. A more meaningful characteristic should be how a religion actually treats nonmembers.

Another criterion is a group's relative isolation. This trait is somewhat more complex than the others we have examined. On the one hand, there are abundant examples of traditional religions establishing communities or monastic centers apart from the larger society that have posed no danger to anyone. On the other hand, some of the worst abuses have taken place in the segregated (usually communal) subsocieties of certain minority religions. From the suicidal violence of the People's Temple to the externally directed violence of certain Identity Christian groups, it was the social dynamics found in an isolated or semi-isolated community that allowed such extreme actions to be contemplated.

In order to flag this characteristic while simultaneously avoiding stigmatizing every religion that sets up a segregated society as being potentially dangerous, it might be best to invert this trait and state it as a counterindicator. In other words, rather than asserting that any religion with a partially isolated community is potentially dangerous, let us instead assert that the relative *lack* of such boundaries indicates that the group in question is almost certainly *not* dangerous.

A final early warning sign is a group's readiness to deceive outsiders (and, to a lesser extent, the systematic deception of insiders). Some critics have said that a recruiter who invites a potential convert to a dinner without mentioning that the event is being sponsored by such-and-such church is deceptive. Others have criticized religions possessing a hierarchical system of knowledge to which only initiates are privy. These kinds of criticisms are silly. When a guru publicly asserts that his organization does not own any guns and police later find a small arsenal in his basement, *that* is deception.

To summarize, the traits designated above as "early warning signs of 'bad religion'" are:

1. The organization is willing to place itself above the law. With the exceptions noted earlier, this is probably the most important characteristic.
2. The leadership dictates (rather than suggests) important personal (as opposed to spiritual) details of followers' lives, such as whom to marry, what to study in college, and so on.
3. The leader sets forth ethical guidelines members must follow but from which the leader is exempt.
4. The group is preparing to fight a literal, physical Armageddon against other human beings.
5. The leader regularly makes public assertions that he or she knows is false or the group has a policy of routinely deceiving outsiders or both.
6. Finally, whereas many benign religions constitute semi-segregated communities, socially dangerous religions are almost always isolated or partially isolated from the larger society.

These six traits are about as close as one can get to legitimate, objective criteria for judging whether a given religious organization is going—or has gone—"bad." With the exception of placing the group's actions above the law, none of these characteristics, taken by themselves, is necessarily cause for alarm. On the other hand, a group possessing more than one or two of the above traits might well bear closer scrutiny. As a corollary to this line of analysis, minority religions possessing none of the above traits are, from a public policy standpoint, almost certainly harmless.

New Religions, Violence, and Suicide

Of all of the negative traits attributed to nontraditional religions, the most troubling is that of violence—particularly their supposed proneness to suicide. Although violent incidents in new religions are actually quite rare (especially in contrast to the much greater violence associated with "mainstream" religions), they have attracted significant popular and scholarly attention.

Two major monographs that appeared in 2000—John R. Hall, Philip D. Schuyler, and Sylvaine Trinh's *Apocalypse Observed* and Catherine Wessinger's *How the Millennium Comes Violently*—developed analyses of NRM-related violence that included thick descriptions of some of the more controversial groups, including the People's Temple, Branch Davidians, Solar Temple, AUM Shinrikyo, and Heaven's Gate. Many other observers have taken similar approaches. As reflected in such titles as *Millennialism, Persecution, and Violence* and *Millennium, Messiahs, and Mayhem* and in numerous scholarly articles, millenarianism has been central to these discussions—though it should immediately be noted that contemporary analysts of NRMs and violence are generally careful to "eschew single-factor explanations" (Bromley 2004, 154). Other factors usually considered in attempts to construct a general model of NRM-associated violence are high-demand organization (meaning that participants do not have the option of being casual, part-time members), charismatic leadership, isolation from the surrounding society, and the threatening role played by external forces such as hostile apostates and intrusive governmental authorities. (For a comprehensive discussion, refer to *Cults, Religion, and Violence* [2002], edited by David G. Bromley and J. Gordon Melton.)

At present, the relatively mature state of this body of literature makes it possible to ask different sorts of questions. Specifically, rather than a straightforward comparison of the five principal groups, what if one focused instead on the three groups that imploded in group suicides—People's Temple, Solar Temple, and Heaven's Gate? Although it is true that both the People's Temple and the Solar Temple also engaged in acts of murder, it could be argued that these violent acts were aspects of the suicide event. It is thus possible to distinguish such suicide-related murders from the otherwise comparable violence initiated by the leadership of AUM Shinrikyo and other groups.

It is often more illuminating to "complexify" rather than to simplify certain phenomena, but for my purposes I will focus on distilling the details of these three groups down to a common core of shared traits. Though this approach is open to criticism—and would certainly never do for a comprehensive explanation—it nevertheless bears fruit as an analytical strategy.

As a preliminary move, it should be noted that neither Shoko Asahara (the leader of AUM Shinrikyo) nor David Koresh (the leader of the Branch Davidians) seriously contemplated suicide. When authorities finally located Asahara in a secret room at AUM Shinrikyo's Mount Fuji center, they also found him with an abundant stash of money that he planned to use to support himself into the foreseeable future. And though Koresh seems to have been willing to die a martyr's death, it also appears he was ready to embrace martyrdom only if all other options (or, perhaps more accurately, all other reasonable options within the horizon of his religious ideology) were closed. The fact that during the siege at Mount Carmel Koresh retained a literary attorney to handle his story should be enough to indicate that he envisioned himself living into the postsiege future—not to mention his explicit assertion to FBI negotiators a few days before the final assault that "I never intended to die in here."

Millenarianism

To turn our attention to the People's Temple, the Solar Temple, and Heaven's Gate, what happens when we ruthlessly cut away everything except the bare-bones structure shared by the three "suicide cults"? Surprisingly, the first trait to drop out is millenarianism. Though it is quite possible to argue that Jim Jones was a millenarian, in point of fact he had no theology in the proper sense, much less a developed eschatology. Well before the establishment of Jonestown, he had become little more than a secular socialist in religious garb. Even as people lined up to drink a mixture of cyanide and Kool-Aid during the final drama, Jones exhorted his followers with the assertion that "this is a revolutionary suicide; this is not a self-destructive suicide," rather than consoling them with visions of the afterlife—though, as Jonathan Z. Smith notes, one can also point to portions of the audiotape made during the event that intimate they would be reunited in a postmortem state (1982, 117). I am aware that this assertion flies in the face of almost all other scholarly approaches to the Jonestown suicides. The point being made here thus calls for more discussion.

Millennial movements in the proper sense, to cite Norman Cohn's classic study, always picture the millennium as something "that is to be accomplished by, or with the help of, supernatural agencies" (1970, 15). Even current definitions of millenarianism typically mention such agencies. However, as in the following excerpt from an encyclopedia of NRMs, the People's Temple is included as a example of a millenarian group, despite Jim Jones's nonbelief in divinities of any sort:

> The terms "millenarianism" and "millennialism" are usually applied to the study of apocalyptic beliefs. They refer to the expectation of imminent world transformation, collective salvation, and the establishment of a perfect, new world of harmony and justice to be brought about by otherworldly beings acting in accordance with a divine or superhuman plan. . . . Millenarian ideas associated with new religions often include the belief that the transformation of the present world will be cataclysmic; the worldview (referred to variously as catastrophic millennialism, apocalypticism or premillennialism) expresses a pessimistic view of humanity, maintaining that the world is fatally flawed and unredeemable by human effort, and that only a divinely ordained world cataclysm can usher in a millennial age of peace and prosperity. Groups such as the Branch Davidians, AUM Shinrikyo and the People's Temple exemplify catastrophic millenarian views. (Wojcik 2004, 388)

One can, of course, redefine religion to encompass secular visions or redefine millenarianism to include secular phenomena (as the editors and some of the contributors do in Thomas Robbins and Susan J. Palmer's 1997 book, *Millennium, Messiahs, and Mayhem*). The problem with such approaches is that as soon as one expands millenarianism to include nonreligious phenomena, then one can legitimately ask: Why stop with survivalism, feminism, and radical environmentalism (three groups examined in the Robbins and Palmer collection)? Almost any group of people that looks forward to a better tomorrow—including educators and mainstream political parties—could conceivably be viewed

as millenarian. At this level of generality, however, millenarianism becomes almost meaningless as a category of analysis.

We should also note that millenarianism in the primary
sense described by Norman Cohn involves a salvation that is
"terrestrial, in the sense that it is to be realized on this earth and
not in some other-worldly heaven" (1970, 15). At the time of their
dramatic "exits," however, *not one* of the three suicide groups examined here envisioned returning to a paradisiacal era that
would be established on this planet.

In spite of the line of argument I have been pursuing in the
preceding paragraphs, I am not necessarily opposed to redefin-
ing millenarianism to encompass either secular phenomena or
extraterrestrial millennia. Rather, my purpose here is simply to
call into question the axiomatic assumption of most analysts that
millennial ideology is a *core* characteristic of contemporary violent groups, *essential* for understanding their violence. And
though readers may be hesitant to restrict the scope of millenarianism, the issues raised in the present discussion should nevertheless cast doubt on the adequacy of this concept as a primary
category for interpreting NRM-related violence—especially if we
are able to find other more compelling factors that can explain
group suicides.

External Provocation and Social Isolation

Shifting our attention from the People's Temple to Heaven's
Gate, we encounter another surprise when we subject Marshall
Applewhite and company's dramatic exit to the same kind of
analysis, namely, pressing external threats, whether real or imagined, are not the essential factors necessary for a group suicide.
In all four of the other new religions to be engulfed by violence,
hostile outsiders were a major factor precipitating each tragedy—
though none was quite as dramatic as the military assault on
Mount Carmel. The press criticism and governmental scrutiny
directed against the Solar Temple and the People's Temple were
mild by comparison.

In the case of Heaven's Gate, the group suicide was set in motion by the seemingly innocuous speculation of UFO buffs that a
large UFO was approaching Earth in the wake of the Hale-Bopp
comet. It seems that Applewhite had already decided some years
prior that he and his followers would make their exit via a group
suicide. Thus, he was predisposed to interpret any indication that

the "space brothers" were coming as a sign that it was time to leave. Although "the Two" (as Applewhite and his partner, Bonnie Lu Nettles, often referred to themselves) had received hostile media coverage in their early years and even feared assassination—at one point, they purchased weapons for fear of being attacked—these were not factors in March 1997 when Applewhite decided they would exit the planet. This is not, of course, to downplay the important role hostile external forces play in the precipitation of most NRM-related violence, only to make the point that this kind of intrusion by the outside world is not essential to all such violence.

To finally shift our attention to the Solar Temple, yet another trait seemingly shared by all of the new religions involved in violence drops out—namely, the group's social isolation. It is the social dynamics of the segregated (usually communal) worlds of certain alternative religions that allow extreme actions to be contemplated, whether the internally directed violence of Heaven's Gate or the externally directed violence of AUM Shinrikyo. The Solar Temple, in contrast, was only semisegregated from the larger society. Although Joseph Di Mambro established his early Pyramid group as a communal organization, the Solar Temple tended to be only partially communal. Thus, for instance, when the Solar Temple was establishing a "survival farm" in Canada, only a half-dozen members actually lived in the group's headquarters. The rest lived outside the house and took their meals there. Yet other members scattered about Quebec traveled to the house once a month for a meeting that took place on the full moon. Perhaps more important, many Solar Temple members were wealthy and socially established—belonging to "the elite of the Francophone west" (Daniels 1999, 147)—people who could have been only partially separated from the larger society without arousing suspicion.

Nevertheless, one could argue that the leader's distance from the voices of all but his closest followers was an essential factor contributing to his radical actions. In fact, Di Mambro tended to stay behind the scenes surrounded by a core of staunch loyalists, even bringing Luc Jouret into the Solar Temple for the purpose of interacting with outsiders. This finally brings us to a core trait of suicide cults, namely, a charismatic leader who surrounds himself with absolutely loyal followers and does not permit any overt disagreement with the group's ideology.

Here the analysis begins to sound rather like a cult stereotype. Focusing on the personality of the leader—usually portrayed, as we have seen, as a warped megalomaniac—is a staple in anticult discussions of NRMs. In contrast, mainstream scholars tend to include an analysis of the leadership as but one factor among others, such as a given group's social dynamics, ideology, and other less personal factors. Of course, the leadership must interact with the membership in order to have any kind of organization at all. But in the NRMs we have been discussing, the leader is clearly the epicenter. And the quest for commonalities among suicide groups has boiled down to commonalities among their leaders. So though I am not unmindful of group dynamics, and would never downplay the importance of external factors, for the sake of simplifying this analysis I will focus narrowly on the leadership.

Di Mambro, Jones, and Applewhite

What can we say about Jim Jones, Joseph Di Mambro, and Marshall Applewhite? If we again try to eliminate everything except shared traits, Applewhite undermines the stereotypical image of the cult leader because he neither demanded to live a better lifestyle than his followers nor attempted to seduce any of them (even before he was castrated). It also seems that Applewhite did not feel particularly bitter toward the people who left Heaven's Gate. And he apparently did not cultivate a distance between himself and his followers. In all of these particulars, he was quite different from Jones and especially from Di Mambro.

What all of these men *did* share was (1) an intolerance of any perspective other than their own, (2) a need for total commitment—if not absolute obedience—from their followers (all three seem to have been "control freaks" to a greater or lesser extent), and (3) a greater or lesser paranoia about external forces threatening them or their group. And although, as we saw with the Solar Temple, it is not essential that the entire group be segregated from the larger society, self-destructive leaders typically surround themselves with loyalists who effectively isolate them from external input. At this point, however, we are faced with the problem of finding what makes these men *different* from other NRM leaders. Although, unlike the three suicide group leaders, David Koresh seems to have regularly interacted with people outside of his community, Shoko Asahara was every bit as isolated from external reality as Di Mambro, Applewhite, and Jones. Furthermore, Asahara demanded total obedience, was extremely intolerant of other views, and was paranoid about real and imagined enemies. Yet Asahara apparently never contemplated suicide.

So where does that leave us? Though we have managed to identify some essential common traits via comparison and contrast, a factor that sets the Solar Temple, the People's Temple, and Heaven's Gate apart from AUM Shinrikyo and the Branch Davidians seems to have eluded us. Discovering this additional factor requires that we shift our focus away from the traits of NRMs frequently discussed in the literature and toward less commonly discussed characteristics. What did Di Mambro, Applewhite, and Jones share that distinguished them from Koresh and Asahara?

Some years ago while researching Heaven's Gate for an analysis of the strategies by which Marshall Applewhite legitimated suicide, I came across several sources that mentioned his health was failing (for example, Perkins and Jackson 1997, 81). Also, Catherine Wessinger points out that Applewhite never considered the option of appointing a successor who could lead the group after his passing, which likely made the group suicide option more attractive (2000, 81). At the time, these seemed like minor factors in explaining the Heaven's Gate tragedy.

In the context of the current discussion, however, these become major factors because they are precisely the traits that set the suicide groups apart from the others. In terms of health, Di Mambro was "suffering from kidney failure and incontinence as well as severe diabetes, and he believed he had cancer" (Wessinger 2000, 221). And Jones—either because he was sedating a genuine physical problem or because he had become a self-destructive addict—was gradually destroying himself with excessive prescription tranquilizers. Thomas Robbins emphasized the importance of a charismatic leader's health in a personal communication to John Hall when the latter was researching and writing *Apocalypse Observed* with Philip Schuyler and Sylvaine Trinh, though Hall quickly passed over the subject after mentioning Robbins's communication in the latter part of his book (2000, 193). It is easy to understand how Hall, focused as he was on other aspects of NRMs, would have failed to perceive the health of the charismatic leader as a major explanatory factor. In the context of the current discussion, however, the observation that Applewhite, Di Mambro, and Jones were in failing health, whereas Koresh and Asahara were not, makes this factor suddenly stand out as important: if the three suicide leaders all perceived themselves as dying, then the notion of bringing the whole group along on their postmortem journeys might strike them as attractive.

In addition to their physical deaths, all three men knew that their respective groups not only had stopped growing but were also likely to decline precipitously in the future, particularly after they died. Neither Applewhite (as noted) nor Jones (apparently) had given serious thought to grooming a successor. Di Mambro, on the other hand, seems for many years to have thought his daughter Emmanuelle would inherit his mantle. By twelve years of age, however, she was already rebelling against the script her father had imagined her fulfilling, effectively frustrating whatever desire he might have had for a legacy. By the time of the "transit," he had also come to nurse an exaggerated hatred for the "barbarian, incompetent and aberrant" Jouret, an obvious person to take over should Di Mambro pass from the scene (Introvigne and Mayer 2002, 177).

To summarize the above discussion into a list of traits, we can say that, based on an analysis of the People's Temple, the Solar Temple, and Heaven's Gate, the essential characteristics of a suicide group are:

1. Absolute intolerance of dissenting views
2. Members must be totally committed
3. Exaggerated paranoia about external threats
4. Leader isolates him- or herself or the entire group from the nonbelieving world
5. Leader's health is failing—in a major way, not just a transitory sickness
6. There is no successor and no steps are being taken to provide a successor, or, alternatively, succession plans have been frustrated
7. The group is either stagnant or declining, with no realistic hopes for future expansion

As noted earlier, there are numerous points of overlap with AUM Shinrikyo and the Branch Davidians. However, despite major areas of overlap, both of these groups lack several essential traits. Specifically, David Koresh did not segregate himself from unbelievers and was in good health immediately prior to the ATF raid on Mount Carmel. Koresh had also fathered a number of children he believed would eventually rule the earth—in effect, his successors. Asahara seems to have been in reasonably good health as well, plus he had already indicated to followers that his children would be his spiritual successors (though it should be noted that this successorship was rather vague at the time of the subway attack and clarified only later). Finally, though neither AUM Shinrikyo in 1995 nor the Branch Davidians in 1993 was experiencing rapid growth, they were also not stagnant; both could have reasonably anticipated future growth. In other words, the Davidians lacked traits 4, 5, 6, and 7, whereas AUM Shinrikyo lacked 5, 6, and 7.

One final point that needs to be addressed before concluding is the problem raised by the suicides of other Solar Temple members in the years following the original murder-suicides. As Massimo Introvigne and Jean-François Mayer argue, "After the second and third tragedies of 1995 and 1997, it became even more apparent that Di Mambro's manipulative behavior could not have been the only explanation for the OTS process of self-destruction" (2002, 178). There were also several Heaven's Gate members who took their own lives in the years following the mass suicide of that group.

These later suicides could be marshaled to support a position that the role of the leadership is less central for interpreting the original group suicides than I have been arguing here. However, this hypothetical position ignores the fact that a number of *new* influences came into play that are *more* important for understanding the actions of members who survived the initial suicide event. Perhaps most important, participants who had been deeply involved in the Solar Temple or Heaven's Gate would have believed a vital part of their lives had been lost in the wake of the departure of the group. They would also have had to endure the ridicule heaped on their religion by the mass media. Finally, in the exit videos left behind by Heaven's Gate and in the "testaments" left behind by the Solar Temple, survivors were explicitly invited to follow the group into the beyond. In other words, surviving members were acting under a new constellation of influences that make their suicides highly problematic as a basis for interpreting the original suicides.

References

Abgrall, Jean-Marie. *Rapport sur l'Eglise de scientology: Les techniques de la scientology, la doctrine dianetique de la, leurs consequences medico-legals.* Submitted in Criminal Prosecution for Fraud, case no. 90: 6119074, Higher Court of Marseilles. 1990.

An Account of the Conflagration of the Ursuline Convent. Boston: "Printed for the Publisher," 1834.

Anthony, Dick. "Religious Movements and Brainwashing Litigation: Evaluating Key Testimony." In *In Gods We Trust,* edited by T. Robbins and D. Anthony. New Brunswick, NJ: Transaction, 1990.

———. "Pseudoscience and Minority Religions: An Evaluation of the Brainwashing Theories of J. M. Abgrall." *Social Justice Research* 12, no. 4 (December 1999): 421–456.

Anthony, Dick, and Thomas Robbins. "Brainwashing and Totalitarian Influence." In *Encyclopedia of Human Behavior,* edited by V. S. Ramchandran. San Diego: Academic Press, 1994.

———. "Conversion and 'Brainwashing' in New Religious Movements." In *The Oxford Handbook of New Religious Movements,* edited by James R. Lewis. New York: Oxford University Press, 2003: 243–297.

Anthony, Dick, Thomas Robbins, and Jim McCarthy. "Legitimating Repression." *Society* 17, no. 3 (March–April 1980).

Arnold, Thomas. *Observations on the Nature, Kinds, Causes, and Prevention of Insanity.* London: Richard Phillips, 1806.

Arrington, Leonard J., and David Bitton. *The Mormon Experience.* New York: Alfred A. Knopf, 1979.

Arrington, Leonard J., and John Haupt. "Intolerable Zion: The Image of Mormonism in Nineteenth Century American Literature." *Western Humanities Review* 22, no. 3 (Summer 1968): 243–260.

Asch, Solomon E. "Studies of Independence and Conformity: A Minority of One against a Unanimous Majority." *Psychological Monographs* (1956).

Associated Press. "Banned Sect Joins Long Chinese History of Religious Repression." July 22, 1999.

Bainbridge, William Sims. "Religious Insanity in America: The Official Nineteenth-Century Theory." *Sociological Analysis* 45, no. 3 (Fall 1984).

Barber, T. X. "Antisocial and Criminal Acts Induced by Hypnosis: A Review of Experimental and Clinical Findings." *Archives of General Psychiatry* 5 (1961): 301–312.

———. *Hypnosis: A Scientific Approach.* New York: Litton, 1969.

Barker, Eileen. *The Making of a Moonie: Brainwashing or Choice?* Oxford: Basil Blackwell, 1984.

———. "Religious Movements: Cult and Anticult since Jonestown." *Annual Review of Sociology,* 12 (1986): 329–346.

Beckford, James. "The Media and New Religious Movements." In *From the Ashes: Making Sense of Waco,* edited by James R. Lewis. Lanham, MD: Rowman and Littlefield, 1994.

Beecher, Lyman. *Plea for the West.* Cincinnati, OH: Truman and Smith, 1835.

Belisle, Orvilla A. *The Prophets; or, Mormonism Unveiled.* Philadelphia, PA: W. M. White Smith, 1855.

Bell, Alfreda Eva. *Boadicea: The Mormon Wife.* Baltimore, MD: Arthur R. Orton, 1855.

Benson, Dr. Samuel. "Testimony of Dr. Samuel Benson." *Katz v. Superior Court,* 73 Cal. App. 3d 952141, Cal. Rptr. 234 (1977).

Berger, Peter L. *The Social Construction of Reality.* Garden City, NY: Doubleday, 1966.

Bergesen, Albert. *The Sacred and the Subversive.* Storrs, CT: SSSR Monograph Series, 1984.

Brigham, Amariah. *Observations on the Influence of Religion upon the Health and Physical Welfare of Mankind.* Boston: March, Capen, and Lyon, 1835.

Bromley, David G. "Violence and New Religions." In *The Oxford Handbook of New Religious Movements,* edited by James R. Lewis. New York: Oxford University Press, 2004.

Bromley, David G., and J. Gordon Melton, eds. *Cults, Religion and Violence.* New York: Cambridge University Press, 2002.

Bromley, David G., and James T. Richardson. *The Brainwashing/Deprogramming Controversy.* New York: Edwin Mellen, 1983.

Bromley, David G., and Anson D. Shupe Jr. *Strange Gods: The Great American Cult Scare.* Boston: Beacon Press, 1981.

Bromley, David, Anson Shupe Jr., and J. C. Ventimiglia. "Atrocity Tales, the Unification Church, and the Social Construction of Evil." *Journal of Communication* 29, no. 3 (1979): 42–53.

Bunker, Gary L., and David Bitton. "Mesmerism and Mormonism." *BYU Studies* 15, no. 2 (Winter 1975): 146–170.

———. *The Mormon Graphic Image, 1834–1914: Cartoons, Caricatures and Illustrations.* Salt Lake City: University of Utah Press, 1983.

Cardno, J. A. "The Aetiology of Insanity: Some Early American Views." *Journal of the History of the Behavioral Sciences* 4, no. 2 (April 1968).

"Cases of Insanity—Illustrating the Importance of Early Treatment in Preventing Suicide." *American Journal of Insanity* (January 1845).

The Charlestown Convent: Its Destruction by a Mob on the Night of August 11, 1834. Boston: Patrick Donahoe, 1870.

Clark, John. "Investigating the Effects of Some Religious Cults on the Health and Welfare of Their Converts." Testimony to the Special Investigating Committee of the Vermont Senate. 1976.

———. "Cults." *Journal of the American Medical Association* 242, no. 3 (1979).

Clark, John G., Jr., Michael D. Langone, Robert E. Schecter, and Roger C. G. Daily. *Destructive Cult Conversion: Theory, Research and Treatment.* Weston, MA: American Family Foundation, 1981.

Cohn, Norman. *The Pursuit of the Millennium.* 1957. Reprint, London: Oxford University Press, 1970.

———. *Cosmos, Chaos and the World to Come: The Ancient Roots of Apocalyptic Faith.* New Haven, CT: Yale University Press, 1993.

Condon, Richard. *The Manchurian Candidate.* New York: McGraw-Hill, 1958.

Conn, J. "The Myth of Coercion under Hypnosis." In *Eriksonian Approaches to Hypnosis and Psychotherapy,* edited by J. Zeig. New York: Brunner-Mazel, 1982.

Conrad, Peter, and Joseph W. Schneider. *Deviance and Medicalization: From Badness to Sickness.* St. Louis, MO: C. V. Mosby, 1980.

Conway, Flo, and Jim Siegelman. *Snapping: America's Epidemic of Sudden Personality Change.* New York: Lippincott, 1978.

———. "Information Disease: Have Cults Created a New Mental Illness?" *Science Digest* 90, no. 1 (1982).

Daniels, Ted, ed. *A Doomsday Reader: Prophets, Predictors, and Hucksters of Salvation.* New York: New York University Press, 1999.

Davis, David Brion. "Some Themes of Counter-Subversion: An Analysis of Anti-Masonic, Anti-Catholic, and Anti-Mormon Literature." *Mississippi Valley Historical Review* 47, no. 2 (September 1960).

Demos, John Putnam. *Entertaining Satan.* New York: Oxford University Press, 1982.

Edwards, Chris. *Crazy for God.* Englewood Cliffs, NJ: Prentice-Hall, 1979.

Eliade, Mircea, ed. *Encyclopedia of Religion.* New York: Macmillan, 1987.

Farber, I. E., H. F. Harlow, and L. J. West. "Brainwashing, Conditioning and the DDD Syndrome." *Sociometry* 29 (1957): 271–285.

Fromm, E., and R. Shor. *Hypnosis: Developments in Research and New Perspectives.* New York: Aldine, 1979.

Frothingham, Charles W. *The Convent's Doom: A Tale of Charleston in 1834.* Boston: Graves and Weston, 1854.

Gauld, A. *A History of Hypnotism.* Cambridge: Cambridge University Press, 1992.

Hall, John R., with Philip D. Schuyler and Sylvaine Trinh. *Apocalypse Observed: Religious Movements and Violence in North America, Europe, and Japan.* London: Routledge, 2000.

Hinkle, Lawrence, and Harold Wolff. "Communist Interrogation and the Indoctrination of 'Enemies of the State.'" *AMA Archives of Neurological Psychology* 76 (1956): 117–127.

Hunter, Edward. *Brainwashing in Red China.* New York: Vanguard, 1951.

———. *Brainwashing: From Pavlov to Powers.* New York: Bookmaster, 1960.

Introvigne, Massimo. "Falun Gong." In *Odd Gods: New Religions and the Cult Controversy,* edited by James R. Lewis. Amherst, NY: Prometheus Books, 2001.

Introvigne, Massimo, and Jean-François Mayer. "Occult Masters and the Temple of Doom: The Fiery End of the Solar Temple." In *Cults, Religion and Violence,* edited by David G. Bromley and J. Gordon Melton. New York: Cambridge University Press, 2002: 170–188.

Kehoe, Alice Beck. *The Ghost Dance: Ethnohistory and Revitalization.* New York: Holt, Rinehart, and Winston, 1989.

Kirsch, I. Foreword to *Hypnosis: A Scientific Approach,* by T. X. Barber. New York: Jason Aronson, 1995.

Lanternari, Vittorio. *The Religions of the Oppressed: A Study of Modern Messianic Cults.* New York: Mentor, 1956.

Lestz, Michael. "Why Smash the Falun Gong?" *Religion in the News* 2, no. 3 (1999).

Levine, Saul. *Radical Departures: Desperate Detours to Growing Up.* New York: Harcourt Brace Jovanovich, 1984.

Lewis, James R. "Reconstructing the 'Cult' Experience: Post-involvement Attitudes as a Function of Mode of Exit and Post-involvement Socialization." *Sociological Analysis* 42, no. 2 (Summer 1986): 151–159.

———. "Apostates and the Legitimation of Repression: Some Historical and Empirical Perspectives on the Cult Controversy." *Sociological Analysis* 49, no. 4 (Winter 1989): 386–396.

Lewis, James R., and David G. Bromley. "The Cult Withdrawal Syndrome: A Case of Misattribution of Cause?" *Journal for the Scientific Study of Religion* 26, no. 4 (December 1987): 508–522.

Lewis, James R., ed. *From the Ashes: Making Sense of Waco.* Lanham, MD: Rowman and Littlefield, 1994.

————. *The Gods Have Landed: New Religions from Other Worlds.* Albany: State University of New York Press, 1995.

Lifton, Robert. *Chinese Thought Reform and the Psychology of Totalism.* New York: Norton, 1961.

Martin, Paul. "Post-cult Recovery: Assessment and Rehabilitation." In *Recovery from Cults,* edited by Michael Langone. New York: Norton, 1993.

Martin, Walter. *The New Cults.* Santa Ana, CA: Vision House, 1980.

Melton, J. Gordon. *The Encyclopedic Handbook of Cults in America.* 2d ed. New York: Garland, 1992.

Milgram, Stanley. *Obedience to Authority.* New York: Harper and Row, 1974.

Miller, Jesse. "The Utilization of Hypnotic Techniques in Religious Conversions." *Cultic Studies Journal* 3 (1986): 243–250.

Monk, Maria. *Awful Disclosures of the Hotel Dieu Nunnery of Montreal.* 1836. Reprint, New York: Arno Press, 1977.

Mooney, James. *The Ghost-Dance Religion and the Sioux Outbreak of 1890.* Abridged ed. 1896. Reprint, Chicago: University of Chicago Press, 1965.

Mosk, Stanley, et al., David Molko and Tracy Leal v. the Holy Spirit for the Unification of World Christianity, 762 P. 2d 46 (Cal. 1988).

Ofshe, Richard. "Report Regarding Mr. Steven Fishman." Submitted for the Court case *U.S. v. Fishman,* 743 F. Supp. (N.D. Cal.90) (1989).

Ofshe, Richard, and Margaret Singer. "Attacks on Peripheral vs. Central Elements of the Self and the Impact of Thought Reform Techniques." *Cultic Studies Journal* 3 (1986): 2–24.

O'Gorman, Edith. *Convent Life Unveiled.* Ca. 1871. Reprint, London: Lile and Fawcett, ca. 1881.

Orne, Martin. "The Potential Uses of Hypnosis in Interrogation." In *The Manipulation of Human Behavior,* edited by A. Biderman and H. Zimmer. New York: Wiley, 1961.

————. "Antisocial Behavior and Hypnosis." In *Hypnosis: Current Problems,* edited by G. Estabrooks. New York: Harper and Row, 1962.

OTS. "To All Those Who Can Still Understand the Voice of Wisdom . . . We Address This Last Message." *Gnosis,* no. 34 (Winter 1995).

Paloutzian, R., J. Richardson, and L. Rambo. "Religious Conversion and Personality Change." *Journal of Personality* 67 (1999): 1047–1049.

Patrick, Ted, with Tom Dulack. *Let Our Children Go!* New York: E. P. Dutton, 1976.

Perkins, Rodney, and Forrest Jackson. *Cosmic Suicide: The Tragedy and Transcendence of Heaven's Gate.* Dallas, TX: Pentaradial Press, 1997.

Pfeifer, Jeffrey E. "The Psychological Framing of Cults: Schematic Representations and Cult Evaluations." *Journal of Applied Social Psychology* 22 (1992): 531–544.

Reed, Rebecca Theresa. *Six Months in a Convent.* Boston: Russel, Odiorne, and Metcalf, 1835.

Richardson, James. "A Social Psychological Critique of 'Brainwashing' Claims about Recruitment to New Religions." In *The Handbook of Sects and Cults in America, Religion and the Social Order* 3B, edited by D. Bromley and J. Hadden. Greenwich, CT: JAI Press, (1993): 98.

Robbins, Thomas, and Dick Anthony. "Sects and Violence." In *Armageddon in Waco,* edited by Stuart Wright. Chicago: University of Chicago Press, 1995.

Robbins, Thomas, and Susan J. Palmer, eds. *Millennium, Messiahs, and Mayhem: Contemporary Apocalyptic Movements.* New York: Routledge, 1997.

Robertson, George. "Island Pond Raid Begins New Pattern." In *Sex, Slander and Salvation,* edited by James R. Lewis and J. Gordon Melton. Stanford, CA: Center for Academic Publishing, 1994.

Robinson, Bruce. "Falun Gong and Falun Dafa." 1999. http://www.religioustolerance.org/falungong.htm.

Rothenberg, Paula. "The Prison of Race and Gender: Stereotypes, Ideology, Language, and Social Control." In *Racism and Sexism,* edited by Paula Rothenberg. New York: St. Martins, 1988.

Schein, Edgar. "The Chinese Indoctrination Program for Prisoners of War: A Study of Attempted 'Brainwashing.'" In *Readings in Social Psychology,* edited by E. Maccoby et al. New York: Holt, 1958.

———. "Brainwashing and the Totalitarianization of Modern Societies." *World Politics* 2 (1959): 430–441.

———. *Coercive Persuasion.* New York: Norton, 1961.

Shapiro, Robert. "Of Robots, Persons and the Protection of Religious Beliefs." *So. Cal. Law Review* 6 (1983): 1277–1308.

Shaw, David. "From Headline to Prime Time." *TV Guide,* 1993.

Singer, Margaret. Testimony in *Robin and Maria George v. Int. Society for Krishna Consciousness of Cal. et al.* Orange County Superior Court, 1983.

———. "Thought Reform Exists: Organized, Programmatic Influence." *Cult Observer* 17, no. 4 (1994): 3–4.

Singer, Margaret, and Janja Lalich. *Cults in Our Midst: The Hidden Menace in Our Everyday Lives*. San Francisco: Jossey-Bass, 1995.

Singer, Margaret, and Richard Ofshe. "Thought Reform Programs and the Production of Psychiatric Casualties." *Psychiatric Annuals* 20, no. 4 (1990): 188–193.

Slotkin, Richard. *Regeneration through Violence: The Mythology of the American Frontier, 1600—1860*. Middletown, CT: Wesleyan, 1973.

Smith, Jonathan Z. *Imagining Religion: From Babylon to Jonestown*. Chicago: University of Chicago Press, 1982.

Snow, David, and Robert Machalek. "The Sociology of Conversion." *Annual Review of Sociology* 10 (1984): 167–190.

Sowards, Bruce A., Michael J. Walser, and Rick H. Hoyle. "Personality and Intelligence Measurement of the Church Universal and Triumphant." In *Church Universal and Triumphant in Scholarly Perspective*, edited by James R. Lewis and J. Gordon Melton. Stanford, CA: Center for Academic Publishing, 1994.

Spanos, Nikos. *Multiple Identities and False Memories: A Sociocognitive Perspective*. Washington, DC: American Psychological Association, 1996.

Sweetser, William. *Mental Hygiene; or, an Examination of the Intellect and Passions*. New York: George P. Putnam, 1850.

Terry, Robert J., and Catherine Manegold. "Krishna Complex Bombed." *Philadelphia Inquirer*, June 18, 1984.

Turner, Alice K. *The History of Hell*. New York: Harcourt Brace, 1993.

Verdier, Paul. *Brainwashing and the Cults*. North Hollywood, CA: Wilshire, 1980.

Wach, Joachim. *Sociology of Religion*. Chicago: University of Chicago Press, 1944.

Ward, Maria. *Female Life among the Mormons*. New York: J. C. Derby, 1855.

Wessinger, Catherine. *How the Millennium Comes Violently: From Jonestown to Heaven's Gate*. Chappaqua, NY: Seven Bridges Press, 2000.

Whitney, Louise Goddard. *The Burning of the Convent*. 1877. Reprint, New York: Arno Press, 1969.

Wojcik, Daniel. "Apocalypticism and Millenarianism." In *Encyclopedia of New Religions: New Religious Movements, Sects, and Alternative Spiritualities*, edited by Christopher Partridge. Oxford: Lion Publishing, 2004: 388–395.

Wong, John, and William T. Liu. *The Mystery of China's Falun Gong: Its Rise and Its Sociological Implications*. Singapore: World Scientific Publishing and Singapore University Press, 1999.

2

Chronology

The contemporary cult controversy did not get under way until the early 1970s. However, in spite of certain unique themes—such as the emphasis on brainwashing—there are clear links between the current debate and earlier periods of religious controversy. Even the portrayal of Catholics and Mormons in the nineteenth century bears certain strong parallels to the manner in which minority religions are viewed in the present period. The following chronology takes account of these parallels by noting the beginnings of some important religious movements and key events in the persecution of minority religions prior to the 1970s.

1830 Founding of the Church of Jesus Christ of Latter-day Saints (LDS)—popularly known as the Mormon Church—in Palmyra, New York.

1831 William Miller begins preaching. Millerism becomes a wildly popular movement that soon evokes harsh criticism from the established churches. Although the movement comes to an end in 1844 with the Great Disappointment, remaining members of the movement found the Adventist Church.

1834 The Ursuline Convent in Charleston, outside of Boston, is attacked and burned to the ground by a Protestant mob.

1838 The governor of Missouri declares, "The Mormons must be treated as enemies, and must be exterminated or driven

1838
cont. from the State if necessary, for the public peace." The state militia raids Haun's Mill, a small Mormon settlement, immediately killing seventeen men, women, and children. Some of the wounded die later.

1844 Joseph Smith is assassinated while in protective custody at the county jail in Carthage, Illinois. Mormon residents of Illinois subsequently abandon their homes and flee westward to territories unknown under the leadership of Brigham Young.

Violent anti-Catholic riots overturn civil order in Philadelphia. The riots leave several dozen people dead and a number of Catholic churches in the city burned to the ground.

1848 The Hydesville rappings at the home of the Fox sisters out of which modern spiritualism originates.

1853 Brigham Young announces the doctrine of plural marriage, a tenet that scandalizes the rest of the nation and sets the stage for further persecution of the LDS Church.

1858 The so-called Utah War of 1858. Federal troops are sent to Utah to establish non-Mormon rule over Mormons.

1860 Ellen White founds the Seventh-Day Adventist (SDA) Church, bringing together various groups that had formed in the wake of the Great Disappointment.

1875 The Theosophical Society is founded in New York City.

1878 *Reynolds v. United States* case reaches the U.S. Supreme Court. The Court decides against polygamy, asserting that although Congress cannot prescribe laws against what one may *believe*, it may legislate against *actions*.

1879 Christian Science is founded in Lynn, Massachusetts, by Mary Baker Eddy. Christian Science was controversial almost from the very beginning. The church's stance against medical treatment brought it into the spotlight again in the 1980s in a series of child-endangerment cases.

1880   The Oneida Community, a highly successful religious communal experiment that had lasted for more than three decades, dissolves. The community had survived fierce external criticism because of its controversial practice of complex marriage, but it could not survive the disbelief of its second generation.

1882   Henry M. Teller, secretary of the interior, orders that all "heathenish dances" and ceremonies be ended because of their "great hindrance to civilization." With the following years, this order—which basically forbids the practice of traditional Native American religions—is gradually implemented.

1887   Congress disincorporates the LDS Church in Utah, appropriating all church property not used for liturgical purposes. The church sued but lost at the Supreme Court level in 1889, in *Mormon Church v. United States* and *Romney v. United States*.

         Founding of the American Protective Association, the largest and most active anti-Catholic organization of the late nineteenth century.

1888   Founding of the Order of the Golden Dawn, an important ceremonial magical group that influences all subsequent magical groups and, indirectly, neopagan witchcraft.

1890   More than 300 peaceful Sioux Ghost Dancers—men, women, and children—are massacred at Wounded Knee by the U.S. military.

         The LDS Church suspends its controversial policy of polygamy under intense pressure from the U.S. government.

1893   The World's Parliament of Religions takes place in Chicago. This event is remarkable for giving Asian

1893
cont.
religions a foothold in North America, particularly Buddhist and neo-Hindu groups.

1894
The Vedanta Society, the oldest Hindu group in the United States, is established in New York.

1906
The Azusa Street Revival, out of which Pentecostalism emerges, takes place.

1909
Birth of snake-handling movement under the leadership of George W. Hensley.

1913
Noble Drew Ali founds the Moorish Science Temple in Newark, New Jersey.

1918
Incorporation of the Native American Church, the first formal organization representing a much earlier pan-Indian religion that, among other things, utilized peyote to enhance religious experiences.

1920
Paramahansa Yogananda, founder of the Self-Realization Fellowship and one of the first Hindu teachers to come to the West, arrives in the United States.

1923
The Arcane School, an important form of Theosophy that influences the New Age movement, is founded by Alice Bailey.

1930
Master Fard Muhammad (W. D. Fard), to whom the Nation of Islam traces its origins, teaches in Detroit.

1931
Edgar Cayce founds the Association for Research and Enlightenment.

1932
Franklin D. Roosevelt appoints John Collier as commissioner of Indian affairs. Collier lifts prohibitions against traditional Native American religious practices.

1934
Elijah Muhammad becomes leader of the Nation of Islam, a Black Muslim group, originally established in Detroit in 1930, that will later become famous with the emergence of Malcolm X as a public spokesperson.

Guy and Edna Ballard begin the public teaching of what will become the I AM Activity.

1935   Victor T. Houteff founds the Shepherd's Rod colony, which will become the Davidian Seventh-Day Adventists, outside Waco, Texas.

1937   Makiguchi Tsunesaburo founds Soka Kyoiku Gakkai, which later becomes Soka Gakkai International.

1938   The first important Supreme Court victory for the Jehovah's Witnesses, in the case of *Lovell v. City of Griffin*, gives Witnesses permission to distribute literature despite an ordinance requiring a permit for such distributions.

1939   In England, Gerald B. Gardner establishes the kernel of what will become the modern neopagan movement.

1940   A significant Supreme Court victory for the Jehovah's Witnesses in *Cantwell v. Connecticut*, a case that extended the freedom of religion clause to state governments and further served to call into the question the 1887 *Reynolds* decision giving government the power to regulate religious actions.

1942   The Way International, a Pentecostal, ultradispensational Christian group, is founded by Victor Paul Wierwille, a minister in the Evangelical and Reformed Church, as a radio ministry under the name of "Vesper Chimes." It assumed its present name in 1974. The Way remained relatively small until the "Jesus movement" of the early seventies.

1943   In this year four cases involving the right of Jehovah's Witnesses to canvass door to door reach the High Court. Three are decided in favor of the Witnesses (*Jones v. Oplika*, *Murdock v. Pennsylvania*, and *Martin v. Struthers*). The fourth case (*Douglas v. Jeannette*) is decided against the Witnesses, but on technical grounds.

Another case involving the refusal of Witnesses to salute the flag, *West Virginia State Board of Education v. Barnette*,

1943 cont. is decided the same year. *Barnette* is decided in favor of the Jehovah's Witnesses, overturning a related Supreme Court decision, *Minersville School District v. Gobitis*, made against the Witnesses in 1940.

1944 An important Supreme Court case involving the charge of mail fraud—based on the supposedly "ridiculous" nature of the group's religious beliefs—*United States v. Ballard*, was decided in favor of the I AM Activity.

1947 The modern UFO era begins when Kenneth Arnold sights nine objects in the sky near Mount Rainier, Washington. The story of Arnold's sighting is reported in newspaper articles almost immediately. The term *flying saucers* is first coined by headline writers for this story. Religious significance is almost immediately attributed to UFOs, particularly in the wake of claims by George Adamski to have received communications from—and even ridden with—the "space brothers."

1949 Paramahansa Yogananda's *Autobiography of a Yogi* is published.

In *Bunn v. North Carolina*, the court rules that public safety outweighs the concern for the free exercise of religion involving the handling of poisonous snakes. The U.S. Supreme Court dismisses the appeal.

1950 Publication of L. Ron Hubbard's *Dianetics: The Modern Science of Mental Health*.

1951 Journalist Edward Hunter formulates the "brainwashing" model to explain Communist Chinese influence over American POWs during the Korean War in his popular book *Brainwashing in Red China*.

1954 Gerald Gardner's *Witchcraft Today* is published, marking the emergence of Wicca as a public movement.

1955 The Church of Scientology begins operation in Washington, D.C. Next to the Jehovah's Witnesses, Scientology has been involved in more religious liberty litigation than any other minority religion in the twentieth century.

Jim Jones founds the Wings of Deliverance, which will later become the People's Temple, in Indianapolis, Indiana.

Publication of the influential *Urantia Book,* which some groups later adopted as scripture.

1956   George King founds the Aetherius Society.

1958   Two former members of the Wisdom, Faith, Love, and Knowledge Foundation show up at the group's main building, confront the leader, Krishna Venta, and blow up the building, killing themselves, Venta, and seven others.

Mark L. Prophet, who had been active in two I AM splinter groups, founds the Summit Lighthouse, in Washington, D.C. Elizabeth Clare Prophet becomes the messenger after Mark's passing in 1973, and Summit Lighthouse eventually expands to become the Church Universal and Triumphant (CUT).

1959   Muhammad Subuh, popularly known as Bapak, brings Subud to the United States.

Transcendental meditation is introduced in the West by Maharishi Mahesh Yogi.

A failed uprising in Tibet against Chinese rulers provokes a campaign of repression that causes religious leaders to flee the country. The exiles introduce Tibetan Buddhism to the West.

1960   Beginnings of neo-Pentecostalism under the leadership of Episcopal priest Dennis Barrett.

1961   In *Braunfeld v. Brown,* a leading "Sunday law" case, the Supreme Court decides against Orthodox Jewish merchants protesting Pennsylvania's Sunday closing laws.

1963   *Sherbert v. Verner,* a key case for what would become known as the "Sherbert-Yoder Test" for deciding free exercise of religion cases. In this case, the Supreme Court decides in favor of a Seventh-Day Adventist who was denied unemployment benefits because she had not been able to accept employment requiring work on Saturday.

Robert de Grimston founds the Process Church of the Final Judgment.

Beginnings of what becomes the channeling movement when Jane Roberts begins to receive messages from the disembodied entity Seth.

1965   President Johnson rescinds the Asian Exclusion Act, a law that had prevented the large-scale immigration of Asians into the United States. The door allowing Asian spiritual teachers to enter the United States is thus thrown wide open.

A. C. Bhaktivedanta Swami, founder of the Hare Krishna movement, journeys to the United States at the behest of his guru to establish Krishna consciousness in the West.

Malcolm X is assassinated.

1966   Anton LaVey announces the formation of the Church of Satan. Highly theatrical but not actually dangerous, the existence of the Church of Satan provides a concrete target for conservative Christians with vague fears about the machinations of the Prince of Darkness.

1967   Catholic charismatic movement begins among students at Duquesne University in Pittsburgh, Pennsylvania.

The Jesus movement begins among counterculturists in California.

1968   The Church of All Worlds, organized by Oberon Zell, is incorporated and in 1971 becomes the first neopagan group to win federal tax-exempt status, the state ruling against it being overturned as unconstitutional.

David Berg, better known as Father David, initiates a coffeehouse ministry in Huntington Beach, California, that eventually becomes the Children of God, later called the Family.

Yogi Bhajan moves to Toronto and then to Los Angeles. The next year, 1969, he founds an ashram and the Healthy, Happy, Holy Organization (3HO) to teach kundalini yoga. Corporately, 3HO is later supplanted by Sikh Dharma.

1969   Benchmark U.S. Court of Appeals decision, *Founding Church of Scientology v. United States,* recognizes Scientology as a bona fide religion. This case marks the high point in a conflict with the Food and Drug Administration (FDA) that had begun dramatically in 1963 with an armed FDA raid during which Church of Scientology "E-Meters" and literature were seized. In 1971, the Court orders the FDA to return the seized materials.

Manson family murders take place, though Charles Manson is not arrested until 1971. The early anticult movement will point to the actions of the Manson family as the most dramatic example of what cults are capable of, despite the fact that Manson and his followers are not a religion and present a very different sociological profile from the groups later stigmatized as "cults."

Paul Erdmann, who adopts the name Love Israel, founds the Church of Armageddon in the state of Washington.

Aumism is founded in France by Gilbert Bourdin, who adopts the name Lord Hamsah Manarah.

1970   The cult controversy proper did not get under way until after the collapse of the sixties counterculture. Rather than reengaging with mainstream society, many former counterculturists continued their quest for an alternative

1970   lifestyle in a wide variety of religions. Hence, the mem-
cont.   bership of many unusual religious groups that had ex-
        isted quietly on the margins of U.S. society experiences
        sudden surges in numbers, laying the groundwork for
        the emergence of the cult issue.

        Chogyam Trungpa Rimpoche, a Tibetan lama, begins to
        establish meditation centers in the United States.

        First visit to the United States by Swami Muktananda.
        His followers are later organized as the Siddha Yoga
        Dham.

        Sun Bear begins to organize what becomes the Bear Tribe.

1971   Ted Patrick begins the practice of deprogramming,
        which, along with the formation of the first anticult or-
        ganization the next year, marks the emergence of the
        modern cult controversy.

        Erhard Seminars Training, more commonly known as est,
        is begun by Werner Erhard. Although not a church or reli-
        gion, est will often be accused of being a "psychotherapy
        cult."

        The Reverend Sun Myung Moon arrives in the United
        States. Although missionaries had been in the country
        since the 1950s, it was only with the arrival of Moon that
        the Unification Church begins to grow dramatically.

        Guru Maharaj Ji, the youthful leader of the Divine Light
        Mission, arrives in the United States.

        Stephen Gaskin founds the Farm in Summertown, Ten-
        nessee.

        Oscar Ichazo founds the Arica Institute.

1972   William Rambur and his wife, together with Ted Patrick
        and other concerned parents, establish the Parent's Com-
        mittee to Free Our Children from the Children of God

Organization (later shortened to FREECOG), the first modern anticult organization.

Richard Alpert (aka Baba Ram Das) publishes *Be Here Now*, regarded by some observers as signaling the beginning of the New Age movement.

Ervil LeBaron, founder of the polygamy-practicing Church of the Lamb of God, orders the murder of his brother Joel LeBaron, founder and leader of the Church of the First Born of the Fullness of Times. More violence follows. In 1979, Ervil is arrested and convicted of murder.

Wisconsin v. Yoder, a key case for what would become known as the "Sherbert-Yoder Test" for deciding free exercise of religion cases. In this case, the Supreme Court decides that a state law mandating high school education is an excessive burden on the Amish religion.

Marshall Applewhite and his partner, the founders of what eventually becomes Heaven's Gate, first attract national attention when thirty people pick up and leave with them after a lecture in Waldport, Oregon.

Franklin Jones, currently known as Avatar Adi Da Samraj, opens a small ashram in Los Angeles that becomes the starting point for Adidam.

Bob Weiner organizes the Maranatha movement.

Jesus People USA (JPUSA) is founded in Chicago, Illinois.

1973   The Divine Light Mission, a rapidly expanding religious group from India that had attracted considerable negative media attention, holds its disastrous Millennium '73 gathering at the Houston Astrodome. Too few people show up, and the mission goes into debt. Although the movement continues, it never recovers its momentum.

Claude Vorilhon, who later adopts the name Rael, founds what becomes the Raelian movement.

1974   "Flirty fishing," the controversial practice of witnessing that could involve sexual relations, is introduced by the Children of God. This practice is eventually abandoned, but not before it attracts extensive negative media attention.

Establishment of Citizen's Freedom Foundation (CFF), a West Coast anticult organization, by William Rambur (one of the founders of FREECOG). CFF, which later changed its name to the Cult Awareness Network, grew to become the umbrella organization for anticult activity in the United States.

The National Council of Churches issues a resolution on deprogramming that is highly critical of the practice.

The Symbionese Liberation Army kidnaps newspaper heiress Patricia Hearst, who is later forced to participate in a bank robbery. She surrenders to authorities the following year, claiming she was a victim of brainwashing.

1975   The Covenant of the Goddess is established as a California nonprofit corporation on Halloween with the intention that it will serve the neopagan movement nationally as a legal church. It is the largest organization serving this purpose.

Michael Aquino founds the Temple of Set as a schism from the Church of Satan.

Claude Rex Nowell establishes Summum, a neo-Egyptian group.

1976   Responding to a petition from his constituents, Senator Bob Dole holds hearings on the Unification Church. The meeting was not a formal congressional hearing and led to no governmental action.

Publication of Ted Patrick's *Let Our Children Go!*—the first and only significant book on deprogramming.

1977   The FBI raids the Washington, D.C., and Los Angeles branches of the Church of Scientology, seizing many files. The raid is declared illegal, but the documents remain in government possession, where they are open to public scrutiny.

Katz v. Superior Court, also called the "Faithful Five–Faithless Four" case (the principal cult conservatorship case), is decided in favor of parents seeking conservatorships for their five adult offspring who are members of the Unification Church—only to have the appeals court overturn the decision almost immediately. Four out of the five individuals leave the church.

JZ Knight, the most popular—as well as the most controversial—channel during the heyday of the New Age movement in the late 1980s, encounters Ramtha, a spiritual entity believed to have lived on earth approximately 35,000 years ago. Knight first publicly operates as a channel the next year.

1978   Jim Jones, leader of the People's Temple, orchestrates a "revolutionary suicide" at the communal agricultural settlement called Jonestown in the South American country of Guyana. More than 900 people—mostly black, some white—die from drinking a deadly poison. Almost overnight, the People's Temple replaces the Manson family as the primary example of what all "cults" are capable of doing.

Louis Farrakhan leaves the American Muslim Mission with several thousand followers and reestablishes the Nation of Islam as instituted by Elijah Muhammad.

An attorney suing the Synanon Church is bitten by a rattlesnake that had been placed in his mailbox by Synanon members.

The Parent-Teacher Association officially adopts an "anticult" stance by issuing a "Resolution on Pseudo-Religious Cults" during its national convention.

1978
cont.
Publication of Flo Conway and Jim Siegelman's *Snapping*, a popular book presenting anecdotal evident for "information disease," a unique mental illness supposedly caused by cultic mind control techniques.

Enactment of the American Indian Religious Freedom Act, a legislative measure intended to affirm traditional Native American religiosity. It is subsequently judged a failure.

1979
A second unofficial hearing on the dangers of cults is sponsored by Senator Bob Dole. The testimony at this hearing is more extensive and volatile, but, in the end, it has no more effect than the first hearing.

Publication of first edition of Starhawk's *Spiral Dance* and Margo Adler's *Drawing Down the Moon*, books that simultaneously document and further stimulate the expansion of the neopagan movement.

The Boston Church of Christ is founded by Kip McKean.

1980
A new concern about the possible presence of Satanism in the United States centered on the sexual abuse of children in Satanic rituals is initiated by the publication of *Michelle Remembers*.

1981
Thomas v. Review Board, a U.S. Supreme Court decision. In this case, a Jehovah's Witness who had quit his job rather than work in an armaments factory had been denied unemployment benefits. The court decided in favor of the Jehovah's Witnesses.

Heffron v. International Society for Krishna Consciousness. This is a Supreme Court decision supporting the state's right to require solicitors to be confined to a booth rather than to wander about at the state fair.

Range purchased in Antelope, Oregon, by followers of Bhagwan Shree Rajneesh (who later adopts the name Osho) that becomes Rajneeshpuram.

1982   The Reverend Sun Myung Moon is convicted and subsequently incarcerated on tax evasion charges. The Unification Church decries the case as religious persecution.

Larson v. Valente Supreme Court case is decided in favor of the Unification Church against a solicitation law that targeted new religious groups.

1983   An insurgent group of racial separatists, mostly Identity believers, known as the Order, or the Silent Brotherhood, begins a wave of crimes preparatory to the launching of attacks on the federal government. Between 1984 and 1986, the members of the Order were captured and tried, and its leader, Robert Matthews, was killed in a shootout with the FBI.

Confrontations between law enforcement authorities and a North Dakota Posse Comitatus leader and Identity believer, Gordon Kahl, result in the deaths of two federal marshals.

A young boy in the House of Judah, a black Hebrew group, is beaten to death, attracting national media attention. The mother of the boy is eventually sentenced to prison for manslaughter.

The American Family Foundation (AFF) begins publication of the *Cultic Studies Journal,* an academic journal publishing research supporting the notion of cultic brainwashing. AFF, a latecomer anticult organization that came into being in the late 1970s, quickly establishes itself as the scholarly wing of the anticult movement.

1984   The Island Pond raid occurs, in which the community's children are taken from the Northeast Kingdom in Vermont. They are almost immediately released.

1985   After years of controversial activity at Rajneeshpuram, his Oregon commune, Bhagwan Rajneesh (Osho) is charged with immigration fraud and deported back to India.

1985   Federal law enforcement authorities besiege and capture
cont.   the commune of a heavily armed paramilitary Identity
          group in Arkansas, the Covenant, Sword, and Arm of the
          Lord, with no loss of life.

          The Way International's tax-exempt status is revoked fol-
          lowing allegations of partisan political involvement and
          certain business activities at its New Knoxville headquar-
          ters. The ruling is reversed by the Supreme Court in 1990.

          The Local Church wins a libel case against authors who
          had accused the church of being a "destructive cult." The
          Spiritual Counterfeits Project, a Christian anticult group
          that published one of the books, was driven to bank-
          ruptcy in the face of an $11 million judgment.

          MOVE, a black communal group in urban Philadelphia,
          is fire-bombed by the city and destroyed. MOVE is sub-
          sequently labeled a "political cult."

1986   *Molko and Leal v. Unification Church* is decided in favor of
          the Unification Church. This was one of the most impor-
          tant cases involving lawsuits leveled against controver-
          sial religions by ex-members. The Court decides in favor
          of the Unification Church and against notions of coercive
          persuasion cited by the plaintiffs. However, three years
          later after a number of appeals, the case was on the verge
          of being tried by the California Supreme Court. Rather
          than go through a new trial, the church finally settled out
          of court in November 1989.

          The Vatican issues the *Vatican Report on Sects and New Re-
          ligious Movements*. The World Council of Churches
          (WCC)/Lutheran World Federation issues a parallel re-
          port, *Summary Statements and Recommendations*.

          John Wimber organizes the Association of Vineyard
          Churches in the Los Angeles area.

1987   The city of Hialeah, Florida, enacts a ban against "animal
          sacrifice" directly aimed at the growing Santeria com-
          munity of the city. One Santeria house challenges the

ban, and in 1993 the Supreme Court unanimously declares the Hialeah ordinance unconstitutional in *Church of Lukumi Bablu Aye v. City of Hialeah.*

This is a benchmark year for media awareness of the New Age movement. Early in the year, Shirley MacLaine's miniseries *Out on a Limb* airs. In August, the media report on the Harmonic Convergence gatherings. In the fall, *Time* publishes an influential issue featuring a cover story on the New Age movement.

The American Psychological Association (APA) rejects the report of the task force on "deceptive and indirect methods of persuasion and control," a group of professionals with anticult leanings who had initiated the task force in an effort to win official support for the notion of cultic mind control. This effort later backfires when the APA rejection of the report is cited in the *Fishman* decision.

1989   In an attempt to avoid negative publicity, two members of Church Universal and Triumphant attempt to acquire otherwise legal weapons in a nonpublic, illegal manner. They are arrested, and the result is a public relations disaster.

Bodies discovered on the grounds of a ranch near Matamoros, Mexico, not far from the Texas border, make headlines. The murders, which are associated with a drug-smuggling operation, are immediately linked to Satanic worship.

The Aquarian Concepts Community is founded by Gabriel of Sedona (Tony Delevin) in Sedona, Arizona.

1990   Members of Church Universal and Triumphant from around the world gather in Montana because of the predicted possibility of an atomic holocaust. Montana is flooded by reporters from around the world eager for sensationalist stories on a "doomsday cult."

The Supreme Court rules against the right of Native American Church members to use peyote in *Employment Division v. Smith.*

1990   After a detailed review of their "coercive persuasion"
cont.   ideas, the U.S. District Court, in *United States v. Fishman*,
        rejects Dr. Margaret Singer and Professor Richard Ofshe
        as expert witnesses on mind control. This is a benchmark
        case that is subsequently used to disqualify Singer and
        Ofshe from testifying in other cult cases.

1991   *Time* publishes a front-page story attacking the Church of
        Scientology. The next year, the church files a major law-
        suit against *Time* after discovering that the maker of
        Prozac—a psychiatric drug that Scientology had been ac-
        tive in opposing—had ultimately been responsible for
        the *Time* article.

        Tony Alamo, cofounder of the Alamo Christian Founda-
        tion (Music Square Church), is arrested.

        Emergence of Soka Gakkai as an independent organiza-
        tion following a formal split with Nichiren Shoshu.

1992   Church Universal and Triumphant's federal tax-exempt
        status is revoked on the basis of a minor item from an
        earlier lawsuit that the church had lost to an ex-member.
        This status is restored two years later.

        The FBI arrests deprogrammer Galen Kelly in connection
        with a conspiracy to abduct Lewis DuPont Smith, heir to
        the DuPont fortune. The arrest represents an important re-
        versal of the longtime policy of law enforcement officials to
        turn a blind eye to deprogramming as a "family matter."

        The FBI releases Kenneth V. Lanning's influential report
        Investigator's Guide to Allegations of "Ritual" Child Abuse.
        This report, which dismisses the reality of Satanic ritual
        abuse, has been described as the most influential docu-
        ment on the subject ever written.

        Li Hongzi establishes Falun Gong as an independent
        organization.

1993   A force of seventy-six agents of the ATF raid the Branch
        Davidian community. The resulting standoff turns into a

fifty-one-day siege that ends when FBI agents launch a new attack on the Davidian complex. A fire ignites in the buildings, and more than eighty members die.

The Family (aka the Children of God) are subjected to a new wave of intensive negative media attention following raids on their homes in France and Argentina on trumped-up charges of child abuse.

In a landmark decision, the Internal Revenue Service ceases all litigation and recognizes the Church of Scientology as a legitimate religious organization.

Margaret Singer and Richard Ofshe file a lawsuit in federal court against the American Psychological Association, the American Sociological Association, and a group of individual scholars for conspiring to discredit them as expert witnesses. Their suit is thrown out of court on August 9.

Reacting to the Supreme Court's decision in *Employment Division v. Smith*, a broad coalition of religious groups support the Religious Freedom Restoration Act (RFRA), a legislative measure explicitly intended to reestablish pre-*Smith* standards for the free exercise of religion.

1994   Fifty-three people, members of the Order of the Solar Temple, are murdered or commit suicide in Switzerland and Canada.

The Movement of Spiritual Inner Awareness (MSIA) attracts the attention of the media after it is discovered that the wife of Michael Huffington—who at the time was running for senator—had been active in MSIA. In the same year, Peter McWilliams drops out of the movement and authors a bitter anti-MSIA book, *LIFE 102: What to Do When Your Guru Sues You.*

Start of the Toronto Blessing when the Reverend Rodney Howard Browne preaches at the Toronto airport Vineyard Church.

A long-standing libel case brought by Cynthia Kisser,

1994
cont. then leader of the Cult Awareness Network, against the Church of Scientology and its international president is dismissed in federal court. The case is similarly dismissed upon appeal in 1997.

After failing to make their case in federal court, Margaret Singer and Richard Ofshe refile their lawsuit against the American Psychological Association and others in California state court. The case is dismissed *with prejudice.*

1995 Poison-gas attack occurs in a Tokyo subway, killing twelve people and injuring many others. Within a few days of the attack, AUM Shinrikyo, a controversial Japanese religious group, is considered the most likely suspect.

When Cynthia Kisser, then director of the Cult Awareness Network, sued the Church of Scientology and its international president for libel in federal court, she simultaneously filed a libel case in Illinois state court. The state case is dismissed with prejudice in 1995.

The siege of an antigovernment group, the Montana Freemen, draws widespread media attention and comparisons with Waco but ends peaceably.

A small remnant of the Order of the Solar Temple commits suicide in France.

Report of the Commission of Inquiry on Sects—usually referred to as the *French Report*—is issued.

1996 Following a declaration of bankruptcy in the wake of losing a deprogramming-related lawsuit, the Cult Awareness Network name, mailing address, and phone number are purchased by the Church of Scientology.

The Liberal Democratic Party (LDP), the principal partner in Japan's ruling coalition, exploits fears generated by AUM Shinrikyo, attacks its chief rival—the New Frontier Party (NFP) that is associated with Soka Gakkai,

Japan's largest new religion—and scores big in the national election.

1997   The bodies of thirty-nine members of Heaven's Gate are found in a posh mansion outside San Diego, all victims of a mass suicide.

Responding to the Solar Temple murder-suicides that took place in Switzerland in 1994, the *Swiss Report* is released in February by the Canton of Geneva. Though more moderate in tone, its substantive proposals are more threatening than the *French Report*.

Additional members of the Order of the Solar Temple commit suicide in Quebec.

The International ("Boston") Church of Christ wins an important case against a newspaper in Singapore, where it is illegal to refer to a religious group as a "cult."

The Belgian parliamentary commission on cults issues its official report. The *Belgium Report* is even more extreme than the *French Report*, naming five mainline Catholic groups, the YWCA, Quakers, Hasidic Jews, and almost all Buddhists as dangerous cults.

1998   Death of the founder of Aumism, Gilbert Bourdin, better known as Lord Hamsah Manarah.

Chen Dao, a Taiwanese UFO group that expects God to manifest in Garland, Texas, attracts intense media attention as the press anticipates another Heaven's Gate–style mass suicide.

The Enquete Commission issues its final report, *New Religious and Ideological Communities and Psychogroups in the Federal Republic of Germany*.

The Ananda Church of Self-Realization files bankruptcy after years of fighting a copyright lawsuit with the Self-Realization Fellowship and lawsuits by disillusioned former members.

1999   Evidence emerges that, counter to earlier claims to the contrary, the FBI did use pyrotechnic military rounds on the day the Branch Davidian community caught fire.

China begins a crackdown on religious groups. Falun Gong responds by staging a peaceful demonstration and subsequently becomes the target of harsh repression. The Chinese legislature passes a resolution banning "cults."

Concerned Christians, a small doomsday group who believed the world would end in December 1999, is accused of being a suicide group and deported from Israel.

2000   The Movement for the Restoration of the Ten Commandments of God, a doomsday religious sect in Uganda, makes headlines in the wake of what was initially thought to be a mass suicide but was later determined to be a mass murder.

2001   Members of Al-Qaida, an extremist Muslim group, run airplanes into the World Trade Center Towers and the Pentagon. Some observers interpret this event as another example of cultic violence.

The About-Picard Law, a draconian piece of legislation giving the government full power to repress unpopular religious groups, is signed into law in France after intense debate.

A giant statue of Gilbert Bourdin, founder of Aumism, is destroyed by French officials.

In a clearly staged-for-television incident, Falun Gong followers supposedly attempt to commit suicide by setting themselves on fire in Tiananmen Square.

Rael, founder-leader of the Raelian movement, testifies in favor of human cloning at a U.S. Congress hearing.

2002   Neo-Phare, also known as the New Lighthouse Movement, founded by Arnaud Mussy, predicts the end of the world and is subsequently surrounded by police in

Nantes, France, who fear the group may commit mass suicide.

Two leaders of Portos, a utopian community near Lubertsy, southeast of Moscow, are convicted for carrying firearms and beating disobedient teenage members.

2003   Brigette Boisselier, head of a cloning business inspired by Rael, announces that Clonaid has successfully cloned the first human being.

Elizabeth Smart, a fifteen-year-old Mormon teenager kidnapped from her Salt Lake City home in 2002, is found. Her kidnapper, self-proclaimed prophet Brian Mitchell, is accused of having brainwashed Smart.

Herbert L. Rosedale, Esq., leader of the anticult movement in the United States, passes away from cancer.

Psychologist Margaret Singer, one of the primary architects of the notion of cultic brainwashing, dies after a long illness.

2004   Russia bans the activities of Jehovah's Witnesses and moves to liquidate them as a legal entity.

Shoko Asahara, founder of AUM Shinrikyo, is sentenced to death for directing the poison-gas attack on the Tokyo subway system in 1995.

Malachi York, leader-founder of the United Nuwaubian Nation of Moors is sentenced to 135 years in prison on charges of child molestation.

An anti-"brainwashing" law is proposed in Italy.

The Local Church's libel suit against John Ankerberg, his coauthor, and the publisher of the *Encyclopedia of Cults and New Religions* proceeds to trial.

3

Controversial Groups and Movements

Groups that have been labeled *cults* constitute a highly diverse set, both organizationally and doctrinally. The only feature that unites them is that they have in some way been involved in a public controversy. In fact, many small and otherwise innocuous minority religions have been drawn into the cult wars as the result of specific conflicts that have no intrinsic relationship with the wider anticult crusade.

For individuals or groups involved in certain kinds of struggles with members of minority religions, the cult stereotype represents a potent ideological resource that—if they are successful in making the label stick—marshals public opinion against their opponent, potentially tipping the balance of power in their favor. Situations in which this strategy can work are not restricted to the kinds of conflicts that are picked up by the news media. For example, the stigma of the cult stereotype has been effectively deployed in child custody cases, in which one parent's membership in a minority religion is portrayed as indicative of her or his unworthiness as a parent.

Relevant social-psychological research also indicates that once a stereotype has been accepted, it structures our perceptions so that we tend to notice information that conforms to our image of the stereotyped group and to neglect or forget other kinds of information. What this means for any given confrontation is that as soon as the label "cult" has been successfully applied (that is, accepted as appropriate by outsiders not directly involved in the conflict), the information that the public gathers is selectively appropriated so that almost every item of data conforms to the stereotype about cults, thus effectively marshaling moral support for the person or group locked in conflict with a minority religion.

In ordinary language, people talk as if there is an objective category of groups called "cults" that can be distinguished from genuine religions. In this commonly accepted view, cults are by definition socially dangerous false religions, led by cynical cult leaders who exploit followers for their own gain. This portrayal is, however, deeply flawed, as has already been indicated in the introductory essay. Although a handful of religious groups may fit the stereotype, "cult" is best understood as a socially negotiated label that frequently means little more than a religion one personally dislikes. For this reason, the inclusion of a particular religious organization in this reference book should *not* be taken as implying that it is thereby legitimate to refer to it as a "cult," as this term is popularly understood.

The following pages contain information on controversial groups and movements that run the gamut from tiny churches with fewer than 100 members to organizations like the Soka Gakkai that number into the millions. Also included are entries on broader, less centrally organized phenomena such as Santeria and the Identity Christian Movement.

Adidam

Adidam—referred to less formally as the "Way of the Heart" by followers—was founded by avatar Adi Da Samraj, born Franklin Jones on Long Island, New York, in 1939. In his autobiography, he says that he was born in a state of perfect freedom and awareness of ultimate reality but sacrificed that reality at the age of two in order to completely identify with human limitations. Jones spent his college and subsequent years pursuing spiritual truth, which eventually led him to Swami Muktananda and other gurus in that lineage. Jones says that he reawakened to his true state in 1970.

One of the central teachings of the Way of the Heart is that no form of seeking happiness is ever permanently successful, because the means of becoming happy are always transitory. In fact, Adi Da points out that seeking means constant activity, and that activity prevents the conscious realization of perfect happiness.

He further asserts that he has realized this most perfect happiness—God, truth, or reality—and has the power to transmit that divine self-realization to others. The Way of the Heart, then, consists of a devotional relationship with Adi Da, who his devotees assert is the source of divine self-realization. All the traditional means of religious life are employed as a means of "radical" understanding and devotional communion with Adi Da—meditation, study, ceremonial worship, community living, moral and ethical observances, and disciplines related to diet, health, sexuality, money, and so on.

Adi Da began to teach this "radical" understanding—a combination of discriminative self-observation and guru devotion—in 1972, opening a small ashram in Los Angeles. His method of working with his students was initially simple and traditional. Over time, however, it became clear that a different approach was necessary, and he switched to a "Crazy-Wise" teaching style. In 1979, he took the name Da Free John. In 1986, he changed his name to Swami Da Love-Ananda. He again changed his name in the late 1980s to Da Avabhasa (the Bright). Finally, in 1995, he became Adi Da.

Adidam became the subject of media attention for a time in the mid-1980s following the filing of a lawsuit by a disaffected former member who alleged that she had been mistreated in various ways while a member. In response to media interest, several other disaffected former members then publicly expressed their own complaints and questions about Adi Da and his way of teaching during the early years of Adidam. Members of Adidam responded by saying that the disaffected former members had simply misunderstood Adi Da's Crazy-Wise way of teaching. The media soon lost interest in the story, Adidam settled its differences with the former members, and the legal conflict was resolved.

The group's Web site is http://www.adidam.org.

Alamo Christian Foundation (Music Square Church)

The Alamo Christian Foundation, a Pentecostal church with doctrine similar to the Assemblies of God, was opened in 1969 in Hollywood, California, by Tony and Susan Alamo. It drew its early strength from the Jesus People movement. The foundation accepts the authority of the King James Version of the Bible and adheres to a strict moral code, condemning drugs, homosexuality, adultery, and abortions.

In the early 1970s, the Alamo Christian Foundation became controversial and was heavily criticized because of what was viewed as heavy-handed proselytizing. Church members worked the streets of Hollywood, inviting potential converts to evening services. The mostly young recruits were taken by bus to the foundation's rural community in Saugus for an evangelistic meeting and meal. Many of those who converted remained in Saugus to be taught the Bible and become lay ministers.

In 1976, the church moved its headquarters to Alma, Arkansas, where Susan Alamo had grown up. There it developed a community of several hundred members and established printing facilities, a school, and a large tabernacle. As the organization expanded further, churches were opened in other cities.

The church developed as an ordered community of people dedicated to evangelism. Converts who wish to receive the church's training and participate in its ministry take a vow of poverty, agreeing to turn over all real property to the church. In return, the church provides the necessities of life. Periodically, members are sent out on evangelistic tours around the United States, frequently using the established church centers as bases of operation. Services are held daily at each of the church centers, and free meals are generally served.

The church publishes a variety of evangelistic tracts that are passed out in the street and mailed. The church also distributes numerous tapes of sermons by Susan and Tony Alamo. Members include a number of talented musicians, and the church has produced a set of records and tapes featuring Tony Alamo and other members. A national television ministry was begun in the 1970s but has been largely discontinued. In 1981, Music Square Church was incorporated. It superseded the foundation in 1982.

To support itself and as part of its rehabilitation program, the church developed several businesses in which members, many of whom were former drug addicts, could begin a process of reintegration into society. A number of former members who later aligned themselves with the anticult movement complained that they should have been paid at least minimum wage for their work hours while members. These complaints led to a series of lawsuits. In 1985, the IRS stripped the Music Square Church of its tax-exempt status. The church went to court to fight this decision.

In 1988, Tony Alamo was accused of beating the eleven-year-old son of a member. Charges were filed and Alamo disappeared. During the next three years, while a fugitive from justice, Alamo moved about the country, frequently making calls to talk shows and even dropping into public offices for visits. Meanwhile, the church's property in Arkansas was seized to pay off court judgments against the organization. Tony Alamo was arrested in July 1991. The current status of the church, whose membership as of 1988 was approximately 400, is problematic.

The group's Web site is http://www.alamoministries.com.

Ananda Cooperative Community

The Ananda Cooperative Community, also known as the Ananda World Brotherhood Village, was founded in 1968 by Swami Kriyananda (J. Donald Walters) in Nevada City, California. Walters was born of American parents in Romania in 1926. He was educated in Romania, Switzerland, England, and the United States. At the age of twenty-two, he became a disciple of Paramahansa Yogananda and received the monastic name Kriyananda. He lived with Yogananda until the master's death in 1952. Kriyananda served as a minister, director of center activities, and vice president of the organization that Yogananda founded, the Self-Realization Fellowship. In 1962, he separated from the Self-Realization Fellowship to write, teach, and lecture on the implications of Yogananda's message for active yoga students and laypersons.

In 1968, Kriyananda founded Ananda Village near Nevada City, California, in response to Yogananda's directive to "cover the earth with world brotherhood colonies, demonstrating that simplicity of living plus high thinking lead to the greatest happiness." Ananda Village is situated at 2,600-feet elevation on 750 acres of wood- and meadowland in the Sierra Nevada foothills of northern California. Members support themselves through a variety of businesses, some of which are privately owned and some of which are owned and operated by the community. The community includes 600 people from many cultural, ethnic, and racial backgrounds. About twenty-five nationalities are represented. A village council is elected annually by Ananda members.

Ananda operates a guest facility called the Expanding Light, which is open year-round for personal retreats, training courses, special events, and holiday programs. Ananda members practice daily meditation using the techniques of *kriya* yoga as taught by Paramahansa Yogananda. Resident members are all disciples of Yogananda. The group is directly involved in a worldwide outreach to those interested in the teachings of Paramahansa Yogananda and his line of gurus.

Ananda has five branch residential communities and fifty centers and meditation groups throughout the world. Ananda's church congregation was established in 1990 and has 1,600 members. The church is open for membership to those who follow the teachings of Paramahansa Yogananda. The goal of the church is to provide fellowship and inspiration for those who want to find God through the practice of ancient *raja* yoga techniques that were brought to the West by Yogananda. In recent years, Ananda's church has been engaged in an ongoing legal conflict with the Self-Realization Fellowship, the U.S. organization founded by Yogananda and with which Kriyananda was formerly affiliated.

The group's Web site is http://www.ananda.org.

Aumism

Founded in 1969 by his holiness Lord Hamsah Manarah, Aumism is considered a religion of unity, representing a synthesis of all religions and spiritual movements. Its headquarters is located in the Holy City of Mandarom Shambhasalem in the Alps of Haute-Provence in France.

Born in a French family practicing traditional Catholicism, Hamsah Manarah was early attracted by mysticism and occult sciences. He later studied law, philosophy, economy, and medicine, while he dedicated his nights to esoteric research. In India, he stayed at Swami Sivananda's ashram, who transmitted the initiation of "Sannyasin" at Rishikesh in the Himalayas. At that time, he gave the name Hamsananda Sarasvati to Manarah. During his numerous trips, Lord Hamsah Manarah was initiated into Jainism; Sufism; different branches of Hinduism; Theravada, Mahayana, and Vajrayana Buddhism; Japanese Shingon; and certain African religions.

It was after this long initiatory journey, which led him to all the holy places of the earth, that Hamsah Manarah, known then

under the name of Shri Mahacharya Hamsananda Sarasvati, settled on a deserted mountain overlooking the small village of
Castellane in the Alps of Haute-Provence. Soon many curious
people arrived. Gradually, what began as a simple camp was
transformed into an ashram (spiritual center) and, eventually,
into the Holy City of Mandarom Shambhasalem. Temples and
statues from every religion were erected there. In 1990, Hamsah
Manarah announced to the world that he was the cosmoplanetary messiah, that is, a messiah whom all the traditions wait for.

Aumism promotes love among humanity and peace in the
world and believes in reincarnation according to the Law of the
Evolution of the Souls. A vegetarian diet is recommended for a
better spiritual journey, although it is not imposed. Aumism is
opposed to drugs, suicide, and what it views as sexual deviations
(polygamy and homosexuality). The Aumist religion has its
headquarters at the Holy City of Mandarom Shambhasalem.
About 50 monks and nuns live there permanently. Aumism is
organized into a church, with priests and priestesses (in the hundreds) and bishops (108). Anyone who receives baptism or the
transmission of the sound *OM* is regarded as an Aumist.

Controversy began in 1990 when Lord Hamsah Manarah revealed himself to the world as the cosmoplanetary messiah. The
international media, which gathered together for the occasion,
spread the news all over the world. The first attacks began at this
time. Since then, the police, the government, ecologists, and anticultists have focused attention on Lord Hamsah Manarah, the
Holy City of Mandarom Shambhasalem, and Aumism. Slanderous articles and reports, as well as fiscal controls and perquisi-
tions, were issued each month to discourage the Aumists. The
pyramidal temple that was supposed to attract the pilgrims from
all over the world was never built; the building permit that had
already been obtained was withdrawn before the beginning of
the work. Today the Aumists are harassed at their jobs, and some
of them have lost their employment.

The group's Web site is http://www.aumisme.org.gb.

AUM Shinrikyo (Aleph)

On March 20, 1995, a poison gas attack occurred on a Tokyo subway that killed twelve people and injured many others. Within a
few days of the attack, AUM Shinrikyo, a controversial Japanese

religious group, was fingered as the most likely suspect. The leadership was eventually arrested and the organization disbanded.

AUM Shinrikyo was founded by Master Shoko Asahara in Tokyo in 1987. A form of Tantric Buddhism, AUM Shinrikyo's teachings emphasized yoga practices and spiritual experiences. Master Asahara, whose original name was Chizuo Matsumoto (b. 1955), had traveled to India seeking enlightenment. Before returning to Japan, he sought out the Dalai Lama and received what he believed was a commission to revive true Buddhism in the land of his birth. By the time of the subway incident, AUM Shinrikyo had acquired a large communal facility near Mount Fuji and a following of approximately 10,000 members in Japan.

In addition to the usual teachings that go hand in hand with mainline Buddhism, Master Asahara was also fascinated with the future. His preoccupation with divination may have grown out of the weakness of his physical senses, as he was born blind in one eye, with only partial use of the other. Before undertaking yoga and meditation practices, Asahara pursued the study of such divinatory practices as astrology. Like many other Japanese spiritualists, he was fascinated by Western biblical prophecies as well as by the prophecies of Nostradamus. Perhaps influenced by the apocalyptic flavor of these predictions, Asahara himself began preaching an apocalyptic message to his followers. In particular, he prophesied a confrontation between Japan and the United States before the end of the century that would in all likelihood destroy his home country.

Asahara was, in fact, so certain about an impending conflict between Japan and the United States that he actually began preparing to wage war. Unable to match the conventional military might of the United States, AUM scientists investigated unconventional weapons, from biological agents to poison gas. This research is reflected in Asahara's last book, *Disaster Approaches the Land of the Rising Sun*, which contains page after page reflecting a very un-Buddhist interest in various forms of poison gas, including sarin.

In retrospect, it is clear that certain highly placed AUM members carried out the subway attack. The attack was motivated by increased police scrutiny of AUM Shinrikyo, with the idea of distracting police attention away from the movement. There had also been smaller-scale acts of violence carried out against the enemies of the group—in one case, poison gas was released near their Mount Fuji center in an attack on local critics. It was this latter assault that led the police to begin investigating AUM Shinrikyo in the first place.

In the end, it was Asahara's own pronouncements that drew police attention to AUM Shinrikyo. In particular, Master Asahara had predicted that gas attacks by terrorists would occur in the not too distant future. This made him an obvious target of suspicion. Hence the subway attack, far from diverting attention away from AUM Shinrikyo, actually had the opposite effect.

No active Web site is available for the group.

Black Judaism

Many African Americans have rejected the Christianity they associate with whites in favor of religions with more distinctively black identities. For centuries, a legend existed that black Jews, descendants of the queen of Sheba, had lived in Ethiopia but had long ago disappeared. The rediscovery in the late nineteenth century of the Falashas, the black Jews of Ethiopia, by French explorer Joseph Halevy, spurred some black people to elect Judaism as an alternative to Christianity.

The first African American Jewish denomination was started by William Saunders Crowdy, who preached that Africans were the descendants of the lost tribes of Israel and thus the true surviving Jews. By 1899, Crowdy had founded churches in twenty-nine Kansas towns. He called his denomination the Church of God and Saints of Christ, which, despite its Christian-sounding name, had from the start identified with Judaism. The Christ of the church's name refers to the awaited Messiah. As it evolved, the doctrine of the Church of God and Saints of Christ became a mixture of Jewish, Christian, and black nationalist precepts.

In 1915, Prophet F. S. Cherry established the Church of God in Philadelphia, Pennsylvania. Cherry was influenced by both the Church of God and Saints of Christ and the Temple of the Gospel of the Kingdom (another early black Jewish group). Cherry taught that God, who is black, originally created black humans, who were the descendants of Jacob. The first white person, Gehazi, became that way as the result of a curse. The church teaches that Jesus was a black man.

Arnold Josiah Ford was a self-proclaimed Ethiopian Jew and the choirmaster for Marcus Garvey, founder of the Universal

Negro Improvement Association. Ford later founded the Beth
B'nai Abraham congregation, which suffered financial problems
and collapsed in 1930. Ford then turned the membership over to
Rabbi Wentworth Matthew. Arthur Wentworth Matthew had
been a minister in the Church of the Living God, the Pillar and
Ground of Truth, a black Pentecostal church that had endorsed
the Universal Negro Improvement Association. In 1919, Matthew
and eight other men organized the Commandment Keepers:
Holy Church of the Living God. In Harlem, he had met white
Jews for the first time and in the 1920s came to know Arnold
Josiah Ford. Matthew began to study Orthodox Judaism, to learn
Hebrew, and to acquire ritual materials from Ford. Ford and
Matthew learned of the Falashas, the black Jews of Ethiopia, and
began to identify with them. When Ford's congregation ran into
financial trouble in 1930, the membership was put into
Matthew's care and Ford moved to Ethiopia.

The Original Hebrew Israelite Nation, or Black Israelites,
emerged in Chicago in the 1960s around Ben Ammi Carter (born
G. Parker) and Shaleah Ben-Israel. Carter and Ben-Israel were
proponents of Black Zionism whose purpose was a return to the
Holy Land. Beginning in the late 1960s, they made attempts to
migrate to Africa and then to Israel. More than 300 members of
the group had migrated to Israel by 1971, when strict immigration restrictions were imposed. Other members of the group continued to arrive using tourist visas.

The Nation of Yahweh, also called the Hebrew Israelites or
the Followers of Yahweh, was founded in the 1970s by Yahweh
ben Yahweh, who was born Hulon Mitchell Jr. Yahweh ben Yahweh was the son of a Pentecostal minister and at one point joined
the Nation of Islam. Yahweh ben Yahweh teaches that there is one
God whose name is Yahweh and who is black. Yahweh ben Yahweh says that he is the son of God, who has been sent to save and
deliver the black people of the United States. Black people are
considered to be the true lost tribe of Judah. In 1991, Yahweh ben
Yahweh and fifteen of his followers were arrested on a variety of
charges, including racketeering and conspiracy to commit murder. At a trial in the spring of 1992, Yahweh ben Yahweh and
seven of his codefendants were convicted of the conspiracy
charges but were not convicted of racketeering.

The group's Web site is http://www.yahwehbenyahweh.
com.

Black Muslims and the Nation of Islam

For many African Americans, Islam has provided an alternative to Christianity, which failed to establish a truly racially inclusive society. The growth of Islam among African Americans is related to the idea that Islam is a religious faith that affirms their African heritage. Most nonimmigrant Muslims in the United States are African American converts.

The Black Muslim movement began when Timothy Drew, who became known as Noble Drew Ali, founded the Moorish Science Temple in Newark, New Jersey, in 1913. Ali was exposed to black nationalist leader Marcus Garvey's ideas after 1917, and they became central to the movement's ideology. The Moorish Science Temple came to real prominence in Chicago in the 1920s. Temple members wore bright red fezzes and converted their slave names into new ones by adding the suffixes *el* or *bey* to them. After Garvey was deported in 1927, the Moorish American Science Temple wooed, and to a great extent won over, Garvey's followers.

The original Nation of Islam arose in Detroit in 1930. In that year Wali Farrad Muhammad (also called W. D. Fard) appeared and eventually established a temple in Detroit. Fard disappeared in 1934, and his top lieutenant, Elijah Muhammad, became the leader of the movement.

Under the leadership of Elijah Muhammad, the Nation of Islam grew into a strong, cohesive unit. Muhammad moved the headquarters to Chicago and opened temples, mosques, schools, housing projects, stores, restaurants, and farms. Many themes taught in the Nation of Islam reflected traditional Islamic teachings: submission to Allah and repudiation of alcohol, sex outside of marriage, the eating of pork, and gambling. Others ran counter to traditional Islam: the white man as devil, the identification of W. D. Fard as Allah and Elijah Muhammad as a prophet, and the quasi-scientific theory of human history and purpose. Muhammad taught that blacks were the original humans, but a rebellious scientist produced and released genetically weakened pale stock.

In the mid-1950s a former nightclub singer named Louis Eugene Wolcott joined the Nation of Islam. He dropped his last name and became known as Minister Louis X. His oratorical and musical skills carried him to a position in charge of the Boston mosque. Malcolm X, the most famous member of the Nation of Islam, was the charismatic leader of the New York temple. He was eventually expelled and shortly thereafter murdered.

When Nation of Islam leader Elijah Muhammad died in 1975, many members thought that Louis X, who was by then known by the name Abdul Haleem Farrakhan, would become the new leader of the Nation of Islam. However, Elijah Muhammad's son, Wallace, was chosen instead. During his first three years as the leader of the Nation of Islam, Wallace Muhammad brought the organization into mainstream Islam and away from the racial and black nationalist policies of his father. The organization went through a series of name changes and was eventually disbanded as an organization distinct from mainstream Islam.

The abandonment by Wallace Muhammad of his father's program was not accepted by all members. At least four splinter groups left Wallace Muhammad's group and formed their own congregations that adhered to Elijah Muhammad's original doctrines. The best known of them is headed by Louis Farrakhan, who, with several thousand followers, left in 1978 and reestablished the Nation of Islam as instituted by Elijah Muhammad.

The group's Web site is http://www.noi.org.

Branch Davidians

In 1979, Vernon Howell, later David Koresh, began participating in study sessions at a Seventh-Day Adventist church in Tyler, Texas, that his mother attended. There was a succession of incidents in which he preached his own version of SDA theology to other church members and took over the pulpit to propound his own theological views. Howell learned of the Branch Davidians—a small group that had splintered from the SDA in the 1930s—and began working as a handyman at their Mount Carmel center in 1981. He became a favorite of the leader, Lois Roden, who eventually named him as her successor.

Vernon Howell enunciated his controversial "New Light" doctrine in 1989. He asserted that as a messiah, he became the perfect mate of all the female adherents. Part of his mission was to create a new lineage of God's children from his own seed.

These children would ultimately rule the world. The New Light doctrine made all female Branch Davidians spiritual wives of Koresh. The doctrine had the effect of annulling the spousal sexual exclusivity of all marriages within the church.

In 1990, Vernon Howell legally adopted the name David Koresh. The word *Koresh* is Hebrew for Cyrus, the Persian king who defeated the Babylonians 500 years before the birth of Jesus. In biblical language, *Koresh* is *a* (not *the*) messiah, one appointed to carry out a special mission for God. By taking the first name David, he asserted his spiritual descent from the biblical King David. By 1992, Koresh had concluded that the apocalypse would occur in the United States rather than Israel, and the group began adopting a survivalist outlook, stockpiling large amounts of food, weapons, ammunition, and fuel. Koresh renamed the Mount Carmel community "Ranch Apocalypse."

The Branch Davidians retained a biblical base for their teachings, but the Bible was supplemented, and in certain respects supplanted, by revelations of the living prophet. They observed a Saturday Sabbath and eschewed meat, alcohol, caffeine, and tobacco. They rejected ostentatious dress and grooming, birthday celebrations, and television viewing. In contrast to Christ, who was sinless and therefore an impossible role model, Koresh was a "sinful messiah." Koresh taught that human sinfulness does not prevent humans from attaining salvation. He informed his followers that Armageddon would begin in the United States with an attack on the Branch Davidians.

Accusations of misbehavior on the part of Koresh and some other residents of the Branch Davidian headquarters began to circulate among anticultists and others. The accusations were those frequently used against many unconventional religions by their opponents: child abuse and possession of firearms. Local authorities investigated the child abuse allegations and found them groundless. The federal Bureau of Alcohol, Tobacco, and Firearms (ATF) of the Department of the Treasury obtained search and arrest warrants on the weapons charges.

On February 28, 1993, a force of seventy-six agents of the ATF raided the Branch Davidian compound. The raid turned into a shoot-out between federal agents and Branch Davidians, who chose to defend themselves. The resulting standoff turned into a fifty-one-day siege that ended on April 19 when federal agents launched a new attack on the Davidian complex. Agents of the federal government used military equipment to batter holes in buildings through which they injected noxious gas in an attempt to force the Davidians outside. A fire ignited in the buildings, and more than eighty members died.

The group's Web site is http://www.sevenseals.com.

Chen Tao

The Taiwanese religious movement known as Chen Tao was briefly in the news when its leader announced that God would appear on television on March 25, 1998, and then in person on March 31, 1998. In Chinese, *chen (zhen)* means "right" or "true," and *tao (dao)* means "way."

The history of Chen Tao goes back roughly four decades to a spiritual self-improvement association based in urban southern Taiwan, called the Association for Research on Soul Light. The group sought to locate, quantify, and cultivate spiritual light energy using technological devices and traditional Chinese practices like Qi Gong; its mixture of Buddhist-Taoism and high technology attracted a good number of students, academics, and white-collar professionals—several thousand by one account.

Among them was sociology professor Hon-ming Chen, who joined the association in the early 1990s. In it he found an explanation for his reportedly lifelong visions of spheres of golden light. Through these golden spheres God the Heavenly Father wished to communicate several things to him: first, that he had a special role to play as spiritual teacher and critic of degraded popular religion, and second, that he was to deliver messages about the end of the world and the return of Christ.

Chen succeeded to prophetic leadership of the group in 1995, refashioning Chen Tao's steady-state cosmology by coupling the Buddhist conception of reincarnation according to merit with a cyclical model of history, bringing in a biblical apocalypse as an exclamation point. According to Chen, the end time is brought about by the collective negative karma of all living beings. God, as a loving father, creates and re-creates the cosmos and sends Christ and Buddha, first to teach us, and then, at the end of each cycle, to save those who have followed the Right Way and attempted to rebalance their karmic books. But God also grants his children complete free will, allowing souls to take on bodies, to be seduced by the lusts of corporeality, and thus to create negative karma for themselves, to injure other living beings, and ultimately to propel the material cosmos to repeated destructions. Evidence provided by the damage to our natural environment and the degradation of our civilization is cited by Chen to bolster his claim that ours are the last days and Christ will soon arrive in God's space aircrafts.

He proclaimed that the Kingdom of God descended first on the group's headquarters in Taiwan in 1995 and then on the North American continent. One site in particular—Garland, Texas—was singled out by Chen as the location of the repeated creations and salvations of humanity. Chen moved to this Dallas suburb in the spring of 1997 and was followed by up to 160 Chen Tao members that fall. In Garland, Chen made public his prophecies concerning the two televised theophanies, statements that for several weeks in the spring of 1998 earned his group headlines around the world. The news media of their own accord, but also at Chen's earnest invitation, came in droves, hyping Chen Tao as the next Heaven's Gate.

When events failed to take place exactly as predicted on March 25, Chen held a press conference at his Garland home at which he stated that the news media and audience worldwide could consider the prophecy nonsense. However, he and his followers hung on until God's appearance on March 31. When the Heavenly Father once again did not appear as promised, press interest dissolved almost entirely, and many followers returned to Taiwan. A small remnant of the group moved to upstate New York in April 1998.

No active Web site is available for the group.

Christian Identity

The Christian Identity movement is a U.S. offshoot of an older religious movement, "British-Israelism" (also known as "Anglo-Israelism"). In an 1840 set of lectures, John Wilson argued that the British peoples were actually the descendants of the migrating ten lost tribes who had forgotten their true "identity." As developed by subsequent writers, British-Israelism posited a revisionist history of Britain and the ancient world and identified England as a divine instrument for the fulfillment of God's purposes.

By the late 1920s, the U.S. branch of British-Israelism had passed into the hands of a Massachusetts lawyer and organizer,

Howard Rand. Rand brought American British-Israelites under the umbrella of a new organization, the Anglo-Saxon Federation of America. His colleague in this enterprise was Henry Ford's publicist, William J. Cameron. Together, they linked the Anglo-Saxon Federation with explicitly right-wing political agendas.

With the end of the Second World War, the stage was set for the emergence of Christian Identity doctrine in southern California. Southern California had absorbed a number of British-Israel influences during earlier decades. The key figures in the emergence of Christian Identity—Bertrand Comparet, William Potter Gale, and, preeminently, Wesley Swift—were all associates of Gerald L. K. Smith. Based in Los Angeles, Smith was the most widely known anti-Semitic agitator of the 1940s and served as the center of an informal national network of those on the extreme right.

Christian Identity millenarian theology rejects the concept of a "rapture," in which the saved will be lifted off the earth before the period of violence (the "tribulation") that climaxes in Armageddon. Instead, Identity followers believe they must survive a period of violence and persecution under the Anti-Christ, a time they often characterize in terms of a race war.

Identity's most distinctive theological hallmark is its view of Jewish origins. Christian Identity asserts that Jews are the direct, biological descendants of Satan. They advance a myth of the Fall in which original sin consists of a sexual coupling between Eve and Satan or his humanoid instrument, begetting Cain, whom they call the first Jew. Hence, in addition to more traditional anti-Semitic motifs, Christian Identity adds a link with primal evil.

By defining the world in racial terms, Identity creates a universe in which the chosen few battle the evil world that surrounds them. In political terms, this vision of cosmic combat leads many Identity believers to identify state and national governments with the Jewish conspiracy and the forces of Anti-Christ. Although the expression of this antipathy is most often limited to the written and spoken word, it has sometimes erupted into acts of open defiance.

In 1983, confrontations between law enforcement authorities and a North Dakota Posse Comitatus leader and Identity believer, Gordon Kahl, resulted in the deaths of two federal marshals. In 1985, federal law enforcement authorities besieged and captured the commune of a heavily armed paramilitary Identity group in Arkansas, the Covenant, Sword, and Arm of the Lord, with no loss of life. In 1983–1984, an insurgent group of racial separatists known as the Order or the Silent Brotherhood engaged in a wave of crimes, mostly in the West, preparatory to the launching of attacks on the federal government. Half of its forty members were Identity believers. Between 1984 and 1986, the members of the Order were captured and tried (its leader, Robert Matthews, was killed in a shoot-out with the FBI), and with the organization's demise, the level of Identity-related violence dropped substantially. Nonetheless, because the movement is fragmented, the possibility of violent episodes in the future cannot be ruled out.

The group's Web site is http://www.aryan-nations.org.

Christian Science
(First Church of Christ, Scientist)

Christian Science was founded in Lynn, Massachusetts, in 1879 by Mary Baker Eddy (1821–1910). Eddy had always been troubled with poor health, which worsened during the 1860s. She tried a number of different alternative treatments, until finally she placed herself under the care of Dr. Phineas Parkhurst Quimby, a mental healer in Portland, Maine. She soon experienced some relief and became his student. However, after his death in 1866, she was periodically disturbed by the return of her illness and the conflicts between his ideas and those she found in the Bible.

The "biblical truth" was imparted while she was slowly and painfully recuperating from an injury that occurred when she slipped on an icy pavement in 1866. Her health was immediately restored, marking the beginning of Christian Science. She claimed that there was no healing agent, either magnetic force or mind, other than God and that God was the only life, which was the only reality of being. In the next few years, she began teaching and writing her first book, *The Science of Man*, and the presentation of her teaching, titled *Science and Health with Key to the Scriptures*.

Christian Science departs from orthodox Christianity in that it believes in what it terms the "allness of God" and hence the unreality of disease, sin, and death. It is believed that Christ does not defeat evil but demonstrates its lack of reality beyond our belief in it. The impersonal aspect of God as principle, mind, life, truth, and love is emphasized by Christian Science, which also distinguishes between the man Jesus and the eternal spiritual selfhood Christ, the Son of God, which the church regards as having been expressed by men and women throughout the centuries.

Christian Science has been attacked since the beginning of the movement. The major challenges to Christian Science came from a medical profession that, at the time of the founding of the church, was just consolidating its position as the normative authority on the treatment of illness in the United States. Numerous court cases were fought over the rights of Christian Scientists to refrain from the use of doctors and the rights of Christian Science practitioners to care for the sick.

During the 1980s, the issue of medical care for children was revived in a series of court cases across the United States, as Christian Science parents were accused of homicide, child abuse, and negligence. Cases of this kind forced judge and jury to consider as possibly criminal the behavior of loving parents who held deep religious beliefs against medical treatment. These cases had mixed results. For instance, a case from California led to the Supreme Court turning back a challenge to the prosecution of parents on the basis of religious freedom, whereas in Florida, a couple was convicted of third-degree murder, but after a long probation they were ordered to give their other children regular medical treatment. David and Ginger Twitchell were convicted of manslaughter in Massachusetts, another couple in California was convicted of child endangerment, while two other parents were acquitted in a similar case. Other cases filed against Christian Science were dismissed in Michigan and Minnesota and left inconclusive the status of parents who rely on Christian Science.

The group's Web site is http://www.tfccs.com.

Church of the First Born of the Fullness of Times; Church of the First Born; Church of the Lamb of God

The Church of the First Born of the Fullness of Times was incorporated in 1955 by brothers Joel, Ross Wesley, and Floren

LeBaron. The Church of the First Born was founded by Ross Wesley LeBaron after he left his brothers' church. The Church of the Lamb of God was founded by another LeBaron brother, Ervil, after he was dismissed from the Church of the First Born of the Fullness of Times.

The LeBaron family and its patriarch, Alma Dayer LeBaron, were members of the Church of Jesus Christ of Latter-day Saints. In 1934, one of Alma's sons, Benjamin LeBaron, claimed to be the One Mighty and Strong, the prophetic figure mentioned in Mormon writings, and several family members substantiated his claims as a prophet. In 1944, the LeBaron family was excommunicated from the Church of Jesus Christ of Latter-day Saints. The family then associated with the "fundamentalist" Mormon colony in Mexico directed by Rulon C. Allred, leader of the Apostolic United Brethren.

In 1955, the LeBarons left Allred's Mexican colony. Benjamin's brothers Joel, Ross Wesley, and Floren established the Church of the First Born of the Fullness of Times. Joel claimed to have the patriarchal priesthood and had a revelation directing Rulon C. Allred to become his councilor. Both Allred and Joel's brother Benjamin rejected Joel's claims.

Also rejecting Joel LeBaron's claim to patriarchal priesthood was his brother, and cofounder of the Church of the First Born of the Fullness of Times, Ross Wesley LeBaron. Ross Wesley left his brother's church and formed the Church of the First Born. The doctrine of the Church of the First Born states that the church was first established by Adam and restored in Joseph. It believes in One Mighty and Strong to come as presented in the doctrine and covenants. Ross Wesley LeBaron disincorporated the church in the early 1980s. Joel's claim to the patriarchal priesthood followed a line of succession through his father, Alma, to Alma's grandfather Benjamin F. Johnson, who was secretly ordained by founder Joseph Smith.

In 1970, the Church of the First Born of the Fullness of Times dismissed Ervil LeBaron, its second-highest-ranking officer and the brother of its leader, Joel LeBaron. Ervil formed the Church of the Lamb of God and claimed full authority over all of the polygamy-practicing groups, even going so far as to claim an authority to execute anyone who would refuse to accept him as the representative of God. Beginning with the establishment of the Church of the Lamb of God, a series of murders and assaults on polygamy-practicing Mormons began.

On August 20, 1972, Joel LeBaron, leader of the Church of the First Born of the Fullness of Times, was shot to death in Ensenada, Mexico. On June 16, 1975, Dean Vest, an associate of Joel LeBaron, was killed near San Diego, California. On May 10, 1977, Dr. Rulon C. Allred, leader of the Apostolic United Brethren, was murdered in his chiropractic office in Salt Lake City while attending patients. On May 14, 1977, an attempt was made on the life of Merlin Kingston, another polygamy leader. Thirteen other polygamy-practicing Mormons were killed before Ervil LeBaron was arrested for the murder of Rulon Allred. Ervil LeBaron was tried, convicted, and sentenced to prison in 1980. He died in prison of natural causes in 1981.

Joel LeBaron headed the Church of the First Born of the Fullness of Times from 1955 until he was murdered in 1972. He was succeeded by his brother Verlan, who led the church until his death in 1981. The current leader of the church is Siegfried Widmar. The Church of the First Born of the Fullness of Times has several hundred members, most of whom live in Mexico.

No active Web sites are available for any of the groups.

Church Universal and Triumphant (Summit Lighthouse)

The Church Universal and Triumphant (CUT) is a Montana-based New Age church led by Elizabeth Clare Prophet. In terms of negative media coverage, by the late 1980s it had become *the* most controversial new religion in North America.

Mark L. Prophet, who had been active in two I AM splinter groups, eventually founded his own group, the Summit Lighthouse, in Washington, D.C., in 1958. The orientation of the prophet's new group was the publication and dissemination of the masters' teachings. In the theosophical tradition, the spiritual evolution of the planet is conceived of as being in the hands of a group of divinely illumined beings (the ascended masters). In the tradition of earlier theosophical leaders, Mark Prophet viewed himself as serving as the mouthpiece for these ascended masters.

Elizabeth Clare Wulf joined the group in 1961, eventually marrying Mark Prophet. Over the course of their marriage, Elizabeth Prophet also became a messenger. After Mark's death in

1973, Elizabeth took over his role as the primary mouthpiece for the masters, as well as leadership of the organization.

The headquarters of Summit Lighthouse moved to Colorado Springs, Colorado, in 1966. In 1974, Church Universal and Triumphant was incorporated, taking over ministerial and liturgical activities, while Summit Lighthouse remained the publishing wing of the organization. After several moves within southern California, the church's headquarters was finally established on the Royal Teton Ranch, in Montana, just north of Yellowstone Park, in 1986.

When "cults" became a public issue in the mid-1970s, Church Universal and Triumphant was not particularly prominent. While still in southern California, several members were kidnapped and deprogrammed. One major lawsuit, brought against the church by ex-member Gregory Mull, cost CUT several million dollars. Despite these struggles and some media attacks, the group remained a relatively minor player in the cult wars until it moved its headquarters to Montana.

Much of the church's negative media attention derives from incidents clustered around its extensive fallout shelters and its preparations for the possibility of a nuclear attack against the United States. At one point in the construction, for instance, fuel stored in several underground tanks (which were sold to the church in defective condition) ruptured and spilled gas and diesel oil into the water table. In 1990, members from around the world gathered in Montana because of the predicted possibility of an atomic holocaust—a gathering that would have gone all but unnoticed had not a local paper painted it in sinister colors and broadcast the news through the Associated Press (AP) wire service to the world.

Also, in 1989, two high-level church members attempted to acquire otherwise legal weapons in a nonpublic, illegal manner (to be stored in the underground shelters). The motivation was to avoid the negative media exposure that would have resulted if members had purchased guns in Montana. The plan backfired and resulted in a public relations disaster. This series of incidents, particularly the gun purchase fiasco, was the basis for subsequent accusations that the Church Universal and Triumphant was a potential Waco.

In more recent years, Elizabeth Prophet has stepped down as the church's leader due to illness. The group is now run by a board of directors. The church has also reactivated its old name, the Summit Lighthouse, as the public face of the organization.

The group's Web sites are http://www.tsl.org and http://www.summitlighthouse.org.

Eckankar

Eckankar is a new religious movement founded by Paul Twitchell in California in 1965. It is currently an international organization headquartered in Minneapolis, Minnesota, with tens of thousands of members. Eckankar began with Paul Twitchell, who claimed that in 1956 he experienced God-realization when he was initiated by a group of spiritual masters known as the "Order of the Vairagi Masters" who live and work on a spiritual plane linked to the mystic East. Twitchell claimed that he was assigned the role of 971st living Eck master by these higher spiritual beings.

Twitchell officially organized and incorporated Eckankar in 1965, soon afterward moving its headquarters to Las Vegas, Nevada. For the next few years, he wrote and published several key books of Eckankar theology. Paul Twitchell died unexpectedly in 1971. His wife, Gail, together with the board of Eckankar, chose his successor as 972nd living Eck master—Darwin Gross. Gross and Gail married shortly afterward. Under their leadership, Eckankar grew and flourished. Its new headquarters was established at Menlo Park, California. Then there was a struggle for leadership in which Gross was deposed and succeeded as 973rd living Eck master by Harold Klemp.

A vision led Klemp and his right-hand man, Peter Skelskey, to move the headquarters of Eckankar to a suburb of Minneapolis, where the multimillion-dollar world Temple of Eck was built in the late 1980s. Under Klemp and Skelskey, Eckankar has continued to grow and change.

Eckankar is "the ancient science of soul travel" and "the religion of the light and sound of God." Its basic cosmology is similar to that of the venerable Radhasoami tradition of India, which teaches initiates to hear divine sounds, see divine lights, and taste divine tastes. These basic techniques have been blended with Rosicrucian and Theosophical tendencies as well. The overall result is that Eckankar is one of the most eclectic new religions in the United States.

Eckankar teaches that God is Sugmad—an impersonal source of all being. Everything that exists is an emanation of this divine spirit. Eck is "soul," a spiritual energy and life force in all things that emanates from Sugmad. It has various levels and on these levels takes different forms, including various intelligences. Eck can be sensed through chanting the mantra "HU," a special name for God in Eckankar. Chanting "HU" is one of Eckankar's central practices and is said to bring one spiritual self-realization or God-realization and to burn off karmic debt.

Eckankar has studiously avoided controversy in the media. The only time conflict happened was during the initial phase of moving its headquarters and building its Temple of Eck in Minnesota. Some citizens of the city of Chanhassen attempted to prevent the city council from permitting it. Articles were written about this controversy in the Twin Cities press, and this was the first time most people outside California had heard of Eckankar.

Within Eckankar there was controversy when Twitchell died and was succeeded by Gross and again when Gross was replaced by Klemp. There was lengthy and complicated litigation between Gross and Eckankar over use of the term itself as well as other related terms used by the organization that it had copyrighted.

The group's Web site is http://www.eckankar.org.

Elan Vital (Divine Light Mission)

Elan Vital grew out of Sant Mat (literally, "the way of the saints"), a nineteenth-century spiritual tradition that developed in northern India. One of the goals of the movement was the instruction of the world in a type of yogic meditation technique that was said to connect the devotee to the universal primordial Force through meditation on the Holy Name (Word) and on the Divine Light that pervades everything.

The Divine Light Mission was founded by Shri Hans Maharaj Ji. When Hans Maharaj Ji died (1966), he was succeeded by his youngest son, Prem Pal Singh Rawat, who was initiated at the age of six and who, two years later, was recognized as the new "perfect master," an embodiment of God on earth and hence an object of worship and veneration, assuming the title of Maharaj Ji. When his father died, he was commissioned as the one to take the knowledge to the world. Although he became officially the autocratic leader of the mission, his whole family shared the authority because of his young age.

In 1971, Maharaj Ji made his first visit to the West, after having been invited by some Americans who became initiates while in India searching for spiritual guidance. Against his mother's wishes, he went to Colorado, where a large crowd heard his first set of discourses given in the United States. A considerable number of people were initiated, and the U.S. headquarters of the mission was established in Denver. By the end of 1973, several hundred centers as well as more than twenty ashrams had emerged, and two periodicals, *And It Is Divine* and *Divine Times*, were begun. However, in November 1973, the Divine Light Mission suffered a major reverse because of the failure of "Millennium '73," an event organized to celebrate the birthday of Maharaj Ji's father and the beginning of a thousand years of peace and prosperity. The event had been scheduled to take place at the Houston Astrodome, and all of the movement's resources were invested in the event. When the anticipated large crowds of people failed to manifest, the movement fell into deep debt, which effectively crippled it.

After the Millennium '73 fiasco, the Divine Light Mission gradually withdrew from the public scene. Many followers left the movement, and many ashrams were discontinued. A number of ex-members became critics of the movement, attacking it with charges of brainwashing and mind control. Maharaj Ji himself was described by the anticultists as immature and unfit to be a religious leader, and his teachings were condemned as lacking in substance.

The movement also suffered from problems within Maharaj Ji's family. Mataji, Maharaj Ji's mother, disapproved of his lifestyle and of his marriage to his secretary, Marolyn Johnson, whom he declared to be the incarnation of the goddess Durga. After accusing her son of breaking his spiritual disciplines, she took control of the mission in India by replacing him with his oldest brother. In 1975, Maharaj Ji took his family to court. He received control of the movement everywhere but in India, where his brother remained the leader. By the end of the 1970s, an estimated 80 percent of the followers had left the mission. In the early 1980s, Maharaj Ji ordered that all of the ashrams be disbanded and that he was no longer to be venerated as God.

When the Divine Light Mission was disbanded, the organization Elan Vital was created in order to relate Maharaj Ji to his students on a one-to-one basis and to support his travels in thirty-four countries worldwide.

The group's Web site is http://www.maharaji.org.

Erhard Seminars Training (est)/The Forum

Erhard Seminars Training, more commonly known as est, was begun in 1971 by Werner Erhard. Although not a church or religion, est is included here because it has often been accused of being a cult.

In November 1970, Werner Erhard (born John Paul "Jack" Rosenberg) enrolled in a two-weekend course called Mind Dynamics. Mind Dynamics featured demonstrations and training in memory feats, enhancement of psychic powers, ESP, precognition, psychic diagnosis, and healing. Erhard was so impressed with Mind Dynamics that he immediately signed up to take instructor training. After a short time, he began to feel restricted by the confines of the Mind Dynamics program, and set up a program of his own. Est was incorporated as a profit-making educational corporation. The training was aimed at the broad public with the fee initially set at $150 for a two-weekend course. Within three years, he had sold $3.4 million of est training sessions.

Est was known for its intensive two-weekend workshops that promoted communication skills and self-empowerment. The purpose of est was to transform one's ability to experience living so that the situations one had been trying to change or had been putting up with cleared up in the process of life itself. The first two hours of est training were devoted to the rules: No one could move from his seat unless told to do so. No smoking, eating, or drinking were allowed in the room. One meal break was scheduled during the day. Students were commonly called "assholes" during the training.

Along with its success, est generated inevitable controversy. In 1977, two articles appeared in the *American Journal of Psychiatry* that described five patients who had developed psychotic symptoms, including paranoia, uncontrollable mood swings, and delusions, in the wake of taking the est training. Claiming psychological damage, several suits were filed against est by trainees and their families.

In 1978, Erhard vowed to end hunger in two decades and started the Hunger Project. The project was accused by *Mother Jones* magazine of collecting several million dollars and donating only a few thousand dollars to a San Francisco church that operated a soup kitchen at Christmas and to OXFAM, a prominent hunger organization. The author of the article concluded that Erhard was using the Hunger Project for self-aggrandizement and for promoting est, a profit-making corporation. In late 1990, Erhard formally broke all ties to the Hunger Project.

The name of the movement was changed to The Forum in 1985. The Forum runs self-awareness seminars, advanced courses, a program for those interested in becoming Forum leaders themselves, a sales course, and the More Time Workshop. In January 1991, Erhard sold the assets of Werner Erhard and Associates to his brother Harry Rosenberg and some other loyal employees.

On March 3, 1991, CBS aired a segment of *60 Minutes* that accused Erhard of beating his wife and children and raping his daughters. Erhard subsequently filed a lawsuit against CBS, claiming that the broadcast contained false, misleading, and defamatory statements. The lawsuit was dropped before a court decision was reached. Erhard left the United States in 1991, beginning a self-imposed exile. Meanwhile, The Forum, under the new name Landmark Education, has once again bounced back to become one of the most successful programs of its kind.

The group's Web site is http://www.landmarkeducation. com.

Falun Gong

Qi Gong is the generic name of a complex of techniques for physical and spiritual well-being, with a tradition in China predating the Christian era. It is often referred to as Chinese yoga. Although spiritual and religious activities in general are viewed with suspicion in Communist China, Qi Gong has been tolerated as a traditional set of physical exercises.

The largest (but by no means the only) such Qi Gong group is Falun Gong. Its founder, Li Hongzi, established his peculiar brand of Qi Gong in 1992. In 1998, Li moved permanently to New York City, where he oversees the expansion of Falun Gong internationally. Small groups exist in the main metropolitan areas of the United States and Canada, and in some thirty other countries.

In 1999, the Chinese regime launched a campaign against spiritual and religious groups, and Falun Gong was targeted as a superstitious and reactionary group by a press campaign. Unlike other groups, Falun Gong reacted with a demonstration of more than 10,000 followers outside Beijing's Zhongnanhai, the residence of China's top leaders, the largest such demonstration in recent Chinese history.

The regime was taken off guard by the failure of its intelligence service to prevent the demonstration and by membership in Falun Gong of a number of medium-level political and military leaders. The authorities reacted with an unprecedented public campaign against the movement. Hundreds of local leaders and members were arrested. China also asked the United States to arrest and extradite Li, a request the United States quickly declined.

Although the persecution scared many followers and drove them underground, millions remain in China and several thousand abroad. Exactly how many members Falun Gong has is a matter of dispute—the government uses a figure of 2 million; Li claims 100 million. "Membership" may not be an entirely applicable concept. Everybody can simply start practicing Falun Gong by following the instructions from one of the many books, cassettes, and Web sites readily available in a variety of languages.

Falun Gong is, basically, a form of Qi Gong. Its main differences with other Qi Gong groups are the unique authority of Master Li as the only living person authorized to define exactly what techniques are to be used and the claim that all previously secret teachings should now be disclosed. It also emphasizes, contrary to what groups tolerated by the Chinese regime claim, that it is essential to add to the practice of the exercises (the Xiu Lian), a spiritual discipline called "cultivation of the Xinxing." This is a simple path based on Buddhism and Confucianism and aimed at promoting the three key values of *zhen* (truthfulness), *shan* (benevolence), and *rhen* (forbearance), both at the individual and the societal level. Falun Gong also teaches the law of karma and reincarnation, the need for "tribulations" in order to test the disciple and to pay off karmic debts, and the existence of both benign deities and demonic forces. The aim of Xiu Lian is to awaken the universal energy of the Falun, so that it may flow harmoniously through the body, thus guaranteeing well-being.

Although Falun Gong does not reject all forms of modern medicine, it teaches that many ailments may be cured through its techniques. There are five key exercises involving movements of the hands and the legs, in ways reminiscent of tai chi practices. While the Chinese regime may be able to eradicate, or at least drive underground, any Falun Gong "organization," Falun Gong as a diffuse and unorganized practice will probably remain popular despite opposition from the government.

The group's Web site is http://www.falundafa.org.

The Family International (Children of God)

The Family International is the successor organization to the Children of God, a Christian group founded by David Brandt Berg (known to followers as Father David). Berg was a former minister in the Christian and Missionary Alliance Church, a conservative holiness denomination in which his mother was an evangelist. In 1967, Berg was informed by his mother about the increasing number of hippies in Huntington Beach, California. He moved there, taking over work previously begun by Teen Challenge, a youth Pentecostal ministry, which centered on the Light Club Mission, a coffeehouse near the Huntington Beach pier.

Berg's critical attitudes toward many establishment structures, including the organized church, and his messages oriented toward total commitment to a Jesus revolution, attracted the attention of a number of street people, many of whom gave up drugs and began to live communally, calling themselves Teens for Christ. In 1969, after Berg received revelation that the group should leave California, which was threatened by an earthquake, he and his followers moved to Tucson, Arizona.

Berg began to be referred to as Moses, after one of the members claimed to have had a revelation, and by February 1970 the members of the group started to call themselves "Moses and the Children of God." They moved to a ranch near Thurber, Texas. While they were staying there, William Rambur, a parent of a member of the group, organized other angry parents into the Parents' Committee to Free Our Children from the Children of God. Accusing the group of keeping their children under drug-induced and hypnotic control, these parents, with the help of Theodore Patrick, initiated the practice of deprogramming, physically kidnapping members of the group, and forcing them to renounce their fidelity to it.

By the middle of the decade, most of the Children had emigrated, spurred in part by Berg's warning of the destructive potential of the comet Kohoutek. Berg continued to exercise his leadership through a series of "Mo Letters," which guided the evolving organization and doctrine of the group. They were often sold on the street in order to spread the group's message. Others were internal documents.

Berg continued to exercise the role of a prophet, whose prophecies, which were increasingly seen as coming from spirit entities, assumed a fundamental role in supporting the ideas of the group. To the radical ideas about sexual freedom was added the most controversial practice of the group, "flirty fishing." This practice was introduced by Berg through a Mo Letter in the beginning of 1974, in which he ordered the women of the group to use their natural sexual appeal and talents to gain new members, to become Christ's fish bait—"hookers for Jesus." This practice was eventually abandoned, but not before it had attracted extensive negative media attention.

The image of the Children of God eventually became extremely negative. Berg decided to change the organization of the group and adopted the use of a family model, asking the followers to call him "Dad" and giving the Children of God the name Family of Love. World Services, which functions as a de facto headquarters, at least for the dispensing of literature, is located in Switzerland. Berg passed on in 1994.

The Family International, as the organization is now known, counts about 7,000–10,000 members widely dispersed around the world. For most of the past several decades, only a few hundred members resided in the United States, where they were occasionally seen on the streets distributing literature. This situation began to change in the early 1990s, when members began returning to the United States in large numbers. They were subjected to a new wave of intensive negative media attention in the summer of 1993, following raids on their homes in France and Argentina on trumped-up charges of child abuse. Although eventually exonerated of all charges, the "sex cult" image created by decades of negative media coverage remains largely unchallenged in the public consciousness.

The group's Web site is http://www.thefamily.org.

Hare Krishna Movement and the International Society for Krishna Consciousness

The International Society for Krishna Consciousness (ISKCON), better known as the Hare Krishna movement, is a transplanted form of conservative Hinduism, representing one of the most conspicuous religious groups in the West since the late 1960s. Its followers practice ecstatic worship; those dedicated to monastic life live a close-knit communalism and are usually noticeable for wearing orange or white robes. The past dozen or so years has seen a dramatic increase in the lay community, chiefly composed of married devotees who raise children, pursue outside professions, and contribute funds and expertise to the mission.

A. C. Bhaktivedanta Swami Prabhupada, born Abhay Charan De (1896–1977), was the founder of the International Society for Krishna Consciousness. Swami Prabhupada was born in Calcutta, where he graduated in 1920 with majors in English, philosophy, and economics. Asked by his guru to write about Krishna Consciousness in English, he authored a commentary on the Bhagavad Gita, and in 1933 was formally initiated into the Gaudiya Mission. His guru also gave him a charge to carry Krishna Consciousness to the West, a charge that he did not take seriously until he retired in 1950.

In 1965, at the age of seventy, he left for the United States. He began his missionary work in New York City on the Lower East Side, where he was chosen by a few hippies as their guru. Within a short time, a center had been opened, and the movement started to grow. Another center was opened in San Francisco in 1967.

Meanwhile, Swami Prabhupada continued to write and translate, working on the *Srimad-Bhagavatam* and the *Caitanya-Caritamrta*. In 1968, a copy of his translation of the Bhagavad Gita, *As It Is,* appeared. By 1972, more than sixty 400-page volumes of his work had been published by the Bhaktivedanta Book Trust. When Swami Prabhupada died in 1977, the twenty-two-person Governing Board Commission, which included eleven people empowered to initiate new disciples, began to lead the international movement. Many senior disciples of Shrila Prabhupada were dissatisfied with the new leadership, particularly when the eleven initiators declared themselves gurus. By the mid-eighties, this internal dissatisfaction had evoked a reform movement, which, eventually, overturned the "guru system," resulting in the decentralization of spiritual authority within ISKCON.

Although the movement has maintained a high profile in the past, it was frequently attacked for threatening common family patterns, with its ascetic, communal, and separatist lifestyle. At present, the majority of its current membership lives outside communal temples, which has decreased its tension with mainstream Western society. Members of the movement were early the target of deprogramming, such as the one of Ed Shapiro by Ted Patrick in the early 1970s. Other anticult activities included arousing public opinion against the group, imposing some restrictions on the group's public soliciting at the airports, efforts to require building permits for the establishment of Krishna temples, and requiring parade permits.

Despite attacks from anticult groups and the media, the society received a favorable welcome from religious scholars, such as J. Stillson Judah, Harvey Cox, Larry Shinn, and Thomas Hopkins, who praised Swami Prabhupada's translations and defended the group against distorted media images and anticult misrepresentations. The American Academy of Religion also welcomed various members of the society.

The movement maintains that the Vedas, the Bhagavad Gita, and the canonical lives of Krishna are literally true and that Krishna is the supreme personal Lord and lives in a paradisiacal world. It also believes that the souls of all individuals are eternal and are trapped in a series of material bodies (reincarnation) owing to ignorance and sensory illusion. The soul overcomes this identification with the temporary body and lives outside of karma, by love for Krishna.

The movement's primary magazine, *Back to Godhead*, ceased publication in the mid-1980s, but was revived in 1991, and is currently published in Alachua, Florida. The movement, which founded more than 50 centers in the United States, and more than 175 centers throughout Canada, the British Isles, Europe, and on other continents, claims 3,000 initiated members and 500,000 lay members who regularly visit a temple at least once a month.

The group's Web site is http://www.iskcon.com.

Heaven's Gate

Marshall Herff Applewhite (aka "Bo" or "Do") and Bonnie Lu Nettles ("Peep" or "Ti") founded one of the most unusual flying saucer religions ever to emerge out of the occult-metaphysical subculture. "The Two," as they were sometimes called, met in 1972. In 1973, they had an experience that convinced them that they were the two witnesses mentioned in Revelation 11. Preaching an unusual synthesis of occult spirituality and UFO soteriology, they began recruiting in New Age circles in the spring of 1975. Followers were required to abandon friends and family, detach themselves completely from human emotions as well as material possessions, and focus exclusively on perfecting themselves in preparation for a physical transition (that is, beaming up) to the next kingdom (in the form of a flying saucer)—a metamorphosis that would be facilitated by ufonauts.

In the early phase of their movement, Applewhite and Nettles taught that the goal of the process they were teaching their followers was to prepare them to be physically taken aboard the spacecraft where they would enter a cocoonlike state, eventually being reborn in a transformed physical body. The notion of resurrection is central to Chapter 11 of the book of Revelation, the biblical passage Applewhite and Nettles came to view as describing their particular ministry. In the early phase of their movement, Applewhite and Nettles prophesied that they would soon be assassinated. They further predicted that they would be resurrected three and a half days later and taken up in a flying saucer. The Two asserted that this event—which they termed "the Demonstration"—would prove the truth of their teachings. As for their followers, they taught that heaven was the literal, physical heavens, and those few people chosen to depart with the Two would, after their physical transformation, become crew members aboard UFOs.

For followers of the Two, the focus of day-to-day existence was to follow a disciplined regime referred to as the overcoming process or, simply, the process. The purpose of this process was to overcome human weaknesses—which was not dissimilar to the goal of certain spiritual practices followed by more mainstream monastic communities. For Applewhite, however, it appears that stamping out one's sexuality was the core issue.

Details about how the group came to attach apocalyptic significance to the Hale-Bopp comet are tantalizingly scanty. Someone outside the group had come to the conclusion that a giant UFO was coming to earth, "hidden" in the wake of Hale-Bopp. This individual then placed his opinion on the Internet. When Heaven's Gate retrieved this information, Applewhite took it as an indication that the long-awaited pickup of his group by aliens was finally about to take place. The decision that the time had come to make their final exit could not have been made more than a few weeks before the mass suicide.

The idea that the group might depart via suicide had emerged in Applewhite's thinking only within the past few years. The earlier idea—an idea that had set Heaven's Gate apart from everyone else—was that a group of individuals selected to move to the next level would bodily ascend to the saucers in a kind of "technological rapture." Applewhite may have begun to rethink his theology after his beloved partner died because, in order to be reunited with Nettles, her spirit would have to acquire a new body aboard the spacecraft. Although the death of Nettles may or may not have been the decisive influence, Applewhite later adopted the view that Heaven's Gate would ascend together spiritually rather than physically.

The group's mirror Web site is http://www.trancenet.org/heavensgate/index.html.

The I AM Religious Activity

The I AM Religious Activity is a popularized form of Theosophy, reformulated to appeal to a broader audience than earlier Theosophical organizations. The founder of the movement was Guy Ballard (1878–1939), who was born in Kansas. He had long been interested in occultism and had studied Theosophical teachings. He married Edna Wheeler (1886–1971) in 1916, and three years later their son, Donald, was born.

The I AM Activity believes that humanity began in America, and that this is the seventh and last cycle of history, under the Lord of the Seventh Ray, Saint Germain. The history of this epoch will also end in America, which will be the vessel of light to bring the world into new and paradisiacal times.

These revelations were spread during the lectures of the three Ballards, who traveled in the 1930s as "accredited messengers" of the masters. Further messages from the ascended masters, especially from Saint Germain and the master Jesus, were sometimes produced in public or private. The main teaching is that the "mighty I AM presence" is God-in-action, which is immediately available. It is also said that one's "individualized presence" is a pure reservoir of energy, from which power can be drawn at will.

Saint Germain and Jesus are considered the mediators between the "I AM presence" and humans. The ascended masters were at one time all human beings who became able to transcend the physical world through purification of their lives. The goal of human life is represented by ascension.

The I AM Activity worked publicly from 1937 to 1940 to establish a group of devoted followers numbering more than 1 million. With the death of Guy Ballard on December 29, 1939, the movement began to decline. Edna Ballard claimed that her husband had become an ascended master. However, the fact that Guy Ballard had experienced a physical death rather than bodily ascension threatened the movement's credibility. The following year, a sensational trial of the leaders of the movement took place, after some members of the Ballards' personal staff accused the Ballards of obtaining money under fraudulent pretenses. The indictment was voided in 1944 by the Supreme Court with a landmark decision on religious liberty. The case was finally dismissed after Justice Douglas, in stating the prevailing opinion, asserted, "Men may believe what they cannot prove. They may not be put to the proof of their religious doctrines or beliefs."

The I AM Activity experienced new growth in the 1980s and is still alive today in a number of cities, where it has temples, reading rooms, and radio programs. The I AM Activity was directed by Edna Ballard until her death in 1971. The current board of directors is formed by Mr. and Mrs. Gerald Craig, who are the "appointed messengers," and Mount Shasta is a major center. Every summer, in an amphitheater on the spotless grounds of the Saint Germain Foundation, the I AM Activity of the Saint Germain Foundation stages a pageant on the life of the "beloved master, Jesus." In this version, the crucifixion is left out, whereas the ascension is what is believed to be important.

The group's Web site is http://www.saintgermainfoundation. org.

Impersonal Enlightenment Foundation (Moksha Foundation)

The Impersonal Enlightenment Foundation (formerly the Moksha Foundation) is a spiritual group founded by Andrew Cohen. Cohen has been a teacher of Enlightenment since the mid-1980s. He was born in New York City in 1955, where he spent his childhood and early adolescence, traveling abroad to complete his education before returning again in his early twenties. Unable to forget a spontaneous spiritual experience that occurred when he was sixteen, Cohen decided to abandon all other aspirations and at the age of twenty-two became a serious spiritual seeker. His meeting with Swami Hariharananda Giri led him to the practice of martial arts and Zen meditation. After pursing many different spiritual teachers and paths, his seeking led him to India where in 1986 he met a little-known spiritual teacher named H. W. L. Poonja. This meeting was a catalyst for a spiritual awakening that completely transformed Cohen's life.

Cohen began teaching in India and then in England, the Netherlands, and Israel. In addition to giving numerous public talks each year, he holds lengthy retreats and many shorter intensives. In 1988, he returned to the United Sates and established a group in Cambridge, Massachusetts. A year later, he moved to Marin County, California, to join a communal group founded by some of his followers. In the mid-1990s, the group moved its headquarters once again, this time to the town of Lenox, in western Massachusetts. Communities of students dedicated to living his teachings have also formed in New York, Boston, Europe, and Australia. During his teaching activity, Cohen developed a different point of view from that of his original master, Poonja, and believed that individuals can express the enlightenment in their lives. He concluded that his teachings had surpassed his master's and has since followed his own beliefs.

Cohen has initiated meetings with teachers, scholars, and leaders in many different fields of inquiry in order to explore and elucidate the fundamental truths at the heart of human life. He is also the founder and editor of *What Is Enlightenment?* a biannual publication devoted solely to the purpose of conducting and promoting significant spiritual inquiry. Cohen is the author of a number of books, including *An Unconditional Relationship to Life, Autobiography of an Awakening, My Master Is My Self,* and *Enlightenment Is a Secret.*

After years of quiet development, Cohen found himself in the public spotlight in the late 1990s. For many years, he had asserted that people in the spiritual subculture should not turn a blind eye to the moral and other failings of spiritual teachers, as if a high state of spiritual development exempted them from ordinary morality. This critical stance did not earn him any friends. Thus, when Cohen's mother turned on her son and wrote a negative book accusing Cohen of being an egotistical guru who controlled his students, many people affected by his critique were willing to accept these accusations at face value.

The group's Web site is http://www.andrewcohen.org.

International Church of Christ (Boston Church of Christ)

The Boston Church of Christ began with a single congregation of the larger Church of Christ denomination. It has also been referred to as the Crossroads Movement (actually a distinct movement from which the Boston Movement developed), Multiplying Ministries, the Disciplining Movement, and the International Church of Christ.

The Crossroads Movement was begun by Charles H. Lucas, who came to Gainesville, Florida, in 1967 to serve as campus minister at the University of Florida. Campus Advance, as the new campus ministry was called, grew quickly. Two practices were characteristic of the ministry: "soul talks" and "prayer partners." Soul talks were evangelistic group Bible studies with prayer and sharing held in student residences. Prayer partners was the practice of pairing up a new Christian with a more mature Christian so that the new Christian could be given one-on-one direction. Both practices emphasized in-depth involvement of members in one another's lives.

In 1972, a freshman at the University of Florida, Kip McKean, was converted through Campus Advance. McKean trained at Lucas's new Crossroads Church of Christ while finishing his education. He left Crossroads and served as campus minister at other mainline Churches of Christ. In 1979, he accepted an invitation to take over the pulpit and campus ministry of a struggling thirty-member church in a Boston suburb, the Lexington Church of Christ. The church was soon renamed the Boston Church of Christ. Within two years, the thirty-member church had grown to a membership of 300.

Kip McKean had a vision to establish churches in key metropolitan centers of the world that could in turn evangelize the cities around them. By 1993, the movement had grown to 42,855 members in 130 congregations worldwide. The church believes that it is unscriptural to have more than one congregation per city. Usually a church affiliated with the Boston Movement will take the name of the city as its name, such as the Los Angeles Church of Christ or the Chicago Church of Christ.

Discipleship is very important to the Boston Movement. In the movement, a disciple is one who is faithfully following Christ and has taken on the lifestyle and purpose of making disciples of all nations. The movement is very exclusive, believing that it is virtually impossible to be among the elect outside the ranks of the Boston Movement.

Whereas the Crossroads members chose their own prayer partners, in the Boston Church of Christ, the leaders of the congregation arrange for older, stronger Christians to give direction to each of the younger, weaker ones. These partners are always of the same sex and are to have daily contact and weekly meetings. These partnerships are not considered optional. "Soul talks" as started in the Crossroads Movement became "Bible talks" in the Boston Movement. They are held weekly at regular times and places and are attended by an average of six to ten members. The Crossroads Church of Christ and the Boston Church of Christ have severed all ties with each other. The mainline Churches of Christ disavowed the Boston Movement in the mid-1980s and are now ardent opponents of it.

The Boston Church of Christ—which has since changed its name to the International Church of Christ—has become the subject of considerable controversy, centering on the level of commitment expected of church members and the authority the church exercises in members' lives. Members are expected to put the church above all else, including job, friends, and family. Each week, the average member attends at least four or five meetings for worship and Bible study. Numerous universities around the country either restrict or bar the movement's activities on their campuses. The movement has experienced some cases of forcible deprogramming of members. A few ex-members have portrayed the movement in a negative light to the media, and two have produced books denouncing their former church. The leadership of the movement has recognized that abuses of authority have occurred and retracted some of its earlier teachings on authority and submission. Despite the controversy, more people have come into the movement than leave it.

No active Web site is available for the group.

Jesus People USA

Jesus People USA (also known as JPUSA, pronounced *je-POO-sa*) is an evangelical Christian communitarian group centered in Chicago. Originating within the Jesus Movement of the early 1970s, the group has continued to play a dynamic role in Christian youth and alternative or underground cultures through its music, magazine, Jesus festivals, and lifestyle; the group also maintains a sizable inner-city ministry.

Jesus People USA began as part of Jesus People Milwaukee, a communal Jesus People group founded by Jim Palosaari in 1971. The following year, this original group temporarily divided into three subministries: Jesus People Europe, led by Palosaari, which traveled to Europe to do youth ministry abroad; Jesus People USA, led by John and Dawn Herrin, which traveled the United States; and the original Milwaukee commune. The proposed reunion never occurred, however; the Milwaukee commune disbanded, and Jesus People Europe returned to the United States to form the basis for the Highway Missionaries and, later, the Servant Community (both now defunct).

The U.S. branch, after traveling to Florida and back, eventually settled in Chicago, where they continued carrying out youth revivals, sponsoring a Christian rock group called the Rez Band, doing street theater and mime work, and publishing a well-produced street paper, *Cornerstone*. During the mid-1970s, the community went through a number of changes; several business ventures were started, including moving, painting, contracting, roofing, music recording, and graphics. Founder John Herrin was ejected from the group, and plurality of leadership was instituted in the form of a council of elders assisted by Dawn Herrin, the ex-wife of the former leader. In addition, the community merged with a communal African American Bible-study group, resulting in an interracial presence often lacking in other Jesus People groups.

JPUSA affirms the existence and practice of the supernatural "gifts of the spirit," such as healing and speaking in tongues, though within the group these gifts tend to be employed privately rather than publicly. In spite of seemingly exclusivist theological beliefs, the group admits a certain latitude by affirming the spiritual unity of all true believers in Christ; Christian humanist strains are also present due to the community's encouragement of both individual and collective forms of musical, literary, and visual artistic expression.

Former members of the community have begun to hold annual reunions; some of these individuals do not recall their time in the community or their departure with favor. Some have accused the group's leaders of excessive control of individuals, mismanagement, and nepotism. Others have complained that longtime members who choose to leave should be financially compensated for their time and effort spent on behalf of the community. Many of these complaints were publicized in *Recovering from Churches That Abuse.* The Jesus People USA community has responded by opening their community to even greater public scrutiny, including making public the correspondence dealing with the allegations; the community also dedicated a double issue of its magazine to examining the book's claims.

The group's Web site is http://www.jpusa.org.

Kashi Church Foundation

The Kashi Church Foundation began in 1976 with the establishment of the Kashi Ashram, located near Sebastian, Florida, by a group of people that had emerged around a young spiritual teacher, Jaya Sati Bhagavati Ma. Ma, born Joyce Green, was formerly a housewife in Brooklyn, New York. Her life began to change radically, however, in December 1972 when she had a vision of someone she, though Jewish, recognized as Jesus Christ. He would reappear three more times. She turned for guidance to residents of a nearby Jesuit seminary who offered her both sympathy and understanding. Then in the spring of 1973, she had a second set of apparitions, this time of a person who called himself Nityananda. He appeared to her almost daily for a year and taught her.

At the time Nityananda appeared, Ma had no knowledge that such a person had actually lived in India, had begun a movement then headed by Swami Muktananda, and had a disciple named Swami Rudrananda who initially brought his teachings to the United States. Nityananda, as he appeared to her, taught her about what he termed *chidakash,* the state in which love and awareness are one. He gave her a new name, Jaya (Sanskrit for "victory" or "glory"), and mentioned a woman named Hilda. Green, who began to call herself Joya Santanya, soon found

Swami Rudrananda and a short time later was led to Hilda Charlton, an independent spiritual teacher in Manhattan who encouraged her to become a teacher.

Through the mid-1970s, Joya Santanya's teaching activity led to the founding of some thirteen small communities where people lived cooperatively and gathered for daily *satsang* for meditation. In July 1976, she moved to Florida where land was purchased and Kashi Ashram was established.

Kashi is an eclectic community tied together by the residents' acceptance of Ma as their guru. The dominant teaching is a form of Adavaita Vedanta, a monistic worldview derived from the Vedas and the Upanishads, popular Hindu scripture. Residents at Kashi come from very different backgrounds and have varying attachments to the religions in which they grew up. The individual's devotion to a particular religion is both recognized and nurtured at Kashi, and shrines have been built to honor the major religions.

Through the 1990s, Ma became best known for her ministry to HIV-positive people, especially those who had been unable to find basic support from their family or help from governmental and church-related facilities. Beginning with a small ministry in Los Angeles and southern Florida, the AIDS-related work has become a major aspect of life at Kashi Ashram.

The community is organized on a semicommunal basis. Each adult member is responsible for an equal share of the budget that is adopted by community consensus. That money covers the residents' room and board, the operation of the school, and the upkeep of the ashram grounds. Thus, all of the members, except for the few who work at the ashram, have outside jobs. The diet is vegetarian with small quantities of fish and milk. No narcotics, alcohol, or tobacco is to be consumed. Chastity is practiced except for married couples trying to have a child.

The group's Web site is http://www.kashi.org.

The Local Church

The Local Church, which is also known as the Little Flock, and the Assembly Hall Movement, was the target of one of the most intense battles in the cult controversy of the early 1980s. The polemics originated from differences of theological language and particular practices unique to the Local Church, although it claimed to be an orthodox evangelical Christian body of believers.

The Local Church was founded in the 1920s in China by Ni Shutsu (1903–1972), who is popularly known by the English translation of his name, Watchman Nee. Nee's movement, which had a modest beginning in Fuzhou, spread through China, with the foundation of congregations based upon the idea that there should be only one local church in each city as the basic expression of the unity of Christianity. Nee was the author of more than fifty books, which were mostly about Christian life and church life. The most important of them are *The Normal Christian Church Life* and *The Spiritual Man*, in which he explained his conception of the tripartite nature of human beings as body, soul, and spirit.

Nee was accused by the new People's Republic of China of being a spy for the U.S. and the nationalist governments and was then exiled from Shanghai and imprisoned in 1952. He died in prison in 1972. During the 1930s, Nee was joined by Witness Lee, a former Protestant minister, who became within a few years one of Nee's most valuable assistants. He was sent by Nee to Taiwan, where the church was to flourish and spread around the Pacific basin.

The movement was brought to the West Coast by members migrating to the United States. Lee himself moved to the United States in 1962, where he founded the Living Stream Ministry. Lee has been a source for innovation in the movement through his introduction of many theological emphases and his initiation of a number of practices such as "pray reading," a devotional practice that uses the words of Scripture as the words of prayer and "calling upon the name of the Lord," an invocation of God by the repetition of phrases such as "O Lord Jesus." These practices have become the subject of controversy.

Much of the controversy between the Local Church and the Evangelical Christians who perceived Lee's theological innovations as departing from acceptable Evangelical thought, began in the early 1970s, when the church in Berkeley was housed in a building across the street from the World Christian Liberation Front (WCLF), with which the church had several emotionally charged encounters. The controversy resulted in the split of the WCLF into two groups, each of which published a book charging Lee with heresy and suggesting that Lee denied the traditional doctrine of the Trinity. Both books also associated the Local

Church with a variety of cultic practices, and one of them accused Lee of mismanagement of church funds and of being the source of psychological damage to members. Lee and many of the congregations filed lawsuits against the publishers of the two books, who apologized to the church.

In 1999, Harvest House, an Evangelical publishing house, published John Ankerberg and John Weldon's *Encyclopedia of Cults and New Religions*. The Local Church regarded the entry on themselves to be libelous and eventually filed suit. The case is proceeding to trial as the present book goes to press.

The group's Web site is http://www.lsm.org.

Maranatha Christian Churches

Maranatha Christian Churches began in 1972 as a campus ministry under the direction of Bob Weiner, formerly a youth pastor for the Assemblies of God, and his wife, Rose Weiner. Bob Weiner dropped out of the Evangelical Free Church's Trinity College at Deerfield, Illinois, and joined the U.S. Air Force. While in the U.S. Air Force he encountered Albie Pearson, a former baseball player turned evangelist-pastor, and received the baptism of the Holy Spirit. Following his discharge from the military, Weiner joined with Bob Cording to form Sound Mind, Inc., to evangelize youth. In 1971, he began to tour college campuses as an evangelist. As a campus minister, Weiner sought to convert students and train them in the fundamentals of the Christian faith.

In 1972, Weiner moved to Paducah, Kentucky, where his wife's father was minister in the United Methodist Church, and began a campus ministry at Murray State University. While focusing on Murray State, he continued to travel as an evangelist and develop other ministries. By 1980, Weiner had established thirty Maranatha Campus Ministries. As members graduated from college, Maranatha Campus Ministries became part of the larger work, which was named Maranatha Christian Churches. In Maranatha's early years, each center had a dorm in which converts could live while attending college, but this is no longer the case. Maranatha's work is still focused in the campus ministry, and all of the congregations are adjacent to a college or university.

During the early 1980s, a variety of accusations were made against Maranatha Campus Ministries concerning their intense program for training new members. Many of these accusations proved unfounded. In other cases, program adjustments were made that have ended any controversies. A program of parent-student contact was broadly implemented that reduced the problems that had arisen because of lack of knowledge by parents of Maranatha and the life shared by its new student members.

General meetings of the fellowship are held weekly, and most members also participate in small group fellowships. Maranatha Christian Churches are Pentecostal in doctrine. Prophecy is an important practice and is seen as ongoing confirmation of God's present activity in the church. Bob and Rose Weiner have written a series of books published by Maranatha Publications that are used as textbooks in the discipleship training work.

Maranatha Leadership Institute in Gainesville, Florida, offered more advanced training for people on a national basis. It often featured a variety of charismatic leaders not otherwise associated with Maranatha. A world leadership conference was held every two years. In 1985, Maranatha began a satellite TV network show as a televised prayer meeting in which sixty churches participated in the broadcast, praying for specific requests phoned in by viewers. In 1990, Maranatha disbanded as an association of churches, though the movement continues.

No active Web site is available for the group.

The Movement for the Restoration of the Ten Commandments of God

The Movement for the Restoration of the Ten Commandments of God was a doomsday religious sect in Uganda that made headlines in the wake of what was initially thought to be a mass suicide in March 2000. The number of bodies increased daily until it exceeded 1,000. About 530 died in an intentionally set fire that gutted their church in Kanungu, Uganda, on Friday, March 17, 2000. In the days following the tragedy, police discovered innumerable other bodies at different sites. All had been murdered prior to the group holocaust, apparently at the behest of the leadership.

Most of the deaths occurred in Kanungu, a small trading center, about 217 miles southwest of Kampala, the capital of Uganda. Though some may still believe that the parishioners had committed suicide, the consensus opinion is that the group leader, Joseph Kibweteere, murdered the members by luring them inside the church and then setting it on fire. The church's windows had been boarded up; its doors were nailed shut with the members inside. They sang for a few hours. Some witnesses reported the smell of gasoline at the scene, an explosion that preceded the fire, and some screams from inside the building.

Before the tragedy, Kibweteere allegedly had said that he overheard a conversation between Jesus Christ and the Virgin Mary. Mary had stated that the world would come to an end unless humans started to follow the Ten Commandments closely. The group initially believed that the end of the world would occur on December 31, 1999. During 1999, members had sold their possessions, presumably in preparation for the end times when they would be transported to heaven. They slaughtered cattle and had a weeklong feast. When the end did not come, Kibweteere changed the date to December 31, 2000. Later, he taught that the Virgin Mary would appear on March 17 and take the faithful to heaven. Devastation would then descend upon the world, and the remaining 6 billion people in the world would be exterminated.

The movement was founded by excommunicated Roman Catholic priests: Joseph Kibweteere, Joseph Kasapurari, John Kamagara, and Dominic Kataribabo; two excommunicated Roman Catholic nuns; and Credonia Mwerinde, an ex-prostitute. Most of the group's members were originally Roman Catholic. The group taught that the Catholic Church was an enemy, badly in need of reform. There own rules came from the Virgin Mary, as channeled through Mwerinde. The leaders taught that the Ten Commandments needed to be restored to their original importance.

The membership appears to have anticipated being taken to heaven by the Virgin Mary on March 17, 2000. They expected the end of the world to occur at that time. They slaughtered some cattle and ordered seventy crates of soda for a feast on March 16. They said good-bye to friends and relatives beforehand.

There was one initial report, never confirmed, that the members had applied gasoline and paraffin to their skin before the explosion and fire. However, it is difficult to see how the observer could have witnessed these preparations if the windows and doors of the church were nailed shut. It is now almost certain that the tragedy was a mass murder, not a mass suicide: the fact that the doors of the church were nailed shut seems to indicate that the leadership wanted to confine the full membership within the church in order to murder the entire group. The discovery of additional bodies that had been murdered and buried in latrines near the church gives weight to the mass-murder theory. The discoveries of many hundreds of murder victims at other locations also point toward mass murder.

The murders may have been precipitated by a failed prophecy. When the end of the world did not occur on December 31, 1999, some members of the sect demanded their money and possessions back. This, in turn, may have triggered the mass murders.

No active Web site is available for the group.

The Movement of Spiritual Inner Awareness

The Movement of Spiritual Inner Awareness (MSIA) is a contemporary religious movement that was founded by John-Roger Hinkins in 1971. Though MSIA has often been characterized as "New Age" and it participates in the larger metaphysical subculture, MSIA's core spiritual practices lie squarely in the Sant Mat (Radhasoami) tradition. In 1963, while undergoing surgery for a kidney stone, Roger Hinkins fell into a nine-day coma. Upon awakening, he found himself aware of a new spiritual personality—"John"—who had superseded or merged with his old personality. After the operation, Hinkins began to refer to himself as "John-Roger," in recognition of his transformed self.

In common with Sant Mat groups, MSIA pictures the cosmos as composed of many different levels or "planes." At the point of creation, these levels sequentially emerged from God along a vibratory "stream" until creation reached its terminus in the physical plane. The Sant Mat tradition teaches that individuals can be linked to God's creative energy and that this stream of energy will carry their consciousness back to God. The Mystical Traveler Consciousness—which formerly manifested through John-Roger (it has since been anchored in John Morton, his spiritual successor)—accomplished this linkup during initiation, although the individual still had to appropriate and utilize the link through the practice of special meditation techniques (referred to as spiritual exercises), particularly meditation on the mantra "Hu."

As a low-intensity group that does not make excessive demands upon either the time or the resources of most members,

MSIA largely escaped the attention of the anticult movement until the late eighties. In 1988, the *Los Angeles Times* published a highly critical article on MSIA. A similar article appeared in *People*. Both pieces dwelt on charges by ex-staff members that Hinkins had sexually exploited them. Depending significantly upon the testimony of disgruntled ex-members and drawing heavily on the "cult" stereotype, MSIA was portrayed as an organization that was created for no other purpose than to serve the financial, sexual, and egotistic needs of John-Roger Hinkins. After a brief moment in the spotlight, reporters turned their attention to other stories, and MSIA disappeared from the pages of the mass media.

Two events occurred in 1994 that once again brought MSIA to the attention of the media circus. First was Michael Huffington's campaign to become a California senator. Arianna Huffington, Michael Huffington's wife, is a member of MSIA. When someone in the media discovered this fact, the link became a focus of a number of sensationalistic articles in which all of the earlier accusations against John-Roger Hinkins and MSIA were dragged out and uncritically repeated. In the same year as the campaign, Peter McWilliams, an MSIA minister who had coauthored a series of popular books with Hinkins, dropped out of the movement and authored a bitter anti-MSIA book, *LIFE 102: What to Do When Your Guru Sues You*, which attracted some media attention.

The group's Web site is http://www.msia.org.

People's Temple

Born in east-central Indiana on May 13, 1931, James Warren Jones married Marceline Baldwin in 1949, moved to Indianapolis in 1951, and soon became a self-taught preacher who promoted racial integration and a veiled communist philosophy within a Pentecostal framework that emphasized faith healing.

Organizationally, People's Temple began as a small church. Jones increasingly modeled the temple after the Peace Mission of American black preacher Father M. J. Divine. Combining the Pentecostalist ethic of a caring community with the social gospel of liberal denominations, the People's Temple established care homes for the elderly, ran a free restaurant to feed the hungry, and maintained a social service center for the down-and-out. In 1960, the unconventional congregation became affiliated with the

Christian Church (Disciples of Christ), which long had been committed to a social ministry.

In 1964, tired of racial intolerance and citing fears of nuclear holocaust, the People's Temple moved to the quiet northern California town of Ukiah. By the early 1970s, the temple was operating churches in San Francisco and Los Angeles. In comparison to both conventional churches and retreatist countercultural communal groups of its day, the People's Temple was an anomaly—a relatively disciplined religiously and politically radical collective. By 1975, the People's Temple was a formidable force in the left-liberal political surge in San Francisco and began to reap political rewards.

During 1972 and 1973, Jones used internal defections and small incidents of external "persecution" as the warrant to establish the People's Temple's "Promised Land"—an "agricultural mission" eventually called Jonestown—in a remote corner of Guyana, an ethnically diverse, socialist-governed South American country bordering the Caribbean. In the summer of 1977, Jones finally ordered the collective migration for which the People's Temple had begun preparing four years earlier. At the time, it was widely believed that they left California because of press exposés, in which opponents raised the key issue of custody over children in the People's Temple.

In November 1978, California Congressman Leo Ryan and a group of concerned relatives and journalists flew to the capital of Guyana, Georgetown. At Jonestown, on the evening of November 17, 1978, Jonestown offered the visitors an orchestrated welcome. But during the festivities, a note was passed to a reporter by community members who wanted to leave. The next day, at the Port Kaituma airstrip, as the travelers started loading two planes, a Jonestown man posing as a defector pulled out a pistol in the smaller plane and started shooting. Simultaneously, a tractor came up pulling a flatbed; from it, the Jonestown sharpshooters shot toward the other plane. Left dead were Congressman Leo Ryan, three newsmen, and defector Patricia Parks.

At Jonestown, Jim Jones told the assembled community that they would no longer be able to survive as a community. With a tape recorder running, Jones argued, "If we can't live in peace, then let's die in peace." One woman spoke against the plan, but others argued in favor. Amid low wails, sobbing, and the shrieks of children, people walked up to take the "potion" laced with cyanide, then moved out of the pavilion to huddle with their families and die.

No active Web site is available for the group.

The Raelian Movement International

The Raelian Movement International was founded in 1973 by a French race-car driver and journalist, Claude Vorilhon (Rael to his followers), born in 1946 in Vichy, France. The movement began with Rael's encounter with extraterrestrials during a walking tour of the Clermont-Ferrand volcanic mountains in France. These beings, whom Rael describes in his book *Space Aliens Took Me to Their Planet*, entrusted him with a message for humanity. This message concerns our true identity: we were "implanted" on earth by a team of extraterrestrial scientists, the "Elohim," who created us from their own DNA in laboratories. Rael's mission is to warn humankind that since 1945 and Hiroshima, we have entered the "age of apocalypse" in which we have the choice of destroying ourselves with nuclear weapons or making the leap into planetary consciousness.

Denying the existence of God and the soul, Rael presents as the only hope of immortality a regeneration through science, and to this end members participate in four annual festivals so that the Elohim can fly overhead and register the Raelians' DNA codes on their machines. This initiation ritual, called "the transmission of the cellular plan," promises a kind of immortality through cloning. New initiates sign a contract that permits a mortician to cut out a piece of bone in their forehead (the "third eye") and mail it packed in ice to Rael, who in turn relays it to the Elohim.

The movement currently claims around 30,000 members worldwide, distributed mainly in French-speaking Europe, Japan, and Quebec. Members are encouraged through summer courses to achieve worldly success in their careers, to have better health through avoiding all recreational drugs and stimulants, and to enlarge their capacity to experience pleasure, which, Rael claims, will strengthen their immune system and enhance their intelligence and telepathic abilities. Rael advises Raelians not to marry or exacerbate the planetary overpopulation problem, but to commune with the wonder of the universe by exploring their sexuality. To this end, Raelians participate annually in the Sensual Meditation Seminar in a rural setting, which features fasting, nudity, sensory deprivation and awareness exercises, and sexual experimentation, the ultimate goal being to experience "cosmic orgasm."

The Raelians have always captured the interest of journalists, who have tended to portray them as delightful, harmless nuts until comparatively recently. The Raelians aroused some controversy in 1992 by distributing free condoms in the playground of the major high schools of Quebec in protest of the Catholic Schoolboard's decision not to have condom machines installed. Anticult organizations have portrayed Rael as a sexual libertine enjoying a luxurious life at the expense of his followers. Raelians have been portrayed in the media in France as Satanists, child sex abusers, and anti-Semites. Lawsuits have been launched by relatives excluded from the wills of deceased Raelians. More recently, the Raelians have been in the headlines as a result of their claim to have successfully cloned human beings.

The group's Web site is http://www.rael.org.

Rajneesh Foundation International (Osho Commune International)

Bhagwan Rajneesh (1931–1990), founder of the Rajneesh Foundation International and the Osho Commune International, was born Rajneesh Chandra Mohan in Kuchwada, India. On March 21, 1953, during his early college days, he announced an experience of *samadhi,* or enlightenment. He went on to receive his MA in philosophy in 1957 and took a professorship at Jabalpur University. Over the following years, the tensions between his work as scholar and his position as unorthodox spiritual teacher became too great, and he resigned from the university in 1966.

In 1970, Rajneesh founded a congregation in Bombay and the next year adopted the title "Bhagwan," or "God." He intended this to signify his method of direct, soul-to-soul teaching, rather than an intellectualized experience. In 1974, his following had grown sufficiently to support the purchase of six acres in Pune, which became his headquarters. Drawing from sources as diverse as humanistic psychology and Sufism, he believed that releasing emotions and developing self-expression in freedom were key elements in the process toward enlightenment. He taught "dynamic meditation," which activated the body through various means, including regulated breathing, chanting, and screaming. He encouraged indulgence in sex as liberating and consciousness raising. Initiates took vows, not to renounce life, but to embrace it with abandon.

Rajneesh's following became almost entirely European and American, as Indians abandoned his teachings as immoral. Seeking a more conducive environment, Rajneesh moved to a 64,000-acre ranch near Antelope, Oregon, in 1981. As his unusual teachings and lavish lifestyle (he had ninety-three Rolls-Royces) became known in the area, and particularly after he proposed building a communal village to be called Rajneeshpuram, opposition became as intense there as in India. In 1985, he was charged with immigration fraud and deported back to India, where he reactivated the Pune compound.

In 1988, Rajneesh dropped "Bhagwan" from his name in favor of "Osho," meaning "one upon whom the heavens shower flowers," and the organization was renamed Osho Commune International. On January 19, 1990, he died suddenly without having appointed a successor. The organization continues under the leadership of some of his close disciples.

The group's Web site is http://www.osho.com.

Rama Seminars

Rama (b. 1950), sometimes called Zen Master Rama, founder of the Rama Seminars, was born Frederick Lenz in San Diego, California. When Lenz was two, the family moved to Stamford, Connecticut, where his father eventually became mayor. Lenz received a BA from the University of Connecticut, then a PhD in 1979 from the State University of New York. While working on his graduate degrees he was a lecturer in English at the New School for Social Research.

Meanwhile, beginning at age eighteen, Lenz studied yoga under Sri Chinmoy, who gave him the name Atmananda. As Atmananda, he taught yoga classes in New York. In 1979, after finishing his degree, he moved to San Diego, California, and opened a Chinmoy meditation center. The following year, he closed the center, moved to Los Angeles, and founded Lakshmi, after the Hindu goddess. He quickly gained a large following after students reported that during meditation sessions he could levitate, disappear, or exude beams of light.

At first teaching under his own name, he began to empha-
size his previous incarnations as a Zen master. He taught what he
called Tantric Zen. In 1983, he announced his new name of Rama,
to indicate his status as the ninth incarnation of the Hindu god
Vishnu. Humanity is at the end of a cycle, in this case a dark age
immediately preceding an incarnation of Vishnu. Rama is one of
the names given a prior incarnation of Vishnu. Although Rama
does not claim to be the same as that prior incarnation, he does
claim to be an embodiment of a portion of that prior incarnation.

By 1985, Rama had about 800 full-time disciples in four centers—San Diego, Los Angeles, San Francisco, and Boston. To accommodate the new growth, he dismantled Lakshmi and rein-
corporated as Rama Seminars. Rama Seminars then took up the
task of enlightening those individuals who began with Lakshmi.
The teachings of the seminar are styled by Rama as Tantric Zen,
a formless Zen that incorporates Chan, Vajrayana Buddhism,
Taoism, and *jnana* yoga.

Rama has been the center of a series of controversies, many
involving former women devotees who claim abuse and sexual
exploitation. Some parents of current and former members
formed an anticult group directed specifically at Rama, called
Lenz Watch, and a number of followers have been kidnapped
and assaulted by deprogrammers. Rama eventually concluded
that at least some such followers were engaged in a prolonged re-
volt against their parents—a conflict they exacerbated by being
his followers. As a consequence they were ejected from the organization, and the controversy around Rama died down.

In 1995, Rama closed down his teaching activities, dissolved
his organization, and turned his full attention to the highly successful businesses in which he was engaged with some of his students. He authored several spiritual novels, including *Surfing the
Himalayas*. Rama died unexpectedly in a drowning accident near
his home in 1998.

No active Web site is available for the group.

Ramtha's School of Enlightenment

A Gnostic esoteric organization founded and headed by JZ
Knight who channels Ramtha, a spiritual entity believed to have
lived on earth approximately 35,000 years ago. Knight was born
Judith Darlene Hampton in Roswell, New Mexico, on March 16,

1946. In Tacoma, Washington, in 1977, Knight had her first encounter with Ramtha one Sunday afternoon. She and her husband had been playing with pyramids, then a rage within the
New Age community, when, without prior warning, Ramtha appeared to the startled housewife as she was alone working in her
kitchen. Ramtha began to speak through her, and over the next
few years she emerged as a channel. During her channeling, she
is in a full trance and Ramtha operates as a second complete personality. Upon awakening, Knight has no memory of what has
been said.

Knight first publicly operated as a channel in November
1978 to a small group in Tacoma and found an immediate public
response. In 1979, she began to travel to gatherings in different
parts of the country and allowed Ramtha to speak through her.
The number of these events, termed "Dialogues," increased dramatically in 1980, and through the early 1980s she expanded the
amount of time she could stay in trance. By the mid-1980s, she
was regularly holding two-day weekend Dialogues drawing
3,000 to 7,000 people.

Knight became the most prominent New Age channeler, and
books, cassettes, and videotapes drawn from Ramtha's teachings
could be found in metaphysical bookstores across North America.
Several celebrities found their way to Ramtha's door, and the size
of his audiences jumped after author Jess Stern included a chapter on him in his book *Soul Mates* (1984) and Shirley MacLaine
spoken glowingly of Ramtha in her book *Dancing in the Light*
(1985).

In 1988, Knight began withdrawing from public appearances and made a significant change in direction in the founding of Ramtha's School of Enlightenment. The school, formally
initiated in May 1988, would become the place of the students'
learning and practice of the spiritual disciplines required if they
were to leave behind their limited existence and assume the essential godlike mastery that was their real goal and purpose in
life.

During the late 1980s and early 1990s, Knight went through
a period of intense criticism. Also in the 1980s, Knight's love of
horses led her to begin a business of raising and selling Arabian
horses. While the business prospered for several years, at one
point in the mid-1980s the bottom fell out of the Arabian horse
market, her business went bankrupt, and Knight was plunged

into debt. At the same time, a number of students who had invested in the business lost their shirts. Many had done so with an understanding that Ramtha had approved and sanctioned their investment.

As Knight recovered financially, she offered to pay back all of the students (as well as the other investors) any money they had lost. Though some refused her offer, she eventually returned the investment to all who accepted it. From 1988 to 1995, Ramtha's School of Enlightenment issued no publications for circulation to the general public but early in 1996 began issuing a broad range of new books and tapes.

The group's Web site is http://www.ramtha.com.

Rastafarianism

The Rastafarian movement originated on the island of Jamaica. After the emancipation of the slaves in 1833, many joined the mission societies. However, when their material position did not improve, they founded or joined movements that had Afro-religious elements in their approach. Mayalism, which included aspects of the black Jamaican religions in its belief system, experienced a revival. Its followers, known as "Angelic People," maintained that the world would come to an end and that Christ was coming, sent by Jah. *Jah* was their word for God—a word used later by the Rastafarians. The so-called mial people (from a syncretistic belief system called Obeah-myal) were the first to envisage a transformed social cosmos.

Marcus Garvey came to the fore in the 1920s with his slogan "Africa for the Africans." It appealed to many blacks, both within and without Africa, and his message was nowhere as influential as on the island of Jamaica where he lived. He said in one of his speeches that the blacks should look to Africa, that when a black king was born the time of their liberation would be near.

Africa represents a spiritual homeland for the Rastafarians. The first Rastafarians appeared in Jamaica in 1930 during the crowning of Haile Selassie as emperor of Ethiopia, seen as the king of kings, lord of lords, conquering lion of the tribe of Judah. The book of Revelation was seen in a new light, especially the words, "And I saw a strong angel proclaiming with a loud voice, 'who is worthy to open the scroll and break its seals?'" (5:2).

"Then one of the elders said to me, 'Weep not lo, the Lion of the tribe of Judah, the Root of David, has conquered, so that he can open the scroll and its seven seals!'" (5).

Since then, the Rastafarian movement has become an important subculture of Jamaica. It is a religion, an ideology, a cultural movement—but not a political innovation. Culturally, it has many African and Jamaican facets, with some Anglo-Spanish contents added. Politically, there was some connection with forces of the black liberation movement that rebelled against Jamaica's neocolonialism. The movement has much to do with deprived economic circumstances.

Leipold Howell was the most influential person in spreading the Rastafarian doctrine. He stated that blacks were the true descendants of Israel but that they were enslaved by the whites, the agents of Babylon. Ras Tafari, he believed, would soon end the rule of the white man and would send ships to return the children of Africa to Ethiopia. Between 1963 and 1978, the political issues were liberation and revolution. The movement moved out of the religious context into the political arena. With this politicizing stance, themes that emphasized the destruction of Babylon became central to their songs.

Conspicuous were their "dreadlocks," long locks of hair that are an essential part of the natural man (Lev. 19:27, 21:5; Num. 6:5). These dreadlocks are symbols of their blackness, dignity, and honor. Because black people are like sheep, calm and unaggressive, they have wool on their heads, whereas the whites have hair. Blacks who debase themselves by becoming like goats and using a comb, scissors, and a razor are responsible for the world's sin.

Many saw the Rastafarian or the Rasta-man type as a mentally retarded drug addict who would have a degrading effect on the moral order if not checked. In Jamaica, the middle-class white and black Jamaican, as well as the Americans, generally avoided the Rastafarians since they considered the "cult" members to be not only mentally deranged or psychopaths but also criminals of the most dangerous type because some of their leaders concealed weapons and explosives. As indicated earlier, however, attitudes toward the Rastafarians changed in Jamaica during the latter part of the seventies with growing appreciation of their cultural contributions.

The group's Web site is http://www.rastafarian.net.

Santeria

Santeria is a magical religion that has its origins among the Yoruba people of West Africa. In the early nineteenth century, the Yoruba were enslaved in great numbers and taken to Cuba and Brazil, where they were able to form Yoruba-speaking communities. Yoruba priests and priestesses created new lineages of initiates dedicated to the Yoruba spirits called *orishas*, which was translated into Spanish as *santos* (literally, "saints"). This led to the people calling the Yoruba traditions in Cuba Santeria, "the way of the saints." Since the Cuban revolution of 1959, more than 1 million Cubans have come to the United States, some of them priests and priestesses of Santeria.

Santeria recognizes a remote and almighty supreme being who is best understood as a personification of fate or destiny. In Santeria, God is invoked by the Yoruba title Olodumare, the owner of all destinies. Individuals are given their own destinies by Olodumare. In order to fulfill these destinies with grace and power, an individual requires guidance from a variety of spirits called *orishas*. Trained priests and priestesses consult oracles to determine the sacrificial foods and actions necessary to secure the power and presence of an *orisha*. One particular *orisha* will begin to assert itself as an individual devotee's patron.

When Santeria first came to the United States with Cuban immigrants, the appeal of the religion was primarily to fellow immigrants. In the United States, the houses of the spirits offered services for cultural survival, mutual aid, and spiritual fulfillment. The houses have also offered spiritual opportunities to a variety of outsiders who have come in contact with the traditions for the first time in the United States. Teaching within Santeria has been done orally in the face-to-face context of initiation. The teachings are secret and available only to those who have been chosen by elders to receive them.

The most controversial element of Santeria in the eyes of outsiders is the slaughter of animals as part of feasts for the *orishas*. Most of the more important ceremonies require a feast to be prepared for the spirits and to be enjoyed by the assembled community. In order to fix the meal to the spirit's specifications, the foods must be prepared and cooked according to strict recipes and properly consecrated with certain prayers and rhythms. Animals for the feast must be slaughtered by a priest or priestess initiated specially to this task in the presence of the community and to the accompaniment of the correct chants. This insistence on animal slaughter has caused a number of problems in the urban centers of the United States, particularly in the crowded neighborhoods of New York and Miami. Problems with the storage of the animals before the ceremony and the disposal of the remains afterward have spurred concerns on the part of municipal authorities.

In 1987, the city of Hialeah, Florida, enacted a ban against "animal sacrifice" directly aimed at the growing Santeria community of the city. One Santeria house decided to challenge the ban and brought the case before the Supreme Court in 1992. In June 1993, the Supreme Court unanimously declared the Hialeah ordinances unconstitutional.

The group's Web site is http://www.church-of-the-lukumi. org.

Satanism and the Church of Satan

Organized Satanist groups were quite rare prior to the 1960s. A new form of Satanism was initiated with the founding of the Church of Satan by Anton LaVey on April 30, 1966, proclaimed the beginning of the Satanic era. Modern Satanism continued to develop in various directions by the several groups that later split off from this organization. The Church of Satan originated from an attempt to reorganize modern occult and magical teachings around a Satanic motif. The church advocates a philosophy of individual pragmatism and hedonism, rather than emphasizing the worship of Satan.

Many of LaVey's teachings focused on self-assertion and the gratification of an individual's physical and mental nature. He considered Satan a Promethean figure representing indulgence, vital existence, undefiled wisdom, kindness to the deserving, and vengeance. The church also taught responsibility to the responsible, the notion that the human being is just another animal, and so-called sins lead to physical or mental gratification. According to LaVey, Satan is a symbol representing these values.

The Church of Satan is based on a philosophy that views each person as living according to his own rules, although illegal acts and drugs are opposed by the church. Sex is considered the strongest instinct and natural. Three principal holidays are celebrated by the church. The first one is the individual's birthday. Halloween and Walpurgisnacht—the latter a supposedly Satanic holiday—are the other two major days. Rituals are regarded as psychodramas and as magical acts focusing upon psychokinetic force.

In 1967, the church received the attention of the media when LaVey performed both the first Satanic wedding and a Satanic funeral for a sailor. Membership grew rapidly, though the active membership was rarely more than 1,000. In 1969, LaVey published the first of three books, *The Satanic Bible,* containing the basic philosophy of the Church of Satan. It was followed by *The Compleat Witch* (1970) and *The Satanic Rituals* (1972). By the 1970s, the Church of Satan had a national membership and groups in many cities around the United States. The *Cloven Hoof,* edited initially by LaVey and later by others, was the newsletter of the church.

The Church of Satan was a rich source of short-lived splinter groups. In 1973, the Church of Satanic Brotherhood was formed by group leaders in Michigan, Ohio, and Florida. Other members of the Church of Satan in Kentucky and Indiana left to form the Ordo Templi Satanis. As more schisms occurred, LaVey disbanded the remaining grottos, the local units of the Church of Satan, in 1975, effectively dismantling his organization as a functioning church.

The headquarters of the church are located in San Francisco, California, where it was founded. LaVey died in 1997, and the leadership passed to his live-in secretary, Blanche Barton, who is also the mother of his son. Peter Gilmore is the current high priest. There have been hot disputes between the original Church of Satan and new Satanist groups since the seventies; this conflict—especially on the Internet—has increased since LaVey's death.

The great majority of contemporary Satanists do not belong to any formal Satanic organizations. Instead, most participate in a loose, decentralized Satanic movement that coheres as a distinct religious community largely by virtue of adherence to certain themes in the thought of Anton LaVey, especially as expressed in *The Satanic Bible.* The Internet has been a major factor facilitating this movement.

It should finally be mentioned that organized Satanism was associated with the ritual-abuse hoax of the late 1980s and early 1990s. During these years, the reality of a vast underground network of evil Satanists abusing children and others was accepted by significant segments of the law enforcement community as well as by numerous therapists. Less responsible members of the mass media, attracted by the sensationalism of these claims, avidly promoted the idea. The ritual-abuse scare began a sharp decline after about 1992. By the mid-nineties, public opinion had shifted, and the reality of this secret network had been rejected by almost everyone except certain groups of conservative Christians.

The group's Web site is http://www.churchofsatan.com.

Scientology, Church of

The Church of Scientology, one of the genuinely new religions to originate in the United States in the twentieth century, was founded by L. Ron Hubbard (1911–1986). Hubbard grew up mostly in Montana, but as a teenager he traveled throughout Asia and the East. In 1929, he enrolled in George Washington University, studying mathematics, engineering, and nuclear physics. He subsequently took up a literary career, publishing numerous stories and screenplays in various genres, including adventure, mystery, and science fiction. Hubbard served in the U.S. Navy during World War II.

By 1950, Hubbard had completed enough of his research to write *Dianetics: The Modern Science of Mental Health*. This book described techniques designed to rid the mind of irrational fears and psychosomatic illnesses. *Dianetics* quickly became a bestseller, and groups were soon formed so that individuals could assist each other in the application of Hubbard's "auditing" techniques. He lectured extensively and wrote more books. In 1951, he announced that the "applied religious philosophy" of Scientology had been born. It was described as a subject separate from dianetics, as it dealt not only with the mind of an individual but also with one's nature as a spiritual being.

In 1954, the first Church of Scientology was established in Los Angeles, California. In 1959, Hubbard moved to Saint Hill Manor, in Sussex, England, and the worldwide headquarters of Scientology was relocated there. In 1966, Hubbard resigned his position as executive director of the church and formed the "Sea Organization," a group of dedicated members of the church who originally lived aboard a fleet of ships. In 1975, these activities outgrew the ships and were moved onto land in Clearwater, Florida. From this time on until his death in 1986, Hubbard continuously wrote and published materials on the subjects of dianetics and Scientology, as well as a number of works of science fiction.

The Church of Scientology has been involved in a considerable number of controversial episodes since 1958, such as battles concerning tax issues, a ten-year battle with the Food and Drug Administration regarding the Electro-meters used to assist auditing, and a conflict with the Australian government. The most notorious series of events in the church began in July 1977, when the FBI conducted a raid on the Washington, D.C., and Los Angeles churches and seized many files. The raid was declared illegal, but the documents remained in government possession and were open to public scrutiny. According to these documents, the church was keeping files on people it considered unfriendly, and there had been various attempts to infiltrate anticult organizations.

After the raid, the church sent a number of top officials incognito to selected government agencies that were collecting data on the church. However, several members were indicted and convicted for theft of government documents. The convicted members were released from their offices in the church, which began a reorganization and closing of the office responsible for initiating the illegal activities.

Problems with the IRS continued through the 1980s and 1990s. L. Ron Hubbard was charged with criminal tax evasion, and the IRS often moved against the church in ways that questioned its tax-exempt status. These problems terminated in a landmark decision in 1993, when the IRS ceased all litigation and recognized the Church of Scientology as a legitimate religious organization. The church has also been extensively attacked in Europe.

The group's Web site is http://www.scientology.org.

Shambhala International

Shambhala International, originally known as Vajradhatu, has been responsible for stimulating the growth of Tibetan Buddhism in the United States. It was found by Chogyam Trungpa Rimpoche (1939–1987), who emphasized Buddhism as a practice to awaken the mind through three aspects: (1) meditation, the state of being in the present moment, which consists of training the mind to exist in the here and now; (2) study, which sharpens the understanding of the experience of meditation and the communication of the experience to others; and (3) work, which allows the meditator to share what has been learned with others.

Trungpa was born in the village of Geje in northeast Tibet and was identified as the tenth incarnation of Trungpa Tulku (one of the Tibetan lineages where the same person is supposed in incarnate over and over, like the Dalai Lama) by the monks of the Buddhist sect known as Karmapa Kargyupa. He was trained at Dudtsi-til Monastery and received his degrees when he was a teenager. He became a monk and, after the invasion of Tibet by China in 1959, went to India where he learned English. He was then allowed to go to the West, and in 1963 he went to Oxford, where he studied art, psychology, and comparative religion.

During his stay in Oxford, Trungpa discovered the Buddhist contemplative center Johnstone House in Scotland. After a severe injury in 1969, he decided to become a layman in order to better communicate to Western people the complicated and sophisticated Tibetan tradition. *Cutting through Spiritual Materialism* is the title of one of Trungpa's early books as well as a major theme of his teaching, according to which the primary mistake of Western followers of a spiritual discipline is their conversion of what they learned to egoistic uses.

After marrying Diana Judith Pybus in 1970, Trungpa immigrated to the United States. In Vermont, some of his followers built the Tail of the Tiger Monastery. He gave several lectures around the country and established many centers, such as the Rocky Mountain Dharma Center at Fort Collins, Colorado, a small facility used primarily for meditative retreats and other short-term programs. In 1973, he established Vajradhatu.

In 1974, Trungpa held the first seminar that led to the formation of the Naropa Institute, which has received the support of Buddhist leaders and scholars throughout North America. During the same year, he received a visit from Gyalwa Karmapa, the international leader of the Kargyupa Buddhists, who performed the famous black hat ceremony and recognized Trungpa as a *vajracarya*, that is, a spiritual master.

In 1976, Trungpa named Thomas Rich, an American disciple, as his dharma successor. Rich, who took the name Osel Tendzin, assumed administrative leadership of the community when Trungpa died. In 1989, the *Los Angeles Times* broke the story that Tendzin had AIDS. It was also reported that for three years he had known of his infection and had continued to have sexual relations with others without telling them of the risk. He was then asked by the organization's board to take a permanent leave of absence. Tendzin died in 1990. Trungpa's son, Sawang Osel Rangdrol Mukpo, succeeded him, returning some stability to the organization.

Since its formation, Shambhala International has grown consistently, although it was early the center of controversy because of Trungpa's unmonklike personal habits, such as eating meat and using both alcohol and tobacco. One controversial episode occurred in the fall of 1975, when a pacifist student attending the classes for advanced students at the Naropa Institute was disturbed by the bloody images in some of the Tibetan material used during the sessions. The same student, who was an outstanding poet, was stripped of his clothes after being ordered by Trungpa to return to a Halloween party at Naropa that he had left earlier in the evening with a friend. The incident became the subject of articles in a national magazine and a book.

The group's Web site is http://www.shambhala.org.

Siddha Yoga Dham Associates

The Siddha Yoga Dham was founded in 1975 by the *siddha* master Swami Muktananda Paramahansa (1908–1982), also known as Baba. He left home at the age of fifteen and began wandering throughout India, studying philosophy and practicing the various branches of yoga. In 1947, he received *shaktipat* initiation, which is the awakening of the spiritual energy known as kundalini, through the grace of the guru, in this case Bhagawan Nityananda. The practice includes meditation, chanting, service, and devotion to the guru. After nine years of intense spiritual practice, he attained full self-realization. He succeeded Nityananda in the *siddha* lineage, and established an ashram, Gurudev Siddha Peeth, near the town of Ganeshpuri, where the first American seekers began to arrive in the 1960s.

In 1970, Baba was invited to undertake his first world tour, which lasted three months and included stops in Europe, New York, Dallas, Los Angeles, and Australia. Shortly after his visit, the first centers were established in the United States. Large centers were established in South Fallsburg, New York, and Oakland, California, and several hundred smaller centers were founded throughout the world.

Among the visitors to Ganeshpuri was Werner Erhard, founder of Erhard Seminars Training, who invited Baba to return to the West for two years. His final journey, lasting three years, was made in 1978. Baba spent the last years of his life in Ganeshpuri. Swami Chidvilasananda, known as Gurumayi, succeeded Baba at his death. She is now the head of the *siddha* lineage and travels the world, giving initiation and teaching.

The Siddha Yoga Dham was involved in two major scandals during the 1980s. After Baba's death, he was accused by some of his associates of taking sexual liberties with female disciples. In addition, in 1986 the *Illustrated Weekly of India* published two stories concerning charges made by Swami Nityananda against his sister Swami Chidvilasananda. However, a defamation case was filed against the magazine, which in 1987 published a full retraction and apology.

The group's Web site is http://www.siddhayoga.org.

Sikh Dharma (Healthy, Happy, Holy Organization)

Yogi Bhajan (b. 1929), a well-educated Sikh from Delhi, India, moved to Toronto in 1968. From Toronto he moved to Los Angeles in December 1968, and in 1969 he founded an ashram and the Healthy, Happy, Holy Organization (3HO) to teach kundalini yoga. Corporately, 3HO was later supplanted by Sikh Dharma, but 3HO was retained as Sikh Dharma's educational wing.

The Sikh religion was founded by Guru Nanak (1439–1538), the first of ten gurus to be recognized by Sikhs. Nanak asserted that there was one God, the Creator, and that he transcended the barriers of race, caste, and creed. His followers were taught to earn an honest living by the sweat of their brow and to share their possessions with those in need. His writings and those of his successors, compiled into the *Siri Guru Granth Sahib*, became the guru for the movement following the death of the tenth guru, Guru Gobind Singh.

3HO Sikhs are vegetarian, usually preferring natural foods. Fish, meat, alcohol, and drugs are prohibited. Several members have opened vegetarian restaurants and groceries. They also prefer natural methods of healing. The traditional holidays of Sikhism are observed by 3HO Sikhs, such as Balsakhi Day, the birthday of Khalsa (April), the martyrdom days of Guru Tegh

Bahadur (November) and Guru Arjun Dev (May), and the birthdays of the ten gurus.

The first controversy involving the Sikh Dharma regarded its relationship to the older Punjabi Sikh community. American Sikhs criticized Punjabi Sikhs for becoming lax in their discipline. An attack followed on Yogi Bhajan by Dr. Narinder Singh Kapany, editor of the *Sikh Sangar,* the magazine of the Sikh Foundation, who condemned Bhajan's emphasis on yoga and diet. Other Sikh leaders echoed Kapany's criticisms in the United States, as well as in India. Although these issues were never resolved, Bhajan's emphasis on orthodoxy was supported by the headquarters of Sikh authority in Amritsar.

Sikh Dharma has received relatively little attention from the anticult movement. Few deprogramming attempts took place. In the early 1980s, militant Sikhs announced a policy of actively opposing any attempts by deprogrammers to attack their organization. No further attempts were reported.

Yogi Bhajan was accused by one ex-member of sexual involvement with several of his staff members, but there was no verification of the charges. In 1984, a number of high-ranking leaders in the Sikh Dharma left the organization, complaining of the intense discipline and being cut off from the Sikh community as a whole and middle-American culture.

Controversy has mainly been focused in other issues, such as members' dress, especially the turban, as in the case of Thomas Costello who, in 1971, faced a military court-martial for refusing to either cut his hair or remove his turban.

Although this case led to a change in army regulations granting permission for Sikhs to wear turbans, in 1983 Gurusant Singh Khalsa was not allowed to enlist in the army because he was a Sikh. In 1984, Karta Kaur Khalsa was threatened with losing her teaching certificate because she refused to take off her turban during classes, but in 1985 the Oregon Court of Appeals declared the law under which she was suspended to be unconstitutional.

The group's Web site is http://www.3ho.org.

Soka Gakkai International

Soka Gakkai International is a Japanese Buddhist group with a comparatively large following in the United States and other

Western countries. Founded in the 1930s, Soka Gakkai has grown to become Japan's largest and most controversial new religion. Although classified as a new religion, Soka Gakkai International's roots lie in thirteenth-century Japan.

Like most other Japanese Buddhist groups, Soka Gakkai International belongs to the Mahayana school. One characteristic of many Mahayana Buddhist texts is that they extol the merit gained by reading, copying, and otherwise propagating that particular scripture. Reading these claims, later generations of Buddhists were led to ask which text was the most potent. This question was the subject of debate in thirteenth-century Japan, when the Buddhist reformer Nichiren concluded that the *Saddharmapundarika* (the *Lotus of the True Law*), better known simply as the *Lotus Sutra*, was the most important of all Buddhist sutras. Nichiren believed that the message contained in the *Lotus Sutra* was so profound that all one had to do was chant "Nam-myoho-renge-kyo "(which can be translated in various ways, including "I dedicate myself to the Lotus Sutra") to develop wisdom and attain enlightenment as described in its pages.

Nichiren and his teachings gave rise to a monastic movement that eventually splintered into different sects. Soka Gakkai began as a movement of lay practitioners attached to the Nichiren Shoshu (the Orthodox Nichiren Sect). The founder, Tsunesaburo Makiguchi (1871–1944), was an educator who was arrested as a "thought criminal" in the prewar period for rejecting the compulsory worship of the emperor and State Shinto as well as criticizing the Japanese militarist regime. He died in 1944, still imprisoned, having refused to compromise his ideals. After the war, Josei Toda (1900–1958) took over as president and built Soka Gakkai into a major religion. This period of rapid growth was accompanied by negative media attention. The group matured under the presidency of Daisaku Ikeda, who became the third president of Soka Gakkai after the passing of Toda.

Soka Gakkai also spread to the United States, where it attracted attention as a consequence of the intensive proselytizing activities that characterized the organization's early years. Although never as controversial as groups like the Hare Krishna movement or the Unification Church, Soka Gakkai (which in the United States went under the name Nichiren Shoshu of America until recently) was not infrequently stereotyped as a brainwashing cult, particularly by anticult authors.

Soka Gakkai has been attacked in Japan because of its support of political activity that challenges the ruling coalition. Exploiting the negative public reaction to AUM Shinrikyo—the Japanese religious group responsible for the 1995 poison-gas attack in the Tokyo subway system—the Liberal Democratic Party, which has always been the dominant party in the ruling coalition) attempted to weaken its principal political rival, the New Frontier Party, which Soka Gakkai supported. In particular, the LDP engaged in a campaign to portray Soka Gakkai as being incompatible with the principles of democracy. In 1999, however, the LDP did an abrupt about-face and allied itself with the New Komeito Party (the successor to the New Frontier Party), the party supported by Soka Gakkai. Unsurprisingly, the media assault on Soka Gakkai subsequently evaporated.

The group's Web site is http://www.sgi.org.

Solar Temple

Joseph Di Mambro, the founder of the Solar Temple, had been fascinated with esotericism from a young age. He joined the Ancient and Mystical Order Rosae Crucis in 1956 and was a member until at least 1968. In the 1960s, he came into contact with several persons who would later play a role in Solar Temple history, including Jacques Breyer, who initiated a "Templar resurgence" in France in 1952. Several groups, including Di Mambro's, trace part of their roots to Breyer's work. *Templar* in this context refers to the Knights Templar, the medieval order to which groups in the neo-Templar tradition claim to trace their lineage. Several major points of doctrine, as well as an initial group of followers, began to come together in the 1960s. In 1971, after dealing with some legal problems in Nîmes connected with a number of petty crimes such as writing bad checks, Di Mambro established himself in Annemasse, near the Swiss border. In 1978, he founded the Golden Way Foundation in Geneva, which would constitute the foundation of the Solar Temple.

Recognizing Luc Jouret's intelligence and charisma, Di Mambro brought him in to become the public face of his organization. Jouret was trained as a medical doctor and was an accomplished practitioner of homeopathy. He also lectured on naturopathy and ecological topics and was active in the wider circuit of the French-speaking New Age movement. He spoke in New Age bookstores and to eclectic esoteric groups in France, Switzerland, Belgium, and Canada. About 1981, he established the Amenta Club, an organization managing his conferences.

The Amenta Club was the outer shell of an esoteric organization. Those who most faithfully attended Jouret's homeopathic practices and conferences were given the invitation to join a more confidential, although not entirely secret, "inner circle": the Archédia Clubs, established in 1984, in which one could already find a definite ritual and an actual initiation ceremony, with a set of symbols taken from Masonic-Templar teachings. The Archédia Clubs were not yet the truly inner part of the organization. Their most trusted members were invited to join an even more "inner" circle, this one truly a secret organization: the International Order of Chivalry Solar Tradition, Solar Tradition for short, later to be called the Order of the Solar Temple.

The temple's teachings stressed occult-apocalyptic themes, bringing together three traditions on the end of the world: (1) the idea found in some (but by no means all) New Age groups of an impending ecological catastrophe; (2) some neo-Templar movements' theory of a cosmic "renovation" revealed by the ascended masters of the Grand Lodge of Agartha; and (3) the political ideas of a final international bagarre propagated by survivalist groups both on the extreme right and on the extreme left of the political spectrum.

On March 8, 1993, a crucial episode in the history of the Solar Temple occurred in Canada. Two temple members, Jean Pierre Vinet, fifty-four, an engineer and project manager for Hydro-Quebéc, and Herman Delorme, forty-five, an insurance broker, were arrested as they were attempting to buy three semiautomatic guns with silencers, illegal weapons in Canada. Daniel Tougas, a police officer of Cowansville and a Temple member, was temporarily suspended from office on charges of having helped the two. On March 9, Judge François Doyon of Montreal committed them to trial, freeing them on parole. Luc Jouret—who according to police reports asked the two to buy the weapons—was also committed to trial, and an arrest warrant was issued against him. (The temple leader could not be found, as he was in Europe at the time.) The event drew the attention of the Canadian press on what newspapers called "the cult of the end of the world."

On October 4, a fire destroyed Joseph Di Mambro's villa in Morin Heights, Canada. Among the ruins, the police found five charred bodies, one of which was a child's. At least three of these people seemed to have been stabbed to death before the fire. On October 5, at one in the morning, a fire started in one of the centers of the Solar Temple in Switzerland, the Ferme des Rochettes, near Cheiry, in the Canton of Fribourg. The police found twenty-three bodies, one of which was a child's, in a room converted into a temple. Some of the victims were killed by gunshots, while many others were found with their heads inside plastic bags. The same morning, at three o'clock, three chalets inhabited by members of the Solar Temple caught fire almost simultaneously at Les Granges sur Salvan, in the Valais Canton. In the charred remains were found twenty-five bodies, along with remainders of devices programmed to start the fires and the pistol used to shoot the people in Cheiry.

No active Web site is available for the group.

Sukyo Mahikari

Mahikari is the Japanese word for "divine true light," believed to be a spiritual and purifying energy. Sukyo Mahikari began in 1959 when Kotama Okada (1901–1974) received a revelation from God concerning how the use of the divine light of the Creator could produce health, harmony, and prosperity. Mahikari is viewed as a cleansing energy sent by SUSHIN, the Creator of heaven and earth that both spiritually awakens and tunes the soul to its divine purpose. In 1963, Okada organized what became known as the Sekai Mahikari Bunmei Kyodan (Church of World True Light Civilization). Okada soon became known as *sukuinushisama* (master of salvation).

God also revealed to Okada the existence of a divine plan. According to his teachings, all of the phenomena of the universe have been controlled by the plan of the Creator. Under this plan, human souls are dispatched to the earth for the specific purpose of learning to utilize its material resources in order to establish a highly evolved civilization governed by spiritual wisdom. These revelations and teachings are to be found in *Goseigen* (The holy words), the Mahikari scriptures, an English-language edition of which was published in 1982.

Okada dedicated his life to teaching the art of the divine light to anyone desiring to be of service to the Creator. Today it is taught in a three-day session at which attendees may learn to radiate the light through the palm of the hand, a process known as *Mahikari no Waza*. At the time of initiation, new members receive an *omitama*, a pendant used to focus the light.

In 1974, following a divine revelation just prior to his death, Okada passed the mission to his daughter, Seishu Okada, the present leader. In 1978, subsequent to another revelation, Seishu Okada changed the name of the organization to Sukyo Mahikari (*Sukyo* means universal laws). Under her guidance, a new international headquarters was established in Takayama, Japan. In 1984, she completed the mission to construct a world main shrine (*suza*) in Takayama.

It is said that there are approximately 800,000 members worldwide and 5,000 members in the North American region (the United States, Puerto Rico, and Canada). There are sixteen centers in the United States, two centers in Puerto Rico, and two centers in Canada. There are associated centers in more than seventy-five countries. As with any large organization, Mahikari has experienced some problems in Japan. Despite a comparatively modest presence in Europe, the group is beginning to be attacked as a dangerous sect. In Belgium, for instance, there have been moves by authorities to force Mahikari to disband.

The group's Web site is http://www.mahikari.org.

The Synanon Church

The Synanon Church was begun in 1958 by Charles E. Dederich in Ocean Park, California, as Synanon Foundation, Inc., a therapeutic group for alcoholics and drug addicts. The group, which within a year grew and moved to Santa Monica, gained a considerable reputation for reeducating drug addicts. During the 1960s, Synanon communities began to appear along the West Coast, as well as in the East, Midwest, and Puerto Rico. In 1968, Dederich settled in Marin County, where three rural Synanon communities were established near the town of Marshall.

Although its religious nature had been tacitly recognized since the beginning of its existence, Synanon was never formally called a religion because many of the people assisted by it had rejected organized religion, while many others outside Synanon regarded it as a therapeutic community. However, as its community life developed, Synanon's religious nature could no longer be denied. The articles of incorporation signed in January 1975 designated the Synanon Foundation as the organization through which the Synanon religion and church are manifest, and in November 1980 the name Synanon Church was formally adopted.

Synanon's theological perspective derives from Buddhism and Taoism, as well as from such Western mystics as Ralph Waldo Emerson and Aldous Huxley. Members of the Synanon community seek to manifest the basic principles of oneness in themselves and in their relations with each other. The "Synanon Game" represents the group's central sacrament and the principal means for the search for unity. It is "played" by a small group of members who meet together as equals in a circle to share in an intense and emotionally expressive context. The outcome of a successful game consists of mutual confession, repentance, and absolution, while offering complete pastoral care.

Synanon members follow the golden rule and help each other, believing that the most effective way to redeem humanity from alienation is to form religious communities based on the beliefs and practices of the Synanon religion and church.

Synanon has been subject of controversy since its inception, and during the past several years more than forty people associated with it have been indicted on various charges by grand juries. In December 1961, Dederich went to jail on a zoning-code violation. Synanon's practices and techniques have been attacked by the *San Francisco Examiner,* against which Synanon filed a libel suit that ended with a large settlement. However, the most controversial event occurred in 1978 when an attorney suing Synanon was bitten by a rattlesnake. In the following year, Dederich suffered three strokes, and as the trial date approached, he found himself unable to pursue the defense of the case. Thus, those charged settled the case by pleading no contest.

The group's Web site is http://www.synanon.net.

Transcendental Meditation and the World Plan Executive Council

The Transcendental Meditation (TM) movement, at one time a widespread fad, is now institutionalized in the World Plan

Executive Council, founded by Maharishi Mehesh Yogi. TM consists primarily of a simple system of daily meditation through the use of a mantra, a word that is repeated over and over again as one sits in otherwise silence.

This type of meditation derives from an old and honored Hindu technique. Maharishi advocated the use of a single mantra, given to each student at the time of their taking the basic TM course. Each mantra is supposed to suit the nature and way of life of the particular individual. These mantras are given out only at *puja* ceremonies, that is to say, at simple Hindu devotional services venerating the lineage of gurus. Maharishi claimed his authority from these gurus.

The World Plan Executive Council has asserted that the practice of TM has extraordinary effects, the validity of which has been tested by scientists who were among the individuals who took the basic TM course. Among the claims made by the council is that the regular practice of TM can produce changes in the body, leading to increased intelligence, improved academic performance, higher job productivity, improved resistance to disease, and better psychological health. TM is generally claimed to transform a person's life.

In 1967, the Beatles, the popular rock group, became followers of Maharishi. In particular, George Harrison, who was later connected with the Hare Krishna movement, after having taken lessons from Indian musician Ravi Shankar and having learned of Maharishi's presence in London, persuaded the other Beatles to attend Maharishi's meetings. In January 1968, they went to Maharishi's center in India with actress Mia Farrow, becoming the first of a number of celebrities who became meditators and who helped make Maharishi become a celebrity among older teens and young adults.

During the early 1970s, the movement experienced considerable growth in Europe and the United States, and by the end of the decade almost 1 million people had taken the basic TM course. However, the World Plan Executive Council suffered several major reverses in the mid-1970s, and around 1976 the number of new people taking the basic TM course in North America dropped drastically. As a response to the decline, the council announced an advanced *siddha* program, which included the teaching of levitation to meditators.

Maharishi and the World Plan Executive Council, besides their success, have often been the target of criticism and controversy centering mainly on three issues. TM's claims to scientific verification have often been challenged, particularly those related to the physical effects of TM that, according to the psychologists studying yoga and meditation, could be produced from a wider variety of practices. Also, other scientists pointed out that positive results could be obtained only from special samples of meditators.

Critics interested in the separation of church and state, supported by evangelical Christians who opposed TM, challenged the use of state funds to spread the practice, arguing that the World Plan Executive Council was in fact a Hindu religious organization and TM a practice essentially religious in nature. TM critics have also charged the movement with an element of deception, claiming that Maharishi, in his effort to bring TM to the United States, created a new image, in part based on the early scientific papers, denying the religious elements and arguing that the practice of TM led to reduced dependence on drugs. In 1978, a federal ruling, asserting that TM was a religious practice, denied access to public funds with which teachers were supported.

During the 1970s, TM was attacked by Bob Kropinski, who took the organization to court, charging fraud and psychological damage from the practice of the *siddha* program. According to Kropinski, while the advertisements promised to teach students the ability to levitate, in fact they taught only a form of hopping while sitting in a cross-legged position. The organization has yet to produce generally verifiable evidence of the *siddha* program involving the ability to levitate, walk through walls, or become invisible.

The group's Web site is http://www.tm.org.

The Twelve Tribes Messianic Communities (Northeast Kingdom Community Church)

The Twelve Tribes Messianic Communities, also known as the Northeast Kingdom Community Church, is a communal, utopian society that emerged from the Jesus People revival in 1972 under the leadership of Elbert Eugene ("Gene") Spriggs, whom the community members consider an apostle, and his wife, Marsha, in Chattanooga, Tennessee. Members adopt Hebrew names and consider themselves as part of the Commonwealth of Israel forming in the last days, bound by the new covenant in the Messiah's blood, as mentioned in Ephesians 2:12. The communities have evolved into a distinct culture emphasizing craftsmanship and handiwork; they have evolved their own devotional music and dance forms and unique, neoconservative patterns of marriage and child rearing. The group condemns abortion and homosexuality and upholds monogamy, premarital chastity, and home schooling.

The belief system is compatible with Evangelical Protestantism but contains certain theological innovations in their views on communal living, marriage, and eschatology. Ongoing collective revelations continue to unveil the community's unique role in their postmillenarian vision of the last days, their relationship to Yahshua—that is, Jesus—and levels of salvation after the Final Judgment. The communities define themselves as the lost and scattered tribes of the ancient Jews undergoing restoration in preparation for eternal life. They believe their community is undergoing a process of purification as the "pure and spotless bride" awaiting her bridegroom and that it will probably take three generations to be ready for the Second Coming. By increasing their ranks through conversions and childbearing, they are "raising up a people" in preparation for the jubilee horn that heralds the return of Yahshua.

Church members have been the target of deprogrammers ever since the founding of communes in Chattanooga, but the most severe and widely publicized conflicts with secular authorities have involved child-beating allegations and child-custody disputes. In 1984, the Vermont State Police, armed with a court order and accompanied by fifty social services workers, raided the Island Pond community homes and took 112 children into custody. District Court judge Frank Mahady ruled that the search warrant issued by the state was unconstitutional, and all the children were returned to their parents without undergoing examinations. Child-custody disputes and investigations by social services continue, partly due to the influence of the anticult movement and disillusioned apostates. The group's commitment to their biblically based disciplinary practices is the primary focus of concern. Parents are instructed to discipline children who do not obey upon "first command" with a thin, flexible "reedlike" rod (as mentioned in Proverbs 23:13) so as to inflict pain but not injury.

Since their "deliverance" from the raid, the group has emphasized cooperation with state authorities and has reached out to neighbors in trying to foster a better understanding. In August 1993, the Island Pond members joined search parties to find a missing pilot whose plane had crashed in Essex County. On June 25, 1994, the church held a ten-year anniversary celebration "to commemorate [our] deliverance from the 1984 Island Pond Raid." Many of those 112 children, now in their teens and twenties, shared their traumatic memories of the raid, denied allegations of abuse, and declared their allegiance to their parents and their community.

The group's Web site is http://www.twelvetribes.com.

Unification Movement (Unification Church)

The Unification Church, formally the Holy Spirit Association for the Unification of World Christianity, refers to an international messianic religious movement led by the Reverend Sun Myung Moon (b. 1920). It also is the core of a complex network of media, industrial, commercial, cultural, and educational enterprises worldwide. Derided in the West as "the Moonies," the UC's emergence has been accompanied by intense and sustained global reaction.

Core beliefs of the Unification Church are contained in its primary doctrinal and theological text, *Divine Principle* (1973), itself derived from two earlier Korean texts, *Woli Kang-ron* (1966) and *Woli Hae-sul* (1955). These texts express aspects of the "new truth" or "principle" revealed through Sun Myung Moon. Utilizing familiar categories of Christian theology, key chapter topics include the Creation, the Fall, Resurrection, predestination, Christology, and history. While polemical opponents have identified departures from orthodoxy, the major novelty is the explicitness with which the text identifies the present as the time of Christ's Second Advent.

An oral tradition consisting mainly of Moon's speeches exists alongside the official doctrinal texts. Many of these speeches are more forthcoming about the Second Advent having arrived in the persons of Reverend and Mrs. Moon. UC members believe them to be the "true parents" of humankind, ushering in the "completed Testament age." Since 1992, when this age is regarded to have begun, pronouncements of this nature have become increasingly public. Widespread and enhanced spiritual sensibility, the liberation of oppressed peoples, the emergence of global culture, and advanced technological development are all associated by the movement with the Second Advent and completed Testament age. So too are ever greater numbers of couples participating in the joint weddings or "blessings" presided over by the "true parents."

The UC has not been subject to the apocalyptic conflagrations associated with such movements as the People's Temple, Branch Davidians, and AUM Shinrikyo. Nevertheless, the scope and duration of reactions accompanying its emergence have rendered it quite possibly the most controversial new religious movement of the latter twentieth century.

Negative reaction was apparent from the UC's Korean mid-1950s origins. There was an intense reaction to UC proselytization efforts on Seoul university campuses, especially Ehwa Women's University, which led to Moon's imprisonment and allegations that the UC was a "sex cult." Although the UC gained a degree of credibility with the Korean military government after 1961, relations were tenuous and successive regimes have been embarrassed by UC "initiatives," the most recent being the Reverend Sun Myung Moon's unauthorized visit to North Korea and Kim Il Sung in late 1991 that was repudiated by Seoul. Korea's Christian population has continually rejected the UC as heretical.

In the United States, the UC has faced widespread suspicion, hostility, and negative press. Kidnapping and deprogrammings were common in the mid-1970s, and a 1977 Gallup survey found that Sun Myung Moon "elicited one of the most overwhelmingly negative responses ever reported by a major poll." During the 1980s, the UC culled some favor under conservative Republican administrations. However, during this period, Moon was convicted and jailed on tax evasion charges regarded by the UC as being motivated by bias. Similar patterns of response have been prevalent elsewhere in the world, notably Europe, the Commonwealth of Independent States, Southeast Asia, and Latin America.

The group's Web site is http://www.unification.net.

Voodoo

Voodoo is a magical religion that originated in Haiti in the late 1700s. The precursor of voodoo was the religion of the Fon people of West Africa who were brought as slaves to Haiti. *Voodoo* (or *vodou*) means "spirit" in the Fon language. In Haiti, the Fon systems of veneration of the spirits came in contact with other African religious traditions and French Catholicism to produce what we call voodoo. It has spread via emigration to New Orleans and major cities in the United States.

The central religious activity of voodoo involves possession of devotees by a number of African deities. In ceremonies led by a priest, each possessed individual enacts a highly specific ritual performance involving dance, song, and speech appropriate to the particular possessing deity. Possession is directed toward healing, warding off evil, and bringing good or evil fortune.

Voodoo recognizes a remote and almighty supreme being who is the personification of fate or destiny. In voodoo, this god is called Bondye. Individuals are given their own destinies by Bondye. In order to fulfill these destinies with grace and power, an individual requires guidance from a variety of spirits called *lwa*. The religion of voodoo is a system of actions toward the development of closer relationships with the *lwa*. Human beings and spirits interact through divination and sacrifice. Trained priests and priestesses consult oracles to determine the sacrificial foods and actions necessary to secure the power and presence of *lwa*. One particular *lwa* will begin to assert itself as an individual devotee's patron. When the spirit wills it, the individual will undergo an initiation into the mysteries of his or her patron spirit. This initiation will mark the member's entry into the priesthood of voodoo and give him or her the authority to found his or her own house and consecrate other priests and priestesses. The spirit will identify with the devotee's inner self, and this intimate relationship will offer the devotee health, success, and wisdom.

Voodoo first came to the United States with Haitian immigrants. In more recent years, white Americans as well as black Americans have been finding their way to voodoo houses. Though there are relatively few white initiates, it is likely that there will be more as the religion becomes better known and spreads further beyond its immigrant roots.

The most controversial element of voodoo in the eyes of outsiders is the slaughter of animals as part of feasts for the *lwa*. Most of the important ceremonies require a feast to be prepared for the spirits and to be enjoyed by the assembled community. In order to fix the meal to the spirit's specifications, the foods must not only be prepared and cooked according to strict recipes but also be properly consecrated with certain prayers and rhythms.

Animals for the feast (fowl, goats, and sheep) must be slaughtered by a priest or priestess initiated specially to this task, in the presence of the community and to the accompaniment of the correct chants. Particularly in the crowded neighborhoods of New York and Miami, animal slaughter as part of voodoo ceremonies has caused some problems, including storage of the animals before the ceremony and the disposal of the remains afterward.

Healing is a high priority of Vodoun and includes psychic and psychological counseling and the dispensing of folk remedies such as rattlesnake oil. Worship is held on the evening of the new moon and consists of ecstatic dance accompanied by flute and drum and led by the priest and priestess. As they dance, members enter trances and often receive revelations and messages from the spirits. Spirituals are also sung. Vodoun teaches the virtues of faith, love, and joy.

No active Web site is available for the group.

The Way International, Inc.

The Way International, Inc., a Pentecostal, ultradispensational Christian group, was founded in 1942 by Victor Paul Wierwille (1916–1985), a minister in the Evangelical and Reformed Church, as a radio ministry under the name of "Vesper Chimes." It assumed its present name in 1974, after being named the Chimes Hour in 1944, and the Chimes Hour Youth Caravan in 1947. Wierwille earned his BD at Mission House Seminary in Minnesota and did graduate work at the University of Chicago and Princeton Theological Seminary, earning an MTh in 1941. In 1948, he was awarded a PhD by the Pikes Peak Bible College and Seminary in Manitou Springs, Colorado.

The first "Power for Abundant Living" (PFAL) class, given in 1953, contained the initial results of Wierwille's research on biblical truth. After one year, he began to study Aramaic, under the influence of Dr. George M. Lamsa, translator of the Lamsa Bible, and began to accept a view of biblical doctrine that was more and more distinct from that of his church. In 1957, he resigned his ministry from the Evangelical and Reformed Church in order to devote himself full-time to his work. He led his ministry, which was chartered as the Way, Inc., in 1955, and then changed to the Way International in 1975, until 1983, when he retired. The headquarters of the Way was established in the family farm outside New Knoxville, Ohio.

The Way grew steadily during the 1950s through the initiation of the PFAL classes and the *Way Magazine* (1954). After experiencing a slow growth in the 1960s, the Way underwent a period of rapid growth in the 1970s, as the ministry suddenly burgeoned at the time of the national Jesus People revival across the United States. The Way expanded its facilities at New Knoxville, which hosted the first national Rock of Ages Festival, an annual gathering of Way members, in 1971.

An eleven-point statement summarizes the beliefs of the Way, which can be considered both Arian and Pentecostal, in that it rejects the Trinitarian orthodoxy of most Western Christianity and denies the divinity of Jesus, as emphasized in Wierwille's *Jesus Christ Is Not God* (1975). The Way believes that Jesus is the Son of God but not God the Son.

The Way International is one of the largest groups to be labeled a "cult." It has also been the target of many deprogrammings, particularly in the early 1980s. It has often been accused by anticult groups of brainwashing and mind control. Additionally, there have been two serious charges that have often been repeated in anti-Way literature: The first charge, in the 1970s, was that the Way was training members in the use of deadly weapons for possible future use against enemies of the organization. These accusations originated from the adoption at the College at Emporia of a Kansas program in gun safety, which was primarily directed to hunters. The second charge came to the fore in the 1980s, as Christian anticultists attacked The Way for its radical departure from orthodox Christianity, its adoption of Arianism, and the denial of the divinity of Jesus and the Trinity.

The Way experienced a period of turmoil after Wierwille's death. Charges of improprieties by Wierwille and many of his close friends resulted in the defection of several leaders, a few of whom established rival groups. As a result, The Way considerably lost support, although it recovered by 1990, when the attendance to the annual Rock of Ages Festival began to return to its former level. The Internal Revenue Service questioned The Way's alleged partisan political involvement and its business activities at New Knoxville. Although its tax-exempt status was revoked in 1985, that ruling was reversed by the Supreme Court in 1990.

The group's Web site is http://theway.com.

Witchcraft (Wicca)

There have been a great many descriptions of Wicca, also referred to as the "Craft," published by now. For the sake of simplicity, we can say that Wicca has the following characteristics:

1. Worship is polytheistic and always includes an exalted concept of a goddess as being close to the ultimate level of divinity.
2. Worship occurs in a small group known as a coven (which may consist of anywhere from three to around twenty members), according to the phases of the moon. These monthly meetings for worship (and the working of practical magic) are referred to as *esbats*. Worship also occurs in larger groups, which may be two covens meeting together or several hundred people, some coming from long distances, for the *sabbats*, of which there are eight in each year.
3. In addition to worship, coven activity focuses on the working of magic, which is highly psychologized, eclectic, and variegated, since the magical training procedures used in any one coven will depend on what training in magic, psychic abilities, psychology, or other disciplines the coven's leaders have had in academia, New Age groups, or other occult groups.
4. Despite the anarchism of neopagan witches, they are just as clear as members of other religions about which individuals and groups belong to their religion and which do not.

The publication of Margaret Murray's *Witch-Cult in Western Europe* (1921) set off a burst of interest in paganism, since Murray proposed that the witch hunters of medieval and early modern times were actually finding the remnants of the pagan religions of northern Europe. The idea of re-creating the kind of witch cult described by Murray was discussed by English occultists during the 1920s and 1930s. However, the first successful attempt to re-create Murray's witch cult was apparently actually carried out by Gerald B. Gardner, a retired British civil servant, and his colleagues among the New Forest occultists, under the leadership of one Dorothy Clutterbuck, a locally prominent homeowner and socialite, during World War II.

In 1953, Gardner initiated Doreen Valiente, who soon became the high priestess of the central coven and rewrote the coven's *Book of Shadows* (liturgical manual) into the form in which it is still used in the movement. *The Book of Shadows* contains rituals for the coven's full moon *esbats;* for the eight *sabbats* at the solstices, equinoxes, and cross-quarter days; and for various rites of passage, as well as some basic magical techniques. The central coven fissured in two in 1957, with Gardner and Valiente each taking a half, but Gardner soon went off on his own again, initiating new priestesses and founding new covens at a fairly rapid pace until his death in 1964, and these have carried on the Craft enthusiastically.

Raymond Buckland, after a long correspondence with Gardner, was initiated in 1963 in Perth, Scotland, by Lady Olwen (Monique Wilson). Buckland then brought the Craft back to the United States and, with his wife, Rosemary, as high priestess, founded the New York coven in Bayside, Long Island, which became the center of the Gardnerian movement and the neopagan movement in the United States for the next twenty years.

The group's Web site is http://www.witchvox.com.

4

Court Decisions, Legislation, and Governmental Actions

Beyond the limited-domain struggles that have taken place around deprogrammings, the principal arenas within which the controversy over new religions has been fought are the courts and the media. Perhaps paradoxically, the anticult movement has suffered defeat in the courts but been victorious in the media. The current state of affairs is comparable to the situation the civil rights movement found itself in during its heyday: although going from victory to victory in the courts, in popular opinion blacks were still viewed as second-class citizens, particularly in the Deep South.

One of the principal reasons minority religions have had such success in the legal arena is that the courts have been compelled to treat such groups seriously as *religions,* entitled to all of the rights and privileges normally accorded mainstream denominations. Critics of new religions would like to draw a sharp line between religions and cults and treat cults as pseudoreligious organizations. The courts, however, are unable to approach such groups differently as long as group members manifest sincerity in their religious beliefs.

This situation explains why none of the legislative efforts to regulate new religious movements have been successful. For example, the New York state legislature once tried to enact a law that would have made starting a pseudoreligion a felony, but it failed to pass because—among other factors—it lacked an objective criterion for distinguishing false from true religions. Without a truly neutral standard, any such law violates the establishment

179

clause of the First Amendment. It is, in fact, the separation of church and state mandated by the First Amendment that has discouraged legislation in this area. This has left the courts to bear the burden of adjudicating the controversy, making an overview of the relevant legal activity far more lengthy and involved than with most other public issues.

Because cases involving contemporary minority religions are often argued in terms of religious liberty issues, earlier religious liberty decisions are directly relevant to the present controversy. Although anticultists have accused cults of "hiding behind the First Amendment," they have been largely unsuccessful at persuading the legal system to set aside First Amendment concerns when dealing with controversial minority religions. The necessity of taking cults seriously as "real" religions explains why it is necessary to refer back to earlier legal decisions involving Mormons, Jehovah's Witnesses, and others.

The following discussion begins with an overview of court cases and legislation not dealing explicitly with contemporary "cult" groups but nevertheless relevant to the controversy because of the religious liberty issue. This will be followed by an examination of the first important "new religion" cases prior to the emergence of the cult controversy as an important public issue. In addition to the initial efforts of governmental bodies to regulate minority religions by passing new laws, deprogrammers and their clients began using conservatorship laws to legitimate their kidnapping activities. Although initially experiencing some limited success, in the long run this strategy was defeated in the courts.

Following the demise of the conservatorship tactic, torts by ex-members claiming damage at the hands of their former religions became the chief strategy by which to weaken controversial minority religions. Once again, this tactic initially had a few notable successes, only to be ultimately frustrated by the defeat of coercive persuasion or "brainwashing" theory in the courts. Of the other legal arenas in which the cult controversy has been fought, perhaps the most important have been the sensitive issues of child abuse and child custody. Other areas have been zoning, solicitation, and taxation issues.

For a long time, it seemed that the new religions and their enemies were more or less evenly matched in the courts, although the balance of power would periodically swing one way or the other. This situation changed dramatically in the mid- to late nineties with the decisive defeat of the "brainwashing" notion in the courts and with the declaration of bankruptcy by the largest anticult organization in the United States.

However, just when it seemed that the anticult movement had suffered final defeat in U.S. courts, a new wave of anticult activity swept across western Europe, Japan, and, later, China. This resurgence of anticultism in Europe was more or less the result of the Solar Temple suicides that took place in Switzerland (as well as Canada) in 1994 and in France in 1995. Correspondingly, Japan reacted to the AUM Shinrikyo's poison-gas attack on the Tokyo subway system in 1995. And in China, the government reacted severely to the peaceable protests of Falun Gong practitioners n 1999, initiating a crackdown on any religious group that did not enjoy official sanctions.

Relevant Court Decisions Not Directly Involving Contemporary New Religions

Mormon Polygamy Cases

Religious beliefs are fully protected under the First Amendment to the Constitution. However, it has become a well-recognized principle of constitutional law that religious conduct may be circumscribed. In *Cantwell v. Connecticut* (discussed below), for instance, the United States Supreme Court acknowledged that religious conduct "remains subject to regulation for the protection of society."

According to the Court, religious practices may be regulated even at the expense of religious freedom. This view dates back to the time of Thomas Jefferson, who proposed legislation in the Virginia House of Delegates recognizing that government may "interfere when [religious] principles break out into overt acts against peace and good order" (quoted in the *Reynolds v. United States* decision). This governmental interference includes allowing for recovery to those who suffer harm as a result of tortious conduct by another. Religious organizations are not exempt from liability for tortious conduct.

Because of the First Amendment, religious liberty cases are almost by definition Supreme Court cases. The first Supreme Court decision having a direct bearing on the contemporary debate over cults was the 1878 case *Reynolds v. United States.* Lurid stories about the plural-wife practices of the Church of Jesus Christ of Latter-day Saints had titillated other Americans for more than three decades—stories implying that Mormon polygamy was a thinly veiled excuse for sexual indulgence. As a consequence, Congress legislated against plural marriage as a form of bigamy in the *Revised Statutes of the United States,* sect. 5352: "Every person having a husband or wife living, who marries another, whether married or single, in a Territory, or other place over which the United States have exclusive jurisdiction, is guilty of bigamy, and shall be punished by a fine of not more than $500, and by imprisonment for a term of not more than five years."

George Reynolds was a member of the LDS Church convicted under this statute. Reynolds asserted that, because plural marriage was prescribed by his religion, his conviction was a violation of the free exercise of religion provision of the First Amendment.

In 1878, this case was considered by the Supreme Court. When Chief Justice Morrison Waite wrote the Court's decision, he was aware that history was being made: this was the first judicial effort to interpret the meaning of the "free exercise of religion." Justice Waite's decision cited, among other things, contemporaneous scholarly opinion that polygamy was detrimental to a free society and concluded that in the First Amendment: "Congress was deprived of all legislative power over mere opinion, but was left free to reach actions which were in violation of social duties or subversive of good order." In other words, although Congress cannot prescribe laws against what one may *believe* ("opinion"), it may legislate against *actions* harmful to society—such as the plural-wife system was judged to be.

This decision was amplified in a second LDS case, *Davis v. Beason,* decided by the Supreme Court in 1889. Samuel D. Davis had had his voter registration in Idaho rescinded merely for belonging to the Mormon Church. Davis argued his case, like Reynolds, on the free exercise provision of the First Amendment. Associate Justice Stephen Field wrote the Court's decision, asserting, like Waite had before him, that not every action prescribed by a religion can be protected by the First Amendment: "History discloses the fact that the necessity of human sacrifices, upon special occasions, had been a tenet of many sects. Should a sect of [this kind] ever find its way into this country, swift punishment would follow the carrying into effect of its doctrines, and no heed would be given to the pretence that, as religious beliefs, their supporters could be protected in their exercise by the Constitution of the United States."

Finally, in the decision of two other LDS cases, Justice Joseph Bradley responded to the free exercise of religion argument by noting that, "No doubt the Thugs of India imagined that their belief in the right of assassination was a religious belief." (Bradley wrote a joint decision for the Supreme Court in *Mormon Church v. United States* and *Romney v. United States*.)

Following *Reynolds* and the other LDS decisions, the standards for measuring the harmfulness of religious conduct were based on socially accepted, traditional notions of religious practice. Because the practice of polygamy was offensive to the notions of traditional religious institutions and because the Court in *Reynolds* assumed that there were innocent victims who suffered harm from such conduct, the religious practice was not allowed to continue.

In *Reynolds*, the Court relied on various excerpts of writings by Thomas Jefferson, one of the proponents of the free exercise clause. Jefferson believed that "religion is a matter which lies solely between man and his God; . . . that the legislative powers of the government reach actions only, and not opinions"; and that government may not opine on the validity of a religion but may only regulate actions that are in violation of social duties or subversive of good order.

The Court in *Reynolds* deferred to contemporary social norms and opinions concerning polygamy and found that it was an odious practice and void under the common law. The Supreme Court upheld the trial court's jury instructions, which reminded the jury of the evil consequences that were supposed to flow from plural marriages. Those "evil consequences" were the subject of numerous books and articles published by anti-Mormons during the second half of the nineteenth century as well as congressional testimony. Thus, the *Reynolds* decision reflects the willingness of the highest court to adopt a standard consistent with majoritarian social norms to the detriment of minority religious practices.

Together, *Reynolds, Davis*, and others, involving the most despised "new religion" of the day, all asserted the absolute right of the government to regulate religious activity. Although, in hindsight, these specific decisions may appear contrary to the spirit of the free exercise clause, at the same time they articulate the obvious point that not every activity deserves the protection of the

First Amendment merely because it has a religious basis. In the context of the contemporary cult controversy, anticult spokespersons have sometimes referred back to the belief-action dichotomy laid out in *Reynolds v. United States*. The *Reynolds* decision was not, however, the final word on the meaning of the free exercise provision.

Jehovah's Witnesses Cases

The Jehovah's Witnesses were the most controversial new religion of the mid-twentieth century. Like the LDS, the Witnesses remain the focus of much contemporary Christian anticultism because of perceived doctrinal deviations from the Evangelical mainstream. The group's aggressive proselytizing in combination with members' refusal to participate in such nationalistic activities as saluting the flag led to persecution and arrests. In response, the Witnesses formed a legal wing for the express purpose of challenging these arrests on First Amendment grounds.

The first important Supreme Court victory for the Jehovah's Witnesses was the 1938 case of *Lovell v. City of Griffin*. The Supreme Court's decision in this case overturned the conviction of a Witness for distributing literature without a permit. The permit ordinance, however, left too much to the discretion of the relevant city official, making it unconstitutional on the basis of the *free speech* (as opposed to the freedom of religion) provision of the First Amendment.

The freedom of religion clause was brought into play two years later in another significant Supreme Court victory for the Witnesses, *Cantwell v. Connecticut*—a case that extended the freedom of religion provision of the federal constitution to the states and served to call into question the 1887 *Reynolds* decision giving government the power to regulate religious actions. *Cantwell's* departure from the LDS cases is reflected in the decision composed by Associate Justice Owen Roberts:

> The Amendment embraces two concepts—freedom to believe and freedom to act. The first is absolute but, in the nature of things, the second cannot be. Conduct remains subject to regulation for the protection of society. The freedom to act must have appropriate definition to preserve the enforcement of that protection. In every case the power to regulate must be so exercised as not,

in attaining a permissible end, unduly to infringe the protected freedom.

The *Cantwell* decision was reinforced by further cases decided three years later. In 1943, four cases involving the right of Jehovah's Witnesses to canvass door-to-door reached the high court. Three were decided in favor of the Witnesses *(Jones v. Oplika, Murdock v. Pennsylvania,* and *Martin v. Struthers).* The fourth case *(Douglas v. Jeannette)* was decided against the Witnesses, but on technical grounds. Associate Justice William O. Douglas wrote the Court's decisions in *Jones* and *Murdock,* referring to the tradition of itinerant evangelism as support for the argument that the solicitation activity of Witnesses was a religious activity, and thus protected by the First Amendment.

Another case involving the refusal of Witnesses to salute the flag, *West Virginia State Board of Education v. Barnette,* was decided the same year. *Barnette* was decided in favor of the Jehovah's Witnesses, overturning a related Supreme Court decision, *Minersville School District v. Gobitis,* made against the Witnesses in 1940. The decision in *Barnette* was made on free exercise of religion rather than free speech grounds.

The Sherbert-Yoder Test

In 1963, the high court decided *Sherbert v. Verner,* a key case for what would become known as the "Sherbert-Yoder Test" for deciding free exercise of religion cases. In this case, the Supreme Court decided in favor of a Seventh-Day Adventist who had been denied unemployment benefits because she had not been able to accept employment requiring work on Saturday. *Wisconsin v. Yoder,* decided six years later, concluded that a state law mandating high school education was an excessive burden on the Amish religion.

Without going into all of the details of these cases, the resulting Sherbert-Yoder Test sets forth criteria for adjudicating conflicts between the interest of the state and the dictates of a religion. These criteria have been summarized by William C. Shepherd (1985) as follows:

1. Are the religious beliefs in question sincerely held?
2. Are the religious practices under review germane to the religious belief system?

3. Would carrying out the state's wishes constitute a substantial infringement on the religious practice?
4. Is the interest of the state compelling? Does the religious practice perpetuate some grave abuse of a statutory provision or obligation?
5. Are there alternative means of regulation by which the state's interest is served but the free exercise of religion is less burdened?

The Sherbert-Yoder test has become the definitive standard for deciding cases involving the free exercise of religion. It would be the crucial criterion for determining the outcome of later cases involving new religious movements.

To get a sense of the importance of the Sherbert-Yoder Test, we might look briefly at a few of decisions made prior to and after *Sherbert*. In 1949 in *Bunn v. North Carolina*, for example, a lower court ruled that public safety outweighed the concern for the free exercise of religion involving the handling of poisonous snakes. The U.S. Supreme Court dismissed the appeal without comment. Only two years before *Sherbert*, in *Braunfeld v. Brown*, the Supreme Court decided against Orthodox Jewish merchants protesting Pennsylvania laws requiring them to close their stores on Sunday.

In 1981, the Supreme Court ruled on *Thomas v. Review Board*. In this case, a Witness who had quit his job rather than work in an armaments factory had been denied unemployment benefits. The court decided in favor of the Jehovah's Witnesses, echoing the decision in *Sherbert*. This case is important as the first major case after *Yoder* to be decided according to the Sherbert-Yoder Test. In 1993, the Court overturned a Hialeah, Florida, ban against "animal sacrifice" aimed at the growing Santeria community of the city as unconstitutional in *Church of Lukumi Bablu Aye v. City of Hialeah*.

The Sherbert-Yoder Test was the standard until the 1990 case of *Employment Division v. Smith*. In this decision, the Supreme Court ruled against the right of Native American Church members to use peyote. The case evoked outrage from church-state scholars and others, who characterized the decision as supplanting religious sincerity with the values of the majority as the standard for determining which religious acts merit the protection of the free exercise clause of the First Amendment.

Reacting to the Supreme Court's decision in *Employment Di-*

vision v. Smith, a broad coalition of religious groups supported and pushed through the Religious Freedom Restoration Act (RFRA), a legislative measure intended to reestablish Sherbert-Yoder standards for the free exercise of religion. RFRA was overwhelmingly endorsed by both houses of Congress.

Earliest Cases Involving Contemporary New Religions

The *Ballard* Decision

Prior to the emergence of the modern cult controversy and even prior to the formulation of *Sherbert v. Verner,* there was one extremely important Supreme Court case involving a contemporary new religion. This 1944 case, *United States v. Ballard,* focused on the belief system of I AM Activity, a neo-Theosophical group from which a whole family of other groups—including Church Universal and Triumphant—trace their roots. The case was built around the charge of mail fraud, based on the "ridiculous" nature of the group's beliefs. In the words of Justice Jackson who wrote the dissenting opinion in *United States v. Ballard:*

> Scores of sects flourish in this country by teaching what to me are queer notions. It is plain that there is wide variety in American religious taste. The Ballards are not alone in catering to it with a pretty dubious product.
>
> The chief wrong which false prophets do to their following is not financial. The collections aggregate a tempting total, but individual payments are not ruinous. I doubt if the vigilance of the law is equal to making money stick by overcredulous people. But the real harm is on the mental and spiritual plane. There are those who hunger and thirst after higher values which they feel wanting in their humdrum lives. They live in mental confusion or moral anarchy and seek vaguely for truth and beauty and moral support. When they are deluded and then disillusioned, cynicism and confusion follow. The wrong of these things, as I see it, is not in the money the victims part with half so much as in the mental and spiritual poison they get.

The founder of the movement, Guy Ballard, had long been interested in occultism and Theosophy. He married Edna Wheeler in 1916, and together they founded the I AM Activity in the 1930s. Ballard's revelations from Saint Germain were spread during the lectures of the Ballards, who traveled in the 1930s as "accredited messengers" of the masters. Further messages from the ascended masters, especially from Saint Germain and the master Jesus, were sometimes produced in public or private.

Saint Germain and Jesus were considered the mediators between the "I AM presence" and humans. The ascended masters were at one time all human beings who were able to transcend the physical world through the purification of their lives. The goal of human life is represented by ascension. In 1938, the I AM Activity was said to have been given a dispensation according to which persons who had devoted themselves so much to the movement that they had not given all they might to personal purification could upon normal death ascend from the after-earth state without reembodiment.

The I AM Activity worked publicly from 1937 to 1940 to establish a group of devoted followers numbering more than 1 million. With the death of Guy Ballard on December 29, 1939, the movement began to decline. Edna Ballard claimed that her husband had become an ascended master. However, the fact that Guy Ballard had experienced a physical death rather than bodily ascension threatened the movement's credibility. The following year, a sensational trial of the leaders of the movement took place, after some members of the Ballards' personal staff accused the Ballards of obtaining money under fraudulent pretenses.

The indictment was voided in 1944 by the Supreme Court with a landmark decision on religious liberty. The case was finally dismissed. Justice Douglas, in stating the prevailing opinion, wrote:

> Heresy trials are foreign to our Constitution. Men may believe what they cannot prove. They may not be put to the proof of their religious doctrines or beliefs. Religious experiences which are as real as life to some may be incomprehensible to others. Yet the fact that they may be beyond the ken of mortals does not mean that they can be made suspect before the law. . . . If one could be sent to jail because a jury in a hostile environment found one's teachings false, little indeed would be left of reli-

gious freedom. . . . The religious views espoused by respondents might seem incredible, if not preposterous, to most people. But if those doctrines are subject to trial before a jury charged with finding their truth or falsity, then the same can be done with the religious beliefs of any sect. When the triers of fact undertake that task, they enter a forbidden domain.

Founding Church of Scientology v. United States

What the Jehovah's Witnesses were to the mid-twentieth century, the Church of Scientology became to the latter part of the century. Like the Witnesses, Scientology early set up a strong legal wing that litigated for religious rights as well as for human rights more generally. One of the first new religions to be embroiled in controversy, Scientology would prevail in most of its legal suits and eventually play a major role in eviscerating the Cult Awareness Network, the most important anticult group in the United States.

The Church of Scientology was one of the genuinely new religions to originate in the United States in the twentieth century. The church was founded by L. Ron Hubbard, a talented writer and adventurer with a consuming interest in the human mind. By 1950, Hubbard had completed enough of his research to write *Dianetics: The Modern Science of Mental Health,* which quickly became a best-seller. In 1951, he announced that the "applied religious philosophy" of Scientology had been born.

Auditing, Scientology's core technique, consists of guiding someone through various mental processes in order to first free the individual of the effects of the "reactive mind" and then to fully realize the spiritual nature of the person. Electrical devices called E-Meters, which rely upon the same basic technology as lie detectors, are used to help the auditor discover emotionally loaded memories. When the individual is freed from the effects of the reactive mind, she or he is said to have achieved the state of "clear."

Somewhat naively, Hubbard contacted the medical and the psychiatric associations, explaining the significance of his discoveries for mental and physical health and asking that the American Medical Association and the American Psychology Association investigate his new technique. Instead of taking this offer seriously, these associations responded by attacking him. The subsequent popular success of *Dianetics* did nothing to improve the image of Hubbard in the minds of the medical-psychiatric establishment and was likely instrumental in prompting the FDA raid against the church.

On January 4, 1963, the Founding Church of Scientology in Washington, D.C., was raided by U.S. marshals and deputized longshoremen with drawn guns, acting in behalf of the Food and Drug Administration. Five thousand volumes of church scriptures, 20,000 booklets, and 100 E-Meters were seized. It took eight years of litigation to finally obtain the return of the materials. Finally, in 1971, the U.S. District Court for the District of Columbia issued the *Founding Church of Scientology v. United States* decision. The Food and Drug Administration was ordered to return the books and E-Meters that had been taken in the 1963 raid. In its decision, the court recognized the church's constitutional right to protection from the government's excessive entanglement with religion.

Deprogramming in Court

The cult controversy proper did not get under way until after the collapse of the sixties counterculture. Rather than reengaging with mainstream society, many former counterculturists continued their quest for an alternative lifestyle in a wide variety of religions. Hence, the membership of many unusual religious groups that had existed quietly on the margins of U.S. society suddenly exploded into public view.

In many cases, friends and family of cult members found it difficult to believe that, without coercion and brainwashing, loved ones would choose to embrace something that they found offensive. They saw "deprogramming" as the natural antidote to this mental programming or brainwashing. By attempting to deprogram the church member, friends and family believed they were helping the member recognize the wrongfulness of his or her choices.

When a person is targeted for deprogramming, he or she is enticed away from the organization or is actually kidnapped and taken to a remote place. While at the remote location, the person is subjected to intensive discussions in which he or she is presented with the "truth" about the religious organization, its tenets and leaders. The process is intense and stressful. Numerous "anticult" organizations promoted kidnapping and deprogramming of church members who had been "deprived of their free will."

These deprogramming activities invade the civil rights of members and deprive the members of choice in their affiliations. Deprogramming also exploits family ties and may further the destruction of family relations. Family members are often the instigators of the kidnapping and deprogramming, and the deprogrammers are the facilitators. In addition to deprogrammers, bodyguards are sometimes hired to prevent the member from escaping. The fact that family members are generally involved makes prosecution of the perpetrators difficult. The state has been reluctant to prosecute a family member for kidnapping. If family members are not prosecuted, judges and juries appear reluctant to convict others who become involved at the request of the family members, the instigators. Further, family members often refuse to testify against the perpetrators, making it virtually impossible to convict.

In deprogramming cases, there is generally testimony by former members. This testimony is filled with a high level of hostility, which increases the prejudice of the judge and jury. The testimony of former members also tends to confuse the legal issues with religious questions. This entanglement of legal and religious issues often confuses the judge and jury and results in placing the religious practices of the church on trial.

In the case of LaVerne Collins (now LaVerne Macchio), a member of Church Universal and Triumphant, LaVerne's mother and sister decided to "rescue" LaVerne from the church because they believed the church was seriously damaging LaVerne and her family. Family members hired deprogrammers and bodyguards to kidnap and deprogram her. At the time of her abduction, LaVerne was thirty-nine years old and the mother and primary caretaker of four children ranging in age from three to fourteen. She was a part-time schoolteacher and had resided in the same house in Ada County, Idaho, for fifteen years. LaVerne was missing for several days, and there was concern in the community for her safety.

After LaVerne's escape from the deprogrammers, charges were filed against LaVerne's mother and sister, the deprogrammers, and the bodyguards for kidnapping and false imprisonment. Later, at LaVerne's request, all charges against family members were dropped. As a result, the deprogrammers were acquitted. The bodyguards, who were to be tried separately, reached an unusual plea bargain with prosecutors: they would enter guilty pleas on either a felony kidnapping charge or a misdemeanor false-imprisonment charge, depending on the outcome of an appeal challenging the judge's ruling to allow the deprogrammers the use of the "necessity defense" at their trial.

When authorities have attempted to resist efforts to kidnap and deprogram members of religious groups by prosecuting those involved, defendants have often been able to assert successfully the defenses of necessity and "choice of evils." The necessity defense has been a major factor in the acquittal of the deprogrammers. The jury appeared to accept the contention that the illegal actions of the defendants were necessary to protect the victim from her own choices and that the church was the greater evil—a view reflecting traditional prejudices.

One element that must be proved under the necessity defense is that there was imminent danger requiring the kidnapping. The standards for determining the nature of the danger and its imminence are colored by the fear and mistrust many have of nontraditional religions. The courts have had difficulty establishing an objective standard by which to measure the danger or threat to the deprogramee. When the "choice of evils" defense is raised, courts have often allowed the jury to consider evidence concerning the supposed evils associated with the church's religious practices.

There is a long line of cases in the area of deprogramming. *People v. Brandyberry,* for example, involved a member of the Unification Church who was kidnapped and held in captivity for several days in an attempt to deprogram her. The trial court balanced the "method of cult indoctrination" and of "coercive persuasion" against the evils of abduction and of forced deprogramming to justify kidnapping; however, the court of appeals evaluated only the imminence of grave injury to the victim. The court of appeals acknowledged that to proceed in the manner permitted by the trial court would invite the jury to "consider the morality and desirability of church doctrine and practices rather than whether in fact the victim was threatened by the prospect of a grave or imminent injury."

The trial judge in *Brandyberry* relied on a decision from the Minnesota Supreme Court, *Peterson v. Sorlien.* The *Sorlien* court allowed parents to deprogram their child without fear of civil liability when the parents reasonably believed that the child was being unduly influenced by the religion and that the child had lost his or her capacity to reason.

Another common issue raised in deprogramming cases is that of involuntary treatment. Deprogrammers have sought orders requiring involuntary treatment for those who have been deprived of their free will and coercively persuaded to join a new religion. They argue that these individuals must be subject to involuntary treatment because they have lost their capacity to reason by virtue of the controlled environment and brainwashing to which they have been subjected. The control of the environment includes control over eating, sleeping, and other basics of life. Most courts have been reluctant to order such involuntary treatment. However, when courts permit the necessity or "choice of evils" defense, an individual's rights under the free exercise clause and right to be free from compulsory medical treatment are often abused.

Victims of deprogramming have also brought civil actions against kidnappers and deprogrammers. These actions have included claims of violations of civil rights, intentional infliction of emotional distress, conspiracy, and false imprisonment. These actions have had mixed results, but generally the cause of action has been allowed. In fact, one appeals court recognized that deprogrammers practice patterns of coercion similar to those alleged against the church (just as many anticult organizations have all of the essential characteristics of the "cults" they attack). However, in most cases, when civil claims are brought against deprogrammers or family members, the defendants try to make the religious practices of the church the focus of the trial. The defenses of necessity and "choice of evils" allow the trier of fact to review the religious organization's practices, and the degree to which those practices comport with the trier of fact's values may affect the outcome of the case.

Legislative Efforts and Conservatorship Cases

Attempting to Legislate against Cults

In the early years of the cult controversy, parents concerned about the religious choices of their adult children lobbied various legislatures. A number of states established committees and hearings to investigate the cult menace. Some resolutions were passed, but legislative bodies were ultimately unable to act against minority religions because of the church-state separation issue. The strongest effort ever made by a U.S. legislature was New York State Assembly Bill AB9566-A, which would have made "promoting a pseudoreligious cult" a felony, introduced by Robert C. Wertz on October 5, 1977:

> A person is guilty of promoting a pseudoreligious cult when he knowingly organizes or maintains an organization into which other persons are induced to join or participate in through the use of mind control methods, hypnosis, brainwashing techniques or other systematic forms of indoctrination in which the members or participants of such organization engage in soliciting funds primarily for the benefit of such organization or its leaders and are not permitted to travel or communicate with anyone outside such organization unless another member or participant of such organization is present.

A number of different groups, including the American Civil Liberties Union, lobbied heavily against the bill and it was ultimately defeated.

Efforts to Amend Conservatorship Laws

Failing to win the support of legislatures, some parents of cult members turned to more desperate measures in the form of the vigilante actions of deprogrammers. To protect themselves, it was sometimes possible to use existing conservatorship laws to legitimate their kidnapping activities. Conservatorships were originally designed to protect very elderly or very disturbed people from being unfairly taken advantage of. Such individuals are reduced to the legal status of children, unable to do such things as independently enter into contracts.

In some early cult conservatorship cases, psychiatrists sympathetic to the plight of concerned parents signed conservatorship orders without ever meeting the adult child—feeling that mere membership in a group like the Hare Krishna movement or the Unification Church was sufficient evidence for declaring her or him incompetent. After this practice was challenged, anticultists pushed for amended conservatorship laws that would de

facto legitimate deprogramming. Once again, such an amendment almost succeeded in the state of New York, where it was defeated only because the governor vetoed it. This measure was introduced on March 25, 1980, as 11122-A. The flavor of this
proposed amendment is captured in its first section, "Persons for
Who a Temporary Conservator May Be Appointed":

> The supreme court and the county courts outside the
> city of New York, shall have the power to appoint one
> or more temporary conservators of the persons and the
> property of any person over fifteen years of age, upon
> showing that such person for whom the temporary con-
> servator is to be appointed have become closely and
> regularly associated with a group which practices the
> use of deception in the recruitment of members and
> which engages in systematic food or sleep deprivation
> or isolation from family or unusually long work sched-
> ules and that such person for whom the temporary con-
> servator is to be appointed has undergone a sudden and
> radical change in behavior, lifestyle, habits and atti-
> tudes, and has become unable to care for his welfare
> and that his judgment has become impaired to the ex-
> tent that he is unable to understand the need for such
> care.

The Faithful Five–Faithless Four Case

The primary conservatorship decision involving a stigmatized
minority religion was *Katz v. Superior Court,* also referred to as the
"Faithful Five–Faithless Four" case. *Katz* was initially decided in
favor of parents seeking conservatorships for their five adult offspring who were members of the Unification Church—only to
have the appeals court overturn the decision almost immediately.
Four out of five of these individuals left the church anyway,
hence the unusual nickname for this case.

Katz was set in motion when the parents approached a California superior court for thirty-day conservatorships for their adult
children. The goal was to forcibly incarcerate the five "Moonies" in
the Freedom Ranch Rehabilitation Center, a deprogramming facility run by the Freedom of Thought Foundation of Tucson, Arizona.
The parents contended that conservatorships were necessary because of their offsprings' "mental illness or weakness and unsound

mind" and propensity "to be deceived by artful and designing persons." The parents' counsel further argued that the five had been victims of "psychological kidnapping."

One expert witness in the case, psychiatrist Samuel Benson, described the putative victims as suffering from a wide variety of pathological symptoms, including "memory impairment," "short attention spans and a decreased ability to concentrate," "limited ability toward abstractions," "defensive attitudes toward id urges," and "various degrees of regression and childlike attitudes." Benson further contended that these symptoms were the direct result of "coercive persuasion"—that is, "brainwashing"—techniques, as reflected in literature on former Korean War and Vietnam War POWs.

Despite countertestimony by the five Unificationists and their own psychological or psychiatric consultants, and despite the obvious constitutional issues that should have been taken into account, the judge decided for the parents, declaring: "We're talking about the very essence of life here, mother, father and children. There's nothing closer in our civilization. This is the essence of civilization."

When some of the conservatees petitioned the order, a California appellate court heard their appeal. The court of appeals found the conservatorship statute unconstitutionally vague: "In the field of beliefs, and particularly religious tenets, it is difficult, if not impossible, to establish a universal truth against which deceit and imposition can be measured." The appellate court also pointed out that there had been no demonstrated emergency that the conservatorship law required. In the absence of demonstrable physical deprivation, the equal protection and due process of law forbid involuntary confinement: "If there is coercive persuasion or brainwashing which requires treatment, the existence of such a mental disability and the necessity of legal control over the mentally disabled person for the purpose of treatment should be ascertained after compliance with the protection of civil liberties provided by the Welfare and Institutions Code. To do less is to license kidnapping for the purpose of thought control."

Finally and perhaps most important, the court of appeals held that the conservatorship orders had violated the Unificationists' rights to freedom of association and freedom of religion. The beliefs and behaviors used as criteria to determine the pathological state of the alleged victims (and to become the targets of the "treatment" to be administered at the Freedom Ranch Rehabilitation Center) were those that stemmed from religious conviction—precisely the arena into which the court system was forbidden to inquire. Hence, "in the absence of such actions as render the adult believer himself gravely disabled," state processes "cannot be used to deprive the believer of his freedom of action and to subject him to involuntary treatment."

The *Katz* decision did not immediately stop other parents from applying for temporary conservatorships for their adult children. There were also ongoing efforts to amend conservatorship laws so as to target members of minority religions. Retrospectively, however, it is evident that *Katz* marked an important watershed, after which the conservatorship tactic went into a gradual decline and eventually died out.

Ex-Member Lawsuits against Minority Religions

The issue of conservatorships for members of controversial religions was eventually completely eclipsed by tort cases brought by ex-members against their former religious group. Because the Constitution does not protect all religiously motivated conduct, courts have come to award damages to individuals who claim to have incurred personal injury because of their religious affiliation. Underlying the rationale for such decisions is the traditional notion that religion should benefit and improve one's life and well-being. When religious beliefs and practices do not fulfill these expectations but instead subject a person to personal harm, those beliefs and practices become suspect and generally open to scrutiny by the courts.

Unfortunately, the willingness of courts to examine nontraditional religious practices in light of mainstream traditions often leads to religion bashing in the judicial forum. Nontraditional beliefs are often found offensive only because of fear and misinformation. Since the emergence of the cult controversy, many minority religious groups have been accused of brainwashing or coercive persuasion. It is claimed that these religious practices subject the individual to a controlled environment in which individuals lose their capacity to reason and think for themselves.

In the early nineties, a judge considered religious practices when sentencing an individual who had pled guilty to charges of murder for hire and conspiracy to tamper with a federal witness. The court sentenced Richard LeBaron to five years for killing a man and his daughter at point-blank range because he had been "brainwashed" by a church to which he had belonged since he was a child. The court believed that because of this brainwashing, LeBaron had lost his capacity to reason and think for himself while committing the crimes, that his thoughts were coerced and not his own, and that he was not totally responsible for his choices and actions.

Religious practices that are assumed to extinguish the individual's capacity to reason and consent foster suspicion and leave the religious organization open to harassment and liability. The courts may, and often do, consider the religious beliefs and practices of nontraditional churches in the context of civil and criminal litigation. Since religious freedom is not absolute, as long as the courts are convinced that certain religious practices cause harm to society or individual church members, all religions will be subject to scrutiny and regulation by the courts and government. When children are involved, the scrutiny is even more exacting. Although the First Amendment was meant to protect individual rights, courts' willingness to delve into religious beliefs and practices affecting a variety of areas has at times resulted in inflaming juries against nontraditional religious practices, which can ultimately tip the scales of justice against the interests of the church. This has particularly been the case in civil suits.

Religious groups, both traditional and nontraditional, have been named in suits for intentional infliction of emotional distress and liability for "outrageous conduct" through spiritual counseling. When counseling by clergy goes awry, the minister or pastor becomes subject to litigation for intentional infliction of emotional distress. The emotional distress arises from beratement for sinful conduct and the member's perception that the pastor's counseling is malicious and intended to demean. A variety of different minority religions have been besieged with lawsuits by ex-members for personal injury claims ranging from fraud to intentional infliction of emotional distress.

In his book *Understanding New Religious Movements* (2003), John Saliba points out that contemporary minority religions have been taken to court for a wide variety of reasons:

1. The mental distress and psychological damage they have caused

2. Kidnapping and brainwashing young adults, thus forcing them to become members
3. The corruption of minors
4. Sexual servitude
5. Defamation
6. Alienation of affections
7. Wanton misconduct and outrageous acts
8. Harassment
9. Wrongful death

Decisions in such cases have varied so widely that general conclusions are difficult to draw. All of the better-known and many of the lesser-known new religions have been involved in such cases. The *Molko-Leal* case will be examined in the present section because of its significance for later developments in the cult controversy. The *Mull* case will be examined partially because of its influence on a later tax case, and partially because I have more direct familiarity with Church Universal and Triumphant than I do with certain other religious movements.

Molko and Leal v. Unification Church

David Molko and Tracey Leal had been members of the Unification Church for approximately six months when they were kidnapped and deprogrammed. Not long after forsaking their new religion, they sued the Unification Church for fraud, intentional infliction of emotional distress, and false imprisonment. They also sought the return of $6,000 worth of donations and payment for the work they did while members. The Unification Church countercharged that the psychological harm Molko and Leal had experienced was caused by deprogramming procedures rather than by church-related activities.

This case dragged on for years. In the first round, charges against the Unification Church were dismissed in 1986. Three years later, after a number of appeals, the case was finally cleared for trial by the California Supreme Court. For a number of different reasons, this case was finally settled out of court in November 1989.

This case is particularly important because of an amicus curiae brief initially filed on behalf of the Unification Church by the American Psychological Association and a number of individual scholars. Margaret Singer, one of the expert witnesses in this case, and Richard Ofshe would later sue the APA and others, citing this amicus curiae brief as the basis for an accusation of a conspiracy against them.

The *Mull* Case

In one prominent case, Gregory Mull, a San Francisco building designer, became a member of Church Universal and Triumphant in 1974 at the age of fifty-seven. He relocated to the Los Angeles area in 1979 and became employed at the church's Malibu headquarters doing design work.

The church loaned Mull a total of $37,000 during the time he was relocating, for which Mull signed two promissory notes. His tenure on church staff lasted about eight months; then he resigned from the organization over a dispute involving repayment of the notes. The church filed an action against Mull in 1981 for repayment of the $37,000; Mull counterclaimed for fraud, duress, undue influence, involuntary servitude, assault, extortion, intentional infliction of emotional distress, and quantum merit, seeking total damages of $253 million. The case was tried in 1986 in Los Angeles Superior Court.

Mull claimed at trial that he was a victim of church mind control and that when he signed the notes, he lacked the legal capacity to do so. He also claimed, in the alternative, that church officials unduly pressured him through psychological and emotional manipulation to sign the notes.

Mull asserted that while he was on staff he was physically debilitated by decreeing (a form of church prayer), a vegetarian diet, and various health practices, such as fasting and enemas. Mull also claimed that, subsequent to his resignation, he had been assaulted at a Church Universal and Triumphant event and that church officials had publicly disclosed private facts, causing him personal suffering. Finally, he claimed that he should be compensated $2 million for his design services while he served on staff.

At the four-week jury trial, the judge allocated one day to evidence involving the promissory notes and the remainder to testimony on a variety of church practices and beliefs. The testimony by numerous expert witnesses, appearing for both sides, and by both present and ex-church members covered reincarnation, the ascended masters, and the church founder's role as a prophet of God, with each side alternately supporting and ridiculing same. The claims of involuntary servitude and extortion were dismissed before trial. The jury gave a general verdict on all of the remaining claims, finding against the church and its leader, Elizabeth Clare Prophet, for $1.5 million in compensatory and punitive damages.

The results in *Mull* are not particularly surprising, given the plaintiff's emotionally charged claims and the willingness of the court to allow evidence that was not relevant to his claims but that the appeals court also ruled was not prejudicial. Given this atmosphere, it was unwise, in hindsight, for the church to have initiated the action to collect the value of the promissory notes from Mull. The case has probably made the church more willing to compromise subsequent claims.

Not all such cases have been decided in favor of plaintiffs. William Purcell, another ex-member of Church Universal and Triumphant, also brought an action against the church and its leaders, claiming fraud, clerical malpractice, psychological malpractice, cancellation of written instruments, involuntary servitude, intentional infliction of emotional distress, and seeking the imposition of a constructive trust. When Purcell filed his suit in 1984, he sought the return of contributions that he had made, claiming that he had made the contributions based on false representations by the defendants. The action was dismissed in 1986 on summary judgment in favor of the church and its leaders.

Child Abuse and Government Intervention in Nontraditional Religions

Child Abuse

On the morning of Sunday, July 26, 1953, a force of 120 Arizona peace officers, together with 100 news reporters, drove across unpaved roads to the Mormon fundamentalist community of Short Creek, Arizona, to arrest 36 men and 86 women and pick up 263 children. It was a sneak attack and was compared by one Associated Press reporter to "a military assault on an enemy position." Sect members were clearly outnumbered, as there were two officers for every home in the community. Although the element of surprise was not completely successful, the officers arrested most of the targeted men and women and the Arizona governor announced on the radio that the purpose of the raid was "to protect the lives and futures of two hundred sixty-three children" and that the religious community was "the foulest conspiracy you could imagine" that was "dedicated to the production of white slaves." Apparently, some officials in the Mormon Church (which had only abandoned polygamy itself fifty years earlier) not only applauded the raid but may also have provided relevant information to the police and other civil authorities.

Shortly after the raid, the mothers and children were bused to Phoenix where they were initially kept in a crowded rest home and were told they would remain there for up to a month before being placed in permanent foster homes. Eventually, juvenile hearings were held in Arizona state courts that resulted in the placement of most of the children in foster homes around Arizona, often accompanied by their mothers. Then in March 1955, an Arizona Superior Court judge ordered that all of the children be restored to their families, which brought an end to Arizona's efforts to segregate children from fundamentalist parents.

One of the primary reasons the "raid" on plural-marriage communities and the subsequent efforts of Arizona and Utah officials to separate parents from their children failed was that state officials eventually recognized that polygamist family ties were so strong that all attempts to punish the practice of polygamous marriage, perpetuated by the parents, through their children, would be counterproductive. They also realized it would not be in the best interests of the children to be separated from their parents, since there was no evidence of child molestation or deviant sexual activities involving the children.

The Short Creek raid bears certain strong parallels with the Northeast Kingdom raid described in the opening sections of this book. In both cases, governmental authorities intervened directly in the affairs of stigmatized religious communities from the high moral ground of protecting children from abuse, only to discover that no such abuse was occurring—except in the imaginations of community critics. Much the same thing happened at Waco, but with far more tragic circumstances.

Although child abuse is technically the jurisdiction of the state rather than the federal government, concern that the Branch Davidian children were being abused was one of the principal reasons cited by authorities as justification for both the initial ATF attack and the concluding FBI assault. On April 21, 1993,

White House spokesperson George Stephanopoulos, defending the holocaust, asserted that there "is absolutely no question that there's overwhelming evidence of child abuse in the Waco compound." This was a very odd line of defense, as if the assertion that the Davidians practiced such abuse justified gassing and incinerating the entire community.

However, on the very day of Stephanopoulos's remarks, the Justice Department publicly acknowledged that it had no solid evidence of child abuse—only *speculation* by mental health professions who had been studying Koresh from a distance. Also on the same day, 1,100 pages of unsealed documents relevant to the case were released. These included only two allegations of child abuse by disgruntled former members. Otherwise, nothing else was reported, certainly nothing like credible evidence.

Certainly during the siege itself, the FBI showed little regard for the children. The weird light and sound show, which included recordings of dentists' drills and dying rabbits, would hardly have promoted any child's sense of well-being. Deteriorating sanitary conditions, caused by decaying bodies and the buildup of sewage, were also given as a justification for attacking Mount Carmel on April 19. The attorney general told Larry King on national television that she feared that "if I delayed, without sanitation or toilets there . . . I could go in there in two months and find children dead from any number of things."

The Texas Department of Human Services had investigated Mount Carmel on child abuse allegations on at least three different occasions. No credible evidence for such accusations was found. The same can be said for the twenty-one children released from Mount Carmel between the ATF raid and the FBI assault— no hard evidence of child abuse. On March 5, Janice Caldwell, director of the Texas Department of Protective and Regulatory Services, stated: "They're in remarkably good shape considering what they have been through. No signs of physical abuse have been found." The March 6 edition of the *Houston Post* noted that "all the youths appear to be in good condition psychologically and physically." In the same article, a social worker asserted that "the children are remarkably well-educated."

The lack of any solid evidence for Branch Davidian child abuse probably explains the reason the attorney general and the FBI dropped this explanation as soon as reporters began to raise questions about specific evidence for abuse. Retrospectively, it is clear that the charge of child abuse leveled against the Davidians was little more than a pretext that legitimated the drastic actions of April 19, 1993.

Child abuse is one of those issues like AIDS and the plight of the homeless that has been uppermost in the public consciousness since the 1990s. As a consequence, accusations of child abuse are more effective at attracting attention than other kinds of charges, particularly if the media can be persuaded to pick up the story. Although one of the principles of our legal system is that a person is innocent until proved guilty, the mass media present their information so that merely reporting sensationalistic accusations is often sufficient to convict the accused in the mind of the general public.

What this means for nontraditional religions accused of child abuse is that such groups lose their chance for a fair hearing as soon as the media labels them "cults." Cults are, by definition, abusive, so that to attempt to assert that such-and-such "cult group" is *non*abusive sounds like a contradiction in terms. Thus, simply succeeding in getting the cult label to stick to any given religious community—whether the community be the Branch Davidians, the Northeast Kingdom Community, or the Short Creek polygamists—is to succeed in convicting the group in the popular imagination.

One of the earliest cases involving children in a religious setting was *Prince v. Massachusetts* (1944). Ms. Prince, a Jehovah's Witness, was the custodian of her nine-year-old niece. She was convicted of violating state child-labor laws for taking her niece with her to sell religious literature. The United States Supreme Court upheld her conviction. It stated that "the family itself is not beyond regulation in the public interest, as against a claim of religious liberty. . . . [N]either rights of religion nor rights of parenthood are beyond limitation."

The state has an interest in protecting juveniles under its traditional role as *parens patriae* (literally, "parent of the country," referring to the state's sovereign role as guardian of persons under legal disability). The state's interest is in restricting any conduct that is harmful to the child. "[T]he state has a wide range of power for limiting parental freedom and authority in things affecting the child's welfare; . . . this includes, to some extent, matters of conscience and religious conviction." The court indicated that parents could become martyrs if they wanted to, but they did not have the right to make martyrs of their children and subject them to emotional, psychological, or physical injury. The Court left no doubt that if a judge perceives that a religious practice or religious belief may be harmful to a child, the Court can and will restrict the religious conduct.

Although the accusation of child abuse has often been used to stigmatize unpopular religious groups, there are other situations of child endangerment where the concern of the state to protect children is more legitimate. Courts have even, at times, restricted the religious practices and beliefs of parents when it is believed that those practices and beliefs harm the child.

In a California case, *Walker v. Superior Court,* a court allowed the prosecution of a mother on charges of involuntary manslaughter and felony child endangerment because she had not sought medical treatment for her daughter when the daughter was dying of acute meningitis. Although certain statutes allowed parents to seek spiritual treatment for children, when the life of the child was seriously threatened, "the right of a parent to rely exclusively on prayer must yield." The court had little tolerance for religious practices and beliefs when the parent endangered the child's life by pursuing his or her own religious interests and not placing the general welfare of the child paramount. Prayer treatment was accommodated only as long as there was no serious risk of harm or danger to the child's life. When a child's life is threatened, religious beliefs take a second seat. The California court quoted the United States Supreme Court in *Prince v. Massachusetts:* "The right to practice religion freely does not include liberty to expose the community or child to communicable disease or the latter to ill health or death." When the religious beliefs and practices of parents interfere with the general welfare of a child, the courts show no reluctance to interfere.

In another example of this pattern, a jury in Minneapolis reviewed the religious practices of the Christian Scientists. An eleven-year-old boy with diabetes died because his mother would not seek treatment because of her religious beliefs. After the child died, the father brought suit and obtained a $14.2 million jury verdict against the church and his ex-wife. The trend in society today is to protect children. When the life of a child is weighed in the balance against the religious freedom of a parent, society tips the scales in favor of the child.

Child Custody Cases

Religious practices and beliefs have also become the subject of child custody cases where nonmembers attempt to highlight nontraditional aspects of a spouse's or ex-spouse's religion to obtain custody of a minor child. Nonmembers seek to show that the religion deviates from social normalcy and, therefore, adversely affects the child's behavior. It is argued that the church's influence is mentally, physically, and emotionally detrimental to the child's well-being. Nonmembers have been successful when the court determines that the practices complained of are not merely religious but detrimental to the child.

In a Kentucky custody case, Melanie Pleasant-Topel was allowed to retain custody of her minor son, Sean Pleasant, but was given strict guidelines by the court as to the religious practices of the Church Universal and Triumphant to which she could expose her son. For example, she was required to follow what U.S. society dictates as a normal and appropriate diet, rather than a vegetarian or nontraditional diet (which the church does not require in any event). She was also required to send him to the school he had been attending rather than to a church school. However, to the extent the custodial member parent raised the child within the framework the court determined normal, the court did not interfere with the custody.

In another case in which a member of Church Universal and Triumphant was involved, the church and its practices were central to the action. The mother, Charlene Viau, had been a member of Church Universal and Triumphant for approximately eleven years. Although the father contended the church was an "armed camp" and raised serious concerns that the church environment would be harmful to the child, the court awarded custody of the minor child to the mother, finding that there was no reasonable likelihood of future impairment to the minor child.

Another child custody action involving this church occurred in Indiana. The court found that the influence of Church Universal and Triumphant would be harmful and detrimental to the children and that the mother's association with the church demonstrated her poor judgment and inability to properly raise the children. Custody of the children was given to the father.

Although these results seem contradictory, individual facts and circumstances often dictate results. Unfortunately, all the relevant circumstances are not always apparent from court records.

In other cases, decisions are often result oriented, and their stated rationale may be misleading. Nevertheless, certain basic principles are almost universally recognized in these types of cases.

In New Mexico, a father who was a devout Sikh in Yogi Bhajan's Sikh Dharma organization sought to change the custody of his children. Until their divorce, both parents had actively practiced the Sikh religion as brought to this country by Yogi Bhajan and involved their children in the religion. Following her remarriage, the custodial mother withdrew from the Sikh religion and discouraged her children from participating in it. The father wanted his children raised in the Sikh religion and sought to modify the custody order to give him custody of the children so that he could control their religious upbringing. The court noted that the paramount concern was the general welfare of the children. The court also recognized that religious restrictions on visitation "have been upheld where evidence of physical or emotional harm to the child has been substantial." The courts have not hesitated to interfere when it is shown that the child suffers anxiety and other emotional distress because of the religious differences of his parents.

In an action in Tennessee to modify visitation, the court noted that the general trend in custody cases is to not allow religious beliefs to be controlling. "The law tolerates and even encourages, up to a point, the child's exposure to the religious influences of both parents even if they are divided in their faiths." Courts will generally not interfere with the religious training a noncustodial parent gives his or her children absent "a clear and affirmative showing that these activities and expressions of belief are harmful to the child." However, courts will not allow conflicting beliefs of parents to cause the children emotional harm; the paramount interest of the court is the general welfare of the child.

Many child custody cases exemplify how the cult stereotype may be used as an ideological resource in specific social conflicts. There is enough ambiguity in the "cult" label to make its application in particular cases a matter of negotiation. Occasions for such negotiation arise in the context of social conflicts. For individuals or groups locked in certain kinds of struggles with members of minority religions, the "cult" stereotype represents a potent ideological resource that—if they are successful in making the label stick—marshals public opinion against their opponent, potentially tipping the balance of power in their favor.

The stigma of the "cult" stereotype has been particularly effective in more than a few child custody cases, in which one parent's membership in a minority religion is portrayed as indicative of her or his unworthiness as a parent. For such "limited domain" legal conflicts, it is difficult to deploy the stereotype unless there is some larger, earlier conflict that led to press coverage in which the particular minority religion in question was labeled a "cult." Lacking earlier "bad press," the cult label can still sometimes be made to stick on the basis of testimony by disgruntled former members.

For the most part, individuals involved in such relatively limited conflicts do not become full-time "anticult" crusaders. Although they may enter into a relationship with the anticult movement, they normally drift away from this involvement within a short time after the termination of their particular struggle. Also, if anticult rhetoric fails to accomplish their end but some other tool works in their particular conflict, they are usually quite ready to dispose of the cult stereotype and adopt an entirely different angle of attack.

One case in which the employment of the cult stereotype was clearly opportunistic involved the mother's association with the Movement of Spiritual Inner Awareness. Her affiliation was effectively used against her by her ex-husband in a dispute involving their mutual offspring. In this particular case, a divorced mother petitioned the court to permit her to relocate in order to take a position in an MSIA-inspired organization offering human-potential seminars. The ex-husband argued that he did not want his son involved in a "cult" and dragged up old rumors about MSIA and MSIA's founder in an effort to prevent his ex-wife from leaving the state. Perceiving that not only would she have a difficult time winning her case but also that her husband might undertake further actions that could result in her son being taken from her, she dropped the case.

What is especially ironic about this case is that for several decades the father has been deeply involved in est—a human-potential group that has very frequently (far more frequently than MSIA) been labeled a "cult." As someone whose participation in est has likely sensitized him to the cult controversy, the ex-husband's utilization of the stereotype is clearly little more than a tactic intended to win support for his side of the case rather than a reflection of deeply held views about the dangers of sinister "cults." The chances of this gentleman becoming a full-time anticult crusader are nil. Here it is clear that the cult stereotype is an ideological resource, deployed without a deep investment in the stereotype per se.

Tax Cases

Churches act as fiduciaries, enter into contracts, purchase property, and otherwise conduct business within the communities where they are located. Churches expose themselves to tax liability when their conduct is not purely religious. Scrutiny becomes particularly focused on churches when they are the recipients of gifts, devises or other transfers of property, or are otherwise benefited. There have been a number of IRS cases involving minority religions in which the Internal Revenue Service has revoked the tax-exempt status of controversial new religions, often at the prompting of enemies of the particular religion involved.

In 1985, for example, the Way International's tax-exempt status was revoked following allegations of partisan political involvement and certain business activities at its New Knoxville headquarters. The ruling was reversed by the Supreme Court in 1990. Most recently, in 1993, the IRS ceased all litigation and recognized the Church of Scientology as a legitimate religious organization. This followed years of contentious litigation between the agency and the church.

Church Universal and Triumphant

I have already had occasion to refer to the Church Universal and Triumphant in earlier sections. CUT is a Montana-based New Age church led by Elizabeth Clare Prophet. An indirect spin-off of the I AM Religious Activity that grew quietly in its early years, by the late 1980s it had become *the* most controversial new religion in North America in terms of negative media coverage.

The church was founded as the Summit Lighthouse by Mark L. Prophet in 1958, and Elizabeth took over his role as the primary mouthpiece for the masters after Mark's death in 1973. The group moved to Montana in 1986. Much of the church's negative media derived from incidents clustered around its extensive fallout shelters and its preparations for the possibility of a nuclear attack against the United States. At one point in the construction, for instance, fuel stored in several underground tanks (which were sold to the church in defective condition) ruptured and spilled gas and diesel oil into the water table. In 1990, members from around the world gathered in Montana because of the predicted possibility of an atomic holocaust—a gathering that would have gone all but unnoticed had not a local paper painted it in sinister colors and broadcast the news through the AP wire service to the world.

On the heals of this extensive publicity, the Church Universal and Triumphant's tax-exempt status was revoked in October 1992. The revocation followed an inquiry that began in 1989 under the Church Audit Procedures Act. Three reasons were given for the revocation: the church was alleged to be involved to an excessive degree in nonexempt commercial activities, it had made an allegedly improper payment on behalf of a church official as part of a court judgment (in the *Mull* case, mentioned in a previous section), and it had allegedly been involved at an official level in a scheme by two church employees to illegally purchase weapons. The IRS claimed Church Universal and Triumphant owed back taxes on business income, employment taxes, and excise taxes.

The church strongly disputed all three reasons given for the revocation, filing a declaratory judgment action to reverse the IRS decision. The church and the IRS entered into extensive settlement negotiations, and the court extended various pretrial hearing dates to accommodate the negotiations. In taking its action against the church, the IRS was clearly influenced by negative publicity, including coverage from the Gregory Mull case, investigative articles in the *Bozeman Daily Chronicle* discussing Church Universal and Triumphant operations, an ex-member's claim that the Church Universal and Triumphant supported international rebel groups, the appearance of Elizabeth Clare Prophet's daughter on the *Oprah Winfrey* show and discussions of alleged church money given to another daughter, a Montana newspaper article about gun ownership by Church Universal and Triumphant members, and the guilty pleas of Vernon Hamilton and Edward Francis to charges that they had illegally purchased weapons.

Initially, the focus of the IRS investigation appeared to be limited to the church's potential liability for unrelated business income tax; the church's tax-exempt status was secondary. However, the information gleaned from newspapers, particularly the illegal gun purchases by Hamilton and Francis, changed the focus to the tax-exempt status of the church. There were, however, irregularities in the agency's investigation that led to a compromise agreement in mid-1994—a compromise that included restoring the church's status as a charitable organization.

The Reverend Sun Myung Moon's Income Tax–Evasion Case

The Unification Church, formally the Holy Spirit Association for the Unification of World Christianity, was one of the most controversial new religions in late-twentieth-century North America. We have already noted a number of cases above in which the UC has been involved. Derided in the West as "the Moonies," the UC is an international messianic religious movement led by the Reverend Sun Myung Moon, a Korean national. Although polemical opponents have identified any number of departures from Christian orthodoxy, the major novelty is the explicitness with which the present is identified as the time of Christ's Second Advent.

After the departure of the Children of God (later known as the Family) from the United States in the mid-1970s, the Unification Church became the most controversial religion on the American scene. This was in part due to the activities of the UC itself, which attracted attention by staging major rallies across the nation in 1976. The California branch of the church was also involved in a deceptive recruiting operation that made the cult stereotype seem particularly applicable. Perhaps most important, however, the leadership of the anticult movement made a conscious choice to focus attention on the Unification Church. The strategy was that, if the government could be moved to act against the UC, this would establish a precedent that could then be turned against other minority religions. However, as we have noted, anticultists were largely unsuccessful in evoking governmental action.

One of the few areas in which the assault on this religion was successful was in a tax case involving the founder, Rev. Sun Myung Moon. In 1982, Moon was convicted and jailed on tax evasion charges for failure to pay a purported tax liability of $7,300 over a three-year period. This liability came about as a result of a church checking account that had been opened in Moon's name by early missionaries in New York rather than as a result of an intentional action on his part. It should also be noted that having a church account in the name of the pastor is a common practice in such denominations as the Baptist Church. This case was regarded by most jurists, civil libertarians, and religious leaders as biased and an intrusion on essential religious freedoms, and the Unification Church decried the case as religious persecution.

The case briefly made headlines, and the anticult movement congratulated itself on finally having achieved a victory in the area of evoking a governmental response. In the long run, however, the results of the case were ambivalent. Clergymen from a wide variety of different congregations came to Rev. Sun Myung Moon's defense, including such national figures as Jerry Falwell. The UC thus acquired contacts and allies it could never have hoped to have made without the case.

Like many other Christian denominations, the Unification Church embraced a theology of redemptive suffering that could speak directly to the conviction and incarceration of the church's founder. Accepting this turn of events as divinely ordained, Moon also stood up well under the conditions of his imprisonment, which were certainly more tolerable than the persecution he had suffered under the North Koreans in the fifties. In the end, the UC probably emerged stronger than it had been prior to the case.

Zoning, Solicitation, and the Like

Minority religions have also encountered less momentous problems with local ordinances governing zoning, solicitation, and so forth. These cases have had ambivalent results. To cite just a few solicitation cases that made it all the way to the Supreme Court, in 1981 in *Heffron v. International Society for Krishna Consciousness*, the high court supported the state's right to require solicitors—including members of the Hare Krishna movement—to be confined to a booth rather than to wander about at the state fair. However, the very next year in *Larson v. Valente*, the Supreme Court decided in favor of the Unification Church against a solicitation law that, it was clear, targeted new religious groups.

Zoning has also been an arena in which minority religions have had to contend with prejudice against "cults." Residents generally resent any "invasion" into their neighborhood that disturbs in any way the status quo. People purchase homes in certain neighborhoods specifically relying on the zoning codes and the general tenor of the neighborhood and are suspicious of new groups using property in the neighborhood for other nontraditional purposes.

Church Universal and Triumphant

The Church Universal and Triumphant has encountered several zoning problems over the years. One high-profile case involved its purchase of a large mansion in Minneapolis in an area that was zoned for single-family residential dwellings but that also allowed for usage by churches and religious organizations. The property and building purchased by the church had previously been used as a duplex. Church Universal and Triumphant proposed to use the building for worship services and as a religious community residence and teaching center.

As soon as the church purchase was completed, the homeowners in the area expressed concern about the church being located in the area. The residents did not understand the religion, particularly since the church and its tenets did not fit into the traditional religious mold. The residents encouraged and then joined a suit by the City of Minneapolis to stop the church from using the property, claiming it offered insufficient parking and the church's religious community and center did not constitute a valid accessory use. In Minnesota, a church sanctuary as well as a monastery and rectory can be situated in a single-family residential zoning area. The court found that the Teaching Center qualified as a church monastery or rectory and that the church was in "substantial compliance" with the zoning code's parking requirements. The Minnesota Supreme Court affirmed this decision.

The hostility encountered by Church Universal and Triumphant in Minneapolis is not unique. When the Church of Jesus Christ of Latter-Day Saints tried to purchase property in Seattle and Portland to construct temples for worship by its members, strong sentiments were expressed in opposition. A comparable situation has generated a long-running conflict with respect to a retreat facility established by the Movement of Spiritual Inner Awareness.

The Movement for Spiritual Inner Awareness

In the mountains overlooking Santa Barbara, California, the Foundation for the Institute of Individual and World Peace (IIWP) (an organization founded by John-Roger Hinkins, founder-leader of the Movement for Spiritual Inner Awareness) purchased some property—later named Windermere—for the purpose of building a peace retreat facility. Bordered on one side by a national forest, the property is also directly adjacent to a semirural neighborhood populated by individuals who moved away from the city for the purpose of enjoying country living. Some of these people view their new neighbor with concern. When they heard about plans to build a facility that, they imagined, would attract large numbers of outsiders from the Los Angeles area who, they imagined, would disturb their peaceful rural setting, some were upset. Eventually, some neighbors organized the Cielo Preservation Organization (named after the main road in the area) to oppose the construction of the retreat—construction that cannot proceed without approval from the county.

Not long after a negative article about MSIA appeared in the *Los Angeles Times,* almost everyone in the neighborhood received a copy. This slanted article immediately became a centerpiece in some of the neighbors' opposition to MSIA's retreat plans. By 1994, the *Times* report had been superseded by the considerable publicity Arianna Huffington's MSIA connections were generating in the southern California media. Thus, in a December 1994 article in the local Santa Barbara paper on the conflict between Windermere and the neighborhood, Huffington and her "cult" connections were brought up and discussed near the beginning of the article: "[John-Roger's] teachings drew national attention during this year's California Senate race between incumbent Diane Feinstein and Rep. Michael Huffington because the Montecito congressman's wife, Arianna, had ties to the John-Roger organization, which some critics claim is a cult. Arianna Huffington has said it is not a cult, and described her past connection with MSIA as a casual one." Despite the cautious wording of this passage, the net effect of mentioning such accusations is that otherwise uninformed readers may conclude that the "cult" label is probably appropriate for MSIA, thus influencing them to side with the retreat's opponents.

This labeling enterprise has been highly successful in generating anti-IIWP and anti-MSIA sentiment in Santa Barbara County. The point here, however, is that the Cielo Preservation Organization is less concerned about the ranch owners' religious persuasion than about preventing, in the words of a local organizer, hordes of "L.A. cowboys" from invading the area, thus spoiling their rural privacy. The claim that the Windermere

Ranch is populated by "weird cultists" is simply one among many accusations hurled at IIWP in an all-out effort to short-circuit their retreat plans rather than representing a deep commitment to the anticult position.

Libel Cases

Considering the often highly charged remarks that have been hurled back and forth in the cult controversy, it is surprising that there have been so few libel cases. These few cases have, however, been significant. Overseas, there was a long-running libel case in England that the Unification Church had brought against the *Daily Mail*. This case was eventually decided in favor of the newspaper. Perhaps the most significant "cult" libel case in the United States was in 1985 when the Local Church won a libel case against authors who had accused the church of being a "destructive cult."

The Local Church Libel Case

The Local Church, also known as the Little Flock, was founded in the 1920s in China by Ni Shutsu, popularly known as Watchman Nee. Accused of being a spy for the U.S. and Nationalist governments, he was sent to prison in 1952, where he died twenty years later. Among Nee's followers was Witness Lee, founder and elder of the church at Yantai. The movement spread around the Pacific basin and was brought to the West Coast of the United States by migrating members. Lee himself moved to the United States, where he founded the Living Stream Ministry and has led the spread of the Local Church.

Although highly orthodox in doctrine, Lee brought innovation to the church by introducing a number of theological emphases as well as new practices such as "pray reading" and "calling upon the name of the Lord." "Pray reading" is a devotional practice using the words of Scripture as the words of prayer. During this practice, which is supposed to allow the Scripture to impart an experience of the presence of God in the person praying, people repeat words and phrases from the Scripture over and over, often interjecting words of praise and thanksgiving. "Calling upon the name of the Lord," on the other hand, represents an invocation of God by the repetition of phrases such as "O Lord Jesus." Both these practices have been subjects of controversy.

A controversy emerged in the 1970s between the Local Church and some members of the larger Evangelical Christian community who regarded the innovations of Lee as departing from acceptable Evangelical thought. This controversy culminated in a series of legal actions in the mid-1980s. A number of anticult writers accused the Local Church of heresy and attacked its unique forms of Christian piety. The lawsuits instituted by the Local Church brought retractions and apologies from all organizations except the Spiritual Counterfeits Project, a Christian anticult group that had published the book *The God-Men*, attacking the church. This case went to trial, and in 1985 a financial settlement was ordered against the Spiritual Counterfeits Project, which was driven to bankruptcy in the face of an $11 million judgment.

The Local Church case sent a chill through the ranks of people who regularly wrote on the cult controversy. Subsequently, writers moved away from referring to a wide variety of minority religions by name and instead shifted to writing about "cults" in general—the only groups it was safe to name were religions that had been decimated or eliminated by violence, such as the People's Temple.

Cynthia Kisser v. the Church of Scientology

In 1990, Michael Rokos, then president of the Cult Awareness Network, resigned when it was discovered that he had been arrested several years earlier for propositioning a young policeman who had been posing as an teenager. After Cynthia Kisser, CAN's executive director, took over the day-to-day running of the organization, members of some of the groups attacked by CAN began investigating her background in hopes of finding a similar skeleton in the closet. Eventually, they discovered that Kisser had worked briefly as a topless dancer in the 1970s.

Even though topless dancing is nowhere near as serious of an act (many people would not even consider it immoral) as propositioning underage boys, critics—including Heber Jentzsch, president of the Church of Scientology, International—seized upon this item of information and hurled it at CAN in an effort to discredit the organization. Kisser responded by suing Jentzsch and the Church of Scientology for defamation of character in 1992. She filed two suits, one in federal court and one in state court. Both were dismissed, the first in 1994, the second in 1995. Kisser's appeal met a similar fate.

In dismissing her federal case, U.S. District Judge James B. Zagel remarked:

> Statements charging Kisser with exposing her breasts in public for remuneration could affect the public's assessment of her as a critic of religious cults. Some might regard such activity as the symptom of a character so deeply flawed that they could expect other symptoms, such as untruthfulness. Some who regard topless dancing as base, immoral or sinful . . . might consider a former topless dancer less likely to understand, appreciate or fairly judge the motives and practices of organizations claiming spiritual inspiration and purpose, or their members' lifestyles.

Zagel further noted that Kisser did not "offer any clear and convincing evidence showing a reckless disregard for the truth," as required by law. Not long after the federal case had been decided, her state case was dismissed with prejudice. Kisser's appeal of the federal decision was finally dismissed in 1997. These defeats took place around the same time that the Cult Awareness Network itself was being dismantled in the courts, in what must stand as the worst losing streak in the anticult movement's short history.

The Defeat of Anticultism in the Courts

For many years the legal struggle between minority religions and their critics went back and forth in the courts, so that, throughout the 1980s, it appeared to longtime observers as though the conflict had reached a kind of stasis. It was thus somewhat surprising when, in the 1990s, the scale tipped decisively in favor of the new religious movements. The defeat of anticultism in the courts took place in two distinct arenas: In the first place, mind control, coercive persuasion, and brainwashing were rejected as a theory that could have a bearing on the outcome of any legal case. In the second place, the Cult Awareness Network was sued out of existence in the wake of a deprogramming-related lawsuit. Subsequently, the Cult Awareness

Network name, mailing address, and phone number were purchased by the Church of Scientology.

The *Fishman* Decision

For many years, Dr. Margaret Singer, a clinical psychologist, had been the most weighty expert witness in court cases involving the notion of coercive persuasion, popularly known as "brainwashing." Part of her legitimacy as an expert derived from her association with other psychological researchers who had examined U.S. soldiers released from POW camps following the Korean War. Singer had testified in such prominent cases as *Katz*, *Mull*, and *Molko-Leal*, to name just a few.

Her demise as an expert witness began, ironically, with an effort by Singer and some of her colleagues to legitimate the anticult position on mind control within the psychological profession. This group had formed a task force on "deceptive and indirect methods of persuasion and control" within the American Psychological Association. This task force submitted its report to the Board of Social and Ethical Responsibility for Psychology of the APA. The report was rejected by the board in May 1987, with the statement that, "in general, the report lacks the scientific rigor and evenhanded critical approach needed for APA imprimatur." Task force members were explicitly warned not to imply that the APA in any way supported the position the report put forward.

The other document that would be brought forward to discredit Singer was an amicus curiae brief filed by the APA and twenty-three scholars in support of the Unification Church in the *Molko-Leal* case. Singer had already testified in this case, and the foreword to the amicus curiae brief cast a harshly critical comment in Singer's direction: "APA believes that this commitment to advancing the appropriate use of psychological testimony in the courts carries with it a concomitant duty to be vigilant against those who would use purportedly expert testimony lacking scientific and methodological rigor." The wording at the end of this statement clearly echoes the decision of the APA board to reject the task force report, although this brief had been filed *before* the report had been rejected.

These two rejections subsequently led to the rejection of Singer as an expert witness in a series of cases, culminating in *United States v. Fishman* in 1990. Stephen Fishman had argued that his criminal behavior, mail fraud, had been caused by the

Church of Scientology's mind-control and thought-reform techniques to which he had been subjected. U.S. District Court judge D. Lowell Jensen reviewed the scientific status of Singer's theories—as well as the related ideas of sociologist Richard Ofshe, whom the defense had also called as an expert witness—in some detail. Ofshe was rejected out of hand as an expert witness. Singer, on the other hand, could testify as a mental health professional, on the condition that she *not* "support her opinion with testimony that involves thought reform, because the Court finds that her views on thought reform, like Dr. Ofshe's, are not generally accepted within the scientific community." This turned out to be a benchmark decision, which was subsequently used to disqualify Singer and Ofshe from testifying in other cult cases.

Singer and Ofshe then sued the APA and the American Sociological Association (ASA), alleging that these two organizations had conspired with twelve individual scholars to discredit them. On August 9, 1993, a federal judge threw their suit out of court. They refiled an almost identical suit in state court in California, but this new suit was thrown out in June 1994. Upon appeal, the case was dismissed with prejudice. With this last dismissal, "cultic mind control" was finally demolished in the courts.

The *Scott* Case and the Demise of the Cult Awareness Network

For many years, the Church of Scientology had invested its legal resources in fighting various governmental agencies—most recently, a host of cases involving the Internal Revenue Service. In 1993, the IRS halted all Scientology-related litigation and extended unqualified recognition to the church and its various affiliated organizations. This action had many different spin-off effects, including the freeing of Scientology's legal resources to fight other enemies. It was thus almost inevitable that the church would turn its big guns on the Cult Awareness Network.

Despite public statements to the contrary, CAN regularly referred worried parents to vigilante deprogrammers. It was in this practice that the Church of Scientology found the weak point that eventually brought the organization down. In a criminal case in the state of Washington, deprogrammer Rick Ross and his associates had been referred to the mother of Jason Scott by the Cult Awareness Network. Scott, a member of a Pentecostal church, had been handcuffed, silenced with duct tape across his mouth, abducted, and forcibly held against his will for days in a failed attempt to destroy his beliefs. The Church of Scientology supported this case in a number of ways, such as by supplying witnesses against Ross and CAN.

When the criminal case failed to convict Ross, the church helped Scott file a civil suit against his kidnappers and the Cult Awareness Network. The jury in this new case found the conduct of some of the defendants "so outrageous in character and so extreme in degree as to go beyond all possible bounds of decency . . . atrocious and utterly intolerable in a civilized community" and approved a $4.875 million verdict against Ross and CAN. When the defendants moved to have the verdict set aside as "unreasonable," U.S. District judge John Coughenour denied the motion, stating: "The court notes each of the defendants' seeming incapability of appreciating the maliciousness of their conduct towards Mr. Scott . . . Thus, the large award given by the jury against both CAN and Mr. Ross seems reasonably necessary to enforce the jury's determination on the oppressiveness of the defendants' actions and deter similar conduct in the future."

The Cult Awareness Network initially filed for bankruptcy under Chapter 11, hoping to continue its operations. However, CAN was finally forced to file Chapter 7 bankruptcy in June 1996. When CAN's resources were auctioned to raise money for the settlement, the Church of Scientology purchased the Cult Awareness Network name, phone number, and post office box address.

The Rebirth of the Cult Controversy on the International Scene

Ironically, just when it seemed that the anticult movement had suffered final defeat in U.S. courts, a new wave of anticult activity swept across western Europe, Japan, and, later, China. Although Europe and Japan had been active in the cult controversy of the preceding three decades, two incidents served to escalate the conflict in these two areas. In Japan, the extreme antisocial acts of AUM Shinrikyo, which culminated in the release of poison gas in the Tokyo subway system in 1995, created widespread fear and distrust in the Japanese populace. Similarly, the Solar

Temple's dramatic murder-suicides in Switzerland in 1994 and in France in 1995 demonstrated that the United States was not the only country in the world that could give birth to dangerous minority religious groups. In both areas of the world, the balance of power was tipped in favor of the forces in Europe and Japan that viewed new religious movements as a purely negative influence in society.

The balance of the present chapter covers this rebirth of the cult controversy on the international scene. The initial material on recent European developments is adapted, with permission, from a paper by Dr. Massimo Introvigne, director of the Center for Studies on New Religions (CESNUR), "Religious Liberty in Europe," which was presented at a press conference held in Washington, D.C., at the National Press Club on December 1, 1997.

An Overview of the European Situation

In the United States, the Jonestown tragedy of 1978 was the catalyst for an increase of anticult activity. The anticult worldview was strengthened, but the activities of the anticult movement were ultimately kept in check by the reactions of academe, mainline churches, and some of the religious minorities themselves. In Europe, as mentioned above, the suicides-homicides of the Order of the Solar Temple, repeated twice in the 1994 and 1995 (and a third time in 1997—but only in Quebec), played a similar role to that played by Jonestown in the United States. The anticult movement was energized, and authorities began considering cults more seriously. Discredited theories such as mind control surfaced again. Parliamentary commissions with a mandate to study the "danger of cults" were established in a number of countries. Although not attempting to examine all of this activity, we will survey some relevant examples.

France

On January 10, 1996, a parliamentary commission in France, composed entirely of members of Parliament (without consulting a single scholar), issued a report titled *Cults in France* after a number of secret hearings. It included a laundry list of 172 "dangerous cults." Although not recommending any new legislation, it suggested a number of administrative actions and the establishment of a national cult observatory (in fact established in 1996).

Although not technically a source of law, the report was quoted in court decisions and led to discrimination against a number of groups. Teachers were fired from public schools after years of honorable service only because they were members of the Jehovah's Witnesses, one of the most dangerous "cults," according to the report. A Roman Catholic theatrical group, the Office Culturel de Cluny, included in the report as a dangerous cult despite letters of protest from a number of French Catholic bishops, was nearly bankrupted due to the refusal of public theaters to air its shows. The City of Lyons decided not to allow the use of public facilities to any group listed in the report as a "cult." Each French Department had a "Mr. Cult" employed by the Ministry of Youth and Sport (often well connected with the French anticult group ADFI) to inform the cultural and sport organizations about the evils of cults.

In 2001, the About-Picard Law, a draconian piece of legislation giving the government full power to repress unpopular religious groups, was signed into law in France after intense debate. In 2004, extending its attacks on religious freedom to non-"cult" groups, the French legislature enacted a public school ban on the wearing of religious symbols, from Jewish yarmulkes to large crucifixes. Its main purpose, however, was to prevent Muslim schoolgirls from wearing the hijab, the head scarves prescribed for women in the Islamic tradition.

Switzerland
Following an intensive anticult campaign in the wake of the Solar Temple and the French Report, the Canton of Geneva released a report in February 1997 written by four lawyers, after interviewing a number of individuals. Although in some chapters the report was written in a more moderate style than the French one, the substantial proposals advocated legislation against "mind control" and against hiring members of "dangerous cults" as government officers.

Belgium
The Belgian parliamentary commission on cults released its report on April 28, 1997. This document was more extreme than the French report, including bizarre allegations against many groups, including five mainline Catholic groups, Quakers, the YWCA, Hasidic Jews, and almost all Buddhists. It also proposed legislation making "mind control" a crime.

Reactions by scholars and mainline churches produced some turmoil in the Belgian Parliament, and in the end it adopted the report itself but not the list of 189 groups included as an appendix. This was a symbolic victory for scholars, but most of what was disturbing was in the main body of the report.

Following the report, legal actions were taken against a Tibetan Buddhist group and a Catholic religious congregation called the Work (a Belgian group now headquartered in Rome, not to be confused with Opus Dei, also mentioned in the report)—notwithstanding vigorous protests by the Vatican and by Belgian bishops. An action was also initiated to force the dissolution of Sukyo Mahikari, a Japanese Shinto-based religious minority whose branches in countries such as Italy and the United States have existed for decades without any trouble for the public order. Based on the testimony of hostile ex-members of some organizations, extreme allegations were made against a dozen groups.

Germany

A parliamentary commission was established including members of Parliament and experts appointed by the different political parties. Hearings were conducted with scholars, anticultists, and members of a number of religious movements. An interim report was released in June 1997. In the meantime, without consulting the parliamentary commission, the government placed the Church of Scientology under the supervision of the Secret Service. Even groups antagonistic to Scientology criticized the decision as a dangerous precedent. Meanwhile, German anticultists named the Jehovah's Witnesses as the second group that should be watched by the Secret Service. Police raids instigated by the same anticultists took place against small independent Pentecostal churches.

Eastern Europe

In Eastern European countries where legal protections or traditions of religious freedom are nonexistent or weak, minority religions are often less able to defend themselves. In some former Soviet Union countries, churches that formerly enjoyed the status of being state sanctioned are engaged in an effort to reestablish their pre-Soviet positions. Alternative religious groups have sometimes suffered from these efforts, especially where the formerly established churches have been able to strike alliances with politicians. In Russia, for instance, laws have been passed that limit religious freedom for religious minorities. In March 2004, the District Court of Moscow banned the activities of Jehovah's Witnesses and moved to liquidate them as a legal entity. Similar efforts to promote former dominant churches at the expense of other religions are also under way in other former Soviet countries as well.

The European Parliament

The European Parliament has entrusted the Committee on Civil Liberties and Internal Affairs with the task of preparing a report. Following criticism of the French and Belgian reports by scholars, the committee initially produced a draft with a number of positive features (such as questioning the usefulness of preparing lists of "cults"). However, caving in to anticult pressure, members introduced amendments during the final debate within the committee, and further amendments may be introduced during the plenary discussion of the European Parliament. Thus, anticult ideas, initially rejected by the committee, may reenter the document.

The European Parliament should not be confused with the Council of Europe, an institution including more European countries but less authoritative and well known in Western Europe. Members of the Council of Europe, unlike those of the European Parliament, are not elected directly by the people. The Committee on Legal Affairs and Human Rights of the Parliamentary Assembly of the Council of Europe also investigated the "cult" problem. The minutes of its meeting held on April 8, 1997, in Paris, with "experts"—including some of the most extreme French anticultists—showed a degree of anticult extremism rare even in the current heated European discussion. The Council of Europe's *Report on Sects and Cults,* which was issued on June 22, 1999, adopted a more moderate tone but still took a hostile stance against minority religious groups.

Some European Case Studies

There are literally hundreds of religious minorities discriminated against in western Europe. They belong to all possible religious and spiritual persuasions. The following case studies involve two comparatively small French groups not well known outside France. They could hardly be more different from each other.

The Evangelical Pentecostal Church of Besançon is an example of how a group whose theology is clearly in the mainstream (and which would be regarded as mainline in most Western countries) is marginalized after an encounter with the anticult movement. As mentioned earlier, a number of Catholic, Protestant, and Jewish groups have suffered the same fate.

The second example—the Aumist Religion (not to be confused with the Japanese group AUM Shinrikyo), headquartered at the Mandarom, in southern France—could hardly be less mainstream. Its theological ideas are at the very fringe of the French religious scene. It is not difficult to understand why the Mandarom has been unpopular. However, constitutional guarantees are aimed, precisely, at protecting unpopular minorities. And even the most unpopular defendant should be guaranteed due process and a fair trial.

The Evangelical Pentecostal Church of Besançon

The Protestant scene in western Europe is slowly becoming as diversified as the one in the United States. Large liberal denominations, members of the World Council of Churches, no longer represent the majority of Protestants in a number of European countries. Literally hundreds of Evangelical and Pentecostal churches are flourishing. The large number of new churches may easily confuse authorities, and anticultists propose simple solutions. In France, the Center against the Mental Manipulations (CCMM), the second largest anticult group after ADFI, explicitly claims that all groups not belonging to the WCC, or to its corresponding French organization, the French Protestant Federation, are suspicious and may be "cults."

The Belgian parliamentary report took the anticult recommendation to target every Christian group not endorsed by the WCC quite literally. Its list included Seventh-Day Adventists, the Amish, the Assemblies of God, Calvary Christian Center, Plymouth Brethren, the Charismatic Renewal in general, and a number of small independent Pentecostal churches.

The French report limited itself, among hundreds of independent churches, to a dozen. Curiously enough, the French report mentioned the Evangelical Pentecostal Church of Besançon (EEPB) and ignored the Evangelical Missionary Federation (FEM), founded on the basis of the success of the Besançon church and now including more than thirty churches. In fact, not unlike other groups, the EEPB seems to have been included in the report for one simple reason. Based on a family conflict between a pastor and his father-in-law, the EEPB has been targeted as a "cult" by the anticult movement, particularly after 1994. Due to the peculiar status of the anticult movement in France, the accusations have been spread by the press (in previous years, quite favorable to EEPB) and up to the parliamentary commission. Among hundreds of independent churches with very similar theologies, only those specifically targeted (often for very local or personal reasons) by the anticult movement have ended up being included in the report.

In fact, the EEPB is just another Evangelical Pentecostal church. Its founder, pastor Rene Kennel, studied at Nogent-sur-Marne's Institut Biblique and started his career in 1950 as a part-time Mennonite preacher. Soon afterward, he welcomed the Pentecostal Gypsy Movement of Pastor Le Cossec (a member of the mainline French Protestant Federation) to his family farm. Impressed by the gypsies' enthusiasm, Kennel started a Pentecostal ministry and in 1967 became a full-time pastor. In 1975, Kennel joined with other pastors to establish the Evangelical Free Pentecostal Federation (FELP). In 1977, he became the pastor of a Pentecostal independent church in Besançon, the present-day EEPB. In 1986, Kennel abandoned his position as president of FELP in order to oversee the planting of daughter churches of EEPB in the region. These churches are the basis of the Evangelical Missionary Federation, incorporated under French law in 1989. The doctrinal statements of the EEPB are quite typical of hundreds of Evangelical Pentecostal churches.

The accusations leveled by the CCMM and the media influenced by it—literal belief in the existence of the devil, in miracles, speaking in tongues—could be easily used against countless Pentecostal or Evangelical churches. It is possible that church leaders, unfamiliar with legal matters, made some mistakes when preparing their bylaws and articles of incorporation, thus exposing the church to potential problems with French tax authorities. On the other hand, it is a fact that the French Revenue Service only took action after anticultists had started targeting EEPB as a "cult." When, in July 1994, a visibly drunk ex-member damaged the furniture of the church belonging to the Evangelical Missionary Federation in Langres, anticultists (and a part of the press) quickly took the side of the apostate, presented as just another "victim" of a "cult." Paradoxically, before and after being labeled a "cult" by the parliamentary commission, the EEPB has always been able to maintain its pastors, for health and retirement insurance purposes, in the lists of CAMAC-CAMAVIC, the social fund for pastors in France that is largely controlled by the Roman Catholic Church and includes ministers of all mainline Christian churches.

In the meantime, however, the fact of being on the parliamentary list of "dangerous cults" threatens the very existence of the EEPB and of the whole FEM. Not only did media pressure against the "cult" continue but—following administrative instructions enacted in the wake of the parliamentary report—the federation's churches were denied use of public meeting halls by local authorities, and the French Revenue Service continuously harassed this struggling minority. The saga of the EEPB confirms that in the present French scenario it is not enough to preach a mainline Christian theology in order to avoid the label of a "cult." A minor incident is enough to result in being blacklisted by the anticult movement. And, unfortunately, the black lists of anticult organizations easily become the black lists of the media and the government.

The French Aumist Religion (the Mandarom)

The French Aumist religion, whose legal structure is called the Association of the Triumphant Vajra, headquartered in its holy city of Mandarom—hence the popular nickname "the Mandarom"—is regarded by anticultists and by a sizable part of the French media not only as *a* cult but as *the* cult, particularly in southern France. This is in itself an interesting phenomenon, taking into account that the Aumist religion is not a very large group, with less than 1,000 members in France and smaller constituencies in Italy, Quebec, Belgium, Switzerland, and Africa. The holy city of the Mandarom—described as the very epitome of the "danger of the cults," as if it was a base threatening a whole country—does not include more than fifty resident monks.

The Aumist religion (the name comes from the sacred Eastern sound *AUM*, the only common element with the Japanese group AUM Shinrikyo) was founded by Gilbert Bourdin, a native of French Martinique. In 1961, he was initiated by the Indian master Sivananda in Rishikesh (later, he received other initiations; for example, from the sixteenth Karmapa of Tibetan Buddhism) and started gathering followers as an ascetic practicing austerities in southern France. He also became quite well known as a yoga teacher and the author of some twenty-two books (some of them translated in several languages). In 1967, he established the Association of the Knights of the Golden Lotus (replaced in 1995 by the current Association of the Triumphant Vajra) and in 1969 founded the holy city of the Mandarom. Gradually, Bourdin revealed himself to be the messiah: the Lord Hamsah Manarah. In 1990, he was publicly crowned as the messiah at the Mandarom; some of the ceremonies were open to the media. At that time, the movement hoped to crown the existing constructions at the Mandarom (temples representing all the great religions of the world and huge statues) with a larger temple-pyramid, a building of great spiritual and cosmic significance for the Aumists.

The public ceremonies of 1990 were interpreted as an arrogant challenge by the anticult movement and the media. The Mandarom with its huge construction project was, simply, too visible. Two TV networks, Antenne 2 and TF1, started a campaign to expose the Mandarom as a "cultic concentration camp." The militant psychiatrist Jean-Marie Abgrall was among the anticult activists involved in this activity. He went on record on TV commenting, about Aumism, that "notwithstanding what they claim, cults are not religious movements, but rather criminal movements organized by gurus who use brainwashing to manipulate their victims," a capsule summary of anticult ideology. The campaign against the Mandarom was largely organized by ADFI, and from 1992 on it was joined by an ad hoc ecological group lead by Robert Ferrato. The latter claimed that the Mandarom was an offense to the ecological equilibrium of the mountain where it was built and called for its destruction. As mentioned earlier, anticult activists are taken more seriously in France than in other countries, and even an extreme character such as Abgrall managed to become one of the two "experts" in the national Observatory of Cults established in 1996.

The Mandarom was raided repeatedly in military-style raids between 1992 and 1995 by tax and police officers. ADFI, Ferrato, and a reporter for the TV network TF1, Bernard Nicolas, played a key role in making an apostate, Florence Roncaglia (whose mother is still with the Mandarom), "remember" that she had been molested and raped by Bourdin in the 1980s. A complaint was filed in 1994. Later, other female apostates also "remembered." Based on Roncaglia's complaint, the Mandarom was raided again on June 12, 1995, and Bourdin was arrested. Coincidentally, on the same date the French Council of State should have rendered its final decision on the question of building permission of the temple-pyramid. The decision was finally unfavorable to the Aumist religion. On June 30, 1995, Bourdin was released; he passed away in 1998.

Though the Pyramid Temple of Unity was a topic of considerable dispute, the destruction of the Statue of the Cosmoplanetary Messiah was a greater harbinger of conflict. Consecrated on August 22, 1990, this thirty-three-meter-high monument erected in the Mandarom was considered to be the receptacle of the energies of the return of God into matter. The statue became the focus of a heated public dispute, which ended when it was destroyed by a controlled implosion during an intervention by security forces on September 6, 2001.

The case of the Mandarom raises important questions. There is little doubt that the claims the Aumists make for their founder are extreme. Generally speaking, claiming to be the messiah does not make any religious leader particularly popular. The Aumist literature combines Eastern themes and Western esotericism, and it is difficult to distinguish between actual and symbolic claims. In short, Bourdin was an unpopular religious leader and Aumism an unpopular minority. This circumstance makes Aumism an excellent case to test religious liberty in France. When a group is protected by its own popularity, there is no need for constitutional or international guarantees.

Scholars are often asked whether there is a risk that groups such as the Mandarom may become involved in violent confrontations with the authorities or commit mass suicides like the Solar Temple. They normally answer that the Aumist doctrine is firmly against violence and suicides. This is, however, only part of the story. Writing on the situation at the Mandarom, Italian scholar Luigi Berzano (a professor of sociology at the University of Turin and a Roman Catholic priest) mentioned the sociological theories of deviance amplification. According to these theories, hostile official responses to a movement regarded as deviant may in fact amplify its deviance. In a sense, the movement is "deformed" by official and anticult harassment. Excessive reaction against a movement, thus, becomes a self-fulfilling prophecy and may cause the very evil it is supposed to avoid.

The Japanese Situation

Japan is presently facing a grave crisis that will determine the future of religious liberty in that country. Unlike the United States, Japan does not have a tradition of religious liberty. To traditionalists anxious about what they perceive as the fractured state of modern Japan, religions (particularly new religions) represent threats to social unity. At the same time, many individuals in positions of authority view new religions as alternate sources of power and legitimation—alternate centers of authority that potentially challenge the authority of the state.

Similar concerns were responsible for the severe persecution of religion that took place in the decades leading up to the Second World War. The persecution of religion in prewar Japan is an unpleasant chapter of national history that many Japanese citizens would rather forget. The most prominent religious body to be persecuted by the militarists was Omoto-kyo, one of Japan's earliest new religions. Accused of plotting to supplant the Imperial government, Omoto leaders were arrested in 1921 but released five years later without judgment. In 1935, however, Omoto leaders were again arrested, and the government undertook to systematically destroy the religion, razing the group's buildings and torturing members. It was not unusual for people to be beaten to within an inch of their lives and then sent home so that they would not die in the custody of the police. Other religions, such as the Jehovah's Witnesses, were treated similarly. Both the first and the second leaders of Soka Gakkai were also imprisoned during this period. Their founder died in jail.

The Role of the Liberal Democratic Party

The current crisis in religious liberty in Japan was precipitated by two groups whose divergent interests come together in the persecution of religions, namely, the Liberal Democratic Party (LDP)—the largest party in the ruling coalition—and an alliance of Communist lawyers. The LDP played an active role in cultivating the atmosphere of distrust that has come to surround religion in the wake of the poison-gas attack on the Tokyo subway system that was attributed to AUM Shinrikyo. This activity has had the further effect of tacitly encouraging antireligious lawyers to expand their attacks on religion.

The LDP's attacks on religion were part of a overall strategy to weaken its principal political rival, the New Frontier Party.

The NFP is supported by Soka Gakkai, Japan's largest new religion. Building on public reaction to the AUM Shinrikyo incident, the LDP was able to push through changes to the Religious Corporation Law (RCL) that give the government more power to directly regulate religion.

The LDP further engaged in a campaign to portray religion in general—and Soka Gakkai in particular—as being incompatible with the principles of democracy. Many examples of this campaign can be cited. For instance, at a press conference held on September 3, 1995, Koichi Kato, secretary-general of the LDP, boldly asserted: "Religion is based on principles taught by a single founder and, because of this essential nature, is irreconcilable with parliamentary democracy." Such a statement reflects either an ignorance of the history of democracy or an irresponsible deployment of rhetoric without concern for accuracy. Later, in March 1996, Kato told the *Los Angeles Times:* "We will not stop our campaign until we get Ikeda [Soka Gakkai's leader] to testify in parliament. He wants to control our country."

Other indications of the ruling party's assault on Soka Gakkai included a televised statement made by Shizuka Kamei on October 22, 1995, in which he flatly stated: "The purpose of revising the Religious Corporation Law is to take measures against Soka Gakkai." Also, when Prime Minister Tomiichi Murayama resigned in January 1996, he told the *Asahi Evening News:* "When I think of the nature of Soka Gakkai, I feel threatened. We need to protect Japan's democracy. To do that, we can't allow leadership to fall to the New Frontier Party." An LDP policy paper released two weeks later added: "The next general election will be a battle to protect the people from religious dictatorship. This will be a race that we cannot lose."

The Liberal Democratic Party's readiness to exploit fears generated by AUM Shinrikyo for short-term political gain was reflected in the title of a negative campaign flyer distributed by the LDP titled "An Emergency Report: More Dangerous Than AUM, Soka Gakkai in NFP's Clothing." On October 2, 1996, Shizuka Kamei, speaking on behalf of an LDP candidate, stated: "There are only two religious groups which tried to control the nation; one is AUM Shinrikyo and the other is Soka Gakkai. AUM used sarin gas and automatic rifles to do so, and Soka Gakkai controls politics using elections. It is indeed a serious problem to undertake election campaign activities in the name of religious practice."

From these statements, it is clear that the LDP was more than willing to sacrifice religious liberty on the alter of political expediency. In 1999, there was an abrupt reversal of the conflict between the LDP and Soka Gakkai when the New Komeito Party (the successor to the New Frontier Party) allied itself with the ruling coalition.

The Religious Corporation Law, the Religion Basic Law, and the New NPO Law

In addition to its deployment of highly charged campaign rhetoric, the Liberal Democratic Party sought to exert increased control over religion via legislation, from revisions to the Religious Corporation Law to new legislation such as the Religion Basic Law (RBL).

Revisions to the RCL were enacted. The revisions placed religions under the direct supervision of the Ministry of Education and required religious corporations to submit detailed records of their financial activities. If authorities suspect a group of expending money on nonreligious activities, they are empowered to question its representatives. Perceived misuse of funds (which would be open to the personal interpretation of authorities) could prompt officials to revoke a religion's corporate status.

One of the most drastic attempts to curtail religious activity was the Religion Basic Law. Although defeated, the mere fact that the ruling party attempted to push through draconian legislation in its efforts to control religious groups is an indicator of the level of hysteria generated by the AUM Shinrikyo incident.

The RBL began by presuming to define religion as "an internal affair of individuals," a definition that would have given authorities wide scope for restricting all sorts of organized religious activities. The RBL than went on to drive a wedge between politics and religion in such as way as to eviscerate Soka Gakkai's ability to support the New Frontier Party. (Although not mentioned by name, it was clear that the RBL was directly assaulting Soka Gakkai in those passages.)

The RBL would also have forbidden religious groups from striking back at critics—particularly the press—via boycotts and other means. One of the provisions of the law was that it forbade religious groups from attempting to "solicit the uninitiated with groundless explanations, in particular those pertaining to an individual's destiny, happiness or unhappiness in the future." Needless to say, the explanations that the RBL characterizes as "groundless" are at the core of every religion. Furthermore, "Should the solicited person refuse membership, the religious organization is barred from further contact with the intention of further solicitation with that individual." In other words, if a religion approached a potential convert more than once, the proselytizer—as well as, presumably, the entire religion—could have been charged with engaging in a criminal act.

The Situation of Academics in Japan

In a free society, there are several institutions that should serve as checks on the power of government. One of these institutions is the press. In Japan, however, the mass media are uncritical servants of the government. Another institution that should serve a critical function in society is academe. In the United States, people rarely listen to what scholars say. Nevertheless, academe is so protected by the tenure system that scholars may say pretty much what they want without fear of losing their positions.

In Japan, by way of contrast, the general public has great respect for academe. However, despite the facade of academic freedom, scholars are directly or indirectly pressured into muting criticisms of the system. During the AUM Shinrikyo incident, for example, a number of academics were told to keep quiet about such events as the ongoing harassment of rank-and-file members of AUM.

One of the most spectacular assaults on the principle of academic freedom occurred when Professor Shimada was fired. The pretext for this action was Shimada's supposed liaison with a female student. It was clear to everyone involved, however, that the firing was a response to Shimada's very public defense of AUM Shinrikyo members against undue government harassment. Shimada's dismissal had a severe dampening effect on the willingness of Japanese scholars to voice criticisms of any government or police action.

Deprogramming and the United Christian Churches of Japan

Although deprogramming disappeared from the public spotlight in the United States in the late seventies, it continued to exist as a cottage industry until the recent demise of the Cult Awareness Network. The practice was imported into Japan after it had already begun its retreat into obscurity in the West. Unlike the U.S. situation, deprogramming has continued to prosper in Japan because deprogrammers have been wise enough to confine their practice to such highly stigmatized groups as the Unification Church and AUM Shinrikyo. In contrast to the U.S. situation, it is not unusual for deprogramming victims in Japan to be locked up for years at a time. In many cases, the deprogrammees are brutalized, and in some cases victims have even been raped.

One of the most unusual aspects of the religious liberty situation in Japan is the participation of the United Christian Churches of Japan (UCCJ) in anticult activity. The UCCJ is, for example, one of the chief participants in Japanese deprogramming activities. Unknown to most of its rank-and-file members, the UCCJ was taken over by violent elements (for example, ministers adhering to liberation theology and other left-leaning theologies) in the late sixties. This takeover is the basis for the current alignment of the UCCJ with the Communist lawyers' group—an alliance that otherwise is incomprehensible.

One of the issues where this alliance is most functional is in both groups' opposition to the Unification Church. From the viewpoint of the UCCJ, the UC represents a heretical variant of Christianity. Simultaneously, the UC is emphatically anticommunist and has been a thorn in the side of the Japanese Communist Party (JCP) for many years. It may even be that the JCP is ultimately responsible for influencing the UCCJ to take a strong stand against the UC.

Whatever the ultimate cause, the UCCJ annually sponsors hundreds of deprogrammings of UC members. The majority of "successfully" deprogrammed ex-UC members become members of UCCJ churches. In addition to new members, one reason the UCCJ continues to sponsor deprogramming is that it provides the organization with much needed income. Fifteen years ago, the UCCJ's anti-UC committee was bringing approximately $10 million a year into the organization's coffers.

Via its connection with JCP lawyers, the UCCJ is able to provide plaintiffs (that is, deprogrammed ex-members) for a series of civil suits against the UC, thus generating income for anti-UC lawyers. The insidious connection between antireligious Communists and Christians thus comes full circle to bring both groups into a moneymaking venture that rivals the actions of the most exploitative capitalists.

Spiritual Sales
Members of the various lawyer bar associations have been banding together and seeking hundreds of ex-members of religions to

claim financial compensation from the religions. Compensation has been for time spent as a volunteer helper, for donations made, and so on. The purpose of the activity seems to be not merely to extract money but also to persecute religions and bring them to their knees.

At present, the primary point of attack for the antireligion lawyers' group is so-called spiritual sales. The spiritual sales issue affects religions as diverse as the Unification Church, Tenchi-seikyo, Hona-Hana, Hongkakuji, and Myokakuji. Although most current cases involve the purchase of particular items, in principle almost any exchange of funds between a church and its parishioners could be construed as a "spiritual sale" and thus open to attack by disgruntled former congregants acting under the direction of unscrupulous lawyers.

These cases all have one very important point in common, namely, that the court assumes it is competent to judge whether a given practice is genuinely religious or a facade for making money. This is clearly a dangerous breakdown in the separation of church and state. *Most alarmingly*, the larger, more established religions in Japan have not recognized the danger in these legal cases, failing to consider that, once precedents are established, the same attack can be made upon any religion.

Spiritual sales are such a key issue that one of the organizations under which antireligious lawyers have gathered is the National Lawyers Association for Measuring Spiritual Sales (originally the Lawyers Association to Measure Religious Sales). The group has thirty-nine branch lawyers' offices around the nation that represent the national office. The lawyers use the various consumer bodies they have set up to advance their cause, including the consumer protection center, the Consumer Law News, and the Small Research Committee for Consumer Problems on Religions.

China

Falun Gong was founded in 1992 by Li Hongzi. Falun Gong was part of a boom in the practice of Qi Gong, a traditional health and personal cultivation practice built around a set of physical exercises that superficially resemble tai chi. At its peak in the eighties and nineties, the boom grew to some 200 million followers. Falun Gong grew rapidly as part of the Qi Gong movement, eventually claiming tens of millions of practitioners.

Falun Gong first made international headlines in April 1999 when approximately 10,000 followers staged a nonviolent protest outside the Communist Party headquarters at Zhongnanhai, in Beijing. This was the largest protest in China since the student-led democracy movement that took place in Tiananmen Square in 1989. The protest came about as a consequence of frequent misportrayals of the movement in the media—misrepresentations that were themselves a result of a semiofficial campaign against Falun Gong. The response to the protest was swift and severe repression: the movement was outlawed, thousands of practitioners followers were imprisoned and tortured, and hundreds were killed.

Chinese authorities outlawed Falun Gong as a "heterodox sect" in laws hurriedly put into place in the summer and fall of 1999. A national propaganda campaign was also undertaken against the movement. Falun Gong books, cassettes, and other material were destroyed. On several occasions, bulldozers crushed movement material—scenes that were replayed repeatedly on national television. Despite demands from the Chinese government, U.S. authorities and Interpol refused to extradite Li Hongzi. Journalists and academicians were required to denounce Falun Gong and other superstitious "sects" in the name of science and modernization. Official sources portrayed Li Hongzi as exploiting his followers, and articles were published that focused on the deaths supposedly caused by followers not seeking regular medicine when sick and on the many followers who supposedly went crazy from Falun Gong.

Most practitioners simply did not accept what they read in official publications. The majority of followers apparently believed that authorities were reacting on the basis of misinformation. As a move to educate the government, small groups of practitioners went to Beijing in hopes of making an appeal to central government authorities (a right granted by China's constitution). When this strategy failed, followers tried other tactics, including peaceful demonstrations in Tiananmen Square by small groups and individuals. Some of these early protests made international news, and authorities thought they had lost face, both in China and internationally. The government soon increased security around Tiananmen Square, as well as around major train and bus stations. Arrested Falun Gong protesters were also sent home to be dealt with by local authorities. Under direction from above, these authorities became more vigilant and brutal.

Human rights groups began reporting an increase in torture and imprisonment from 1999 onward. Also, practitioners living in other countries began to appeal to the governments of the countries where they resided on behalf of Falun Gong members in China. The majority of the foreign practitioners were Chinese who had left the country—frequently to study overseas—in the 1980s and 1990s. Especially in North America, practitioners were able to evoke significant sympathy for the Falun Gong members in China. Both the Canadian and the U.S. governments repeatedly asked Chinese authorities to cease its campaign of persecution.

On January 23, 2001, some individuals portrayed as Falun Gong members were filmed setting fire to themselves in Tiananmen. This clearly staged-for-TV incident left five people dead. Although this pseudoincident did not leave a lasting negative impression of the movement outside of China, it succeeded in convincing a significant portion of the Chinese public that Falun Gong was truly dangerous. Despite the heavy persecution, foreign members, taking advantage of the extra protection provided to them as foreign nationals, began traveling to Tiananmen to stage protests as a way of continuing to promote their cause in the international media.

5

Documents and Data

Statistics

General estimates of the extent of the new religions phenomenon vary considerably. The two basic quantitative questions in this area are: How many groups? And how many people? These questions are not as simple as they might at first appear. A more fundamental question involves classification: Where does one draw the line between alternative and nonalternative religions? What one finds when one actually tries to determine where to draw such a line is that the difference between "mainstream" and "alternative" is a matter of degree rather than a sharply defined distinction.

The indeterminacy of this dividing line allows anticultists like the late Margaret Singer to assert, without fear of direct contradiction, that as many as 20 million people have been involved in 3,000 to 5,000 thousand cults in the United States (Singer and Lalich 1995). In contrast, Gordon Melton estimates 500 to 600 alternative religions in the United States (1992). Similarly, Peter Clarke estimates 400 to 500 new religions in the United Kingdom (1984). The situation is rather different in Japan, where new religions have been thriving since the end of World War II. Japanese sociologists estimate anywhere from 800 to several thousand such groups (Arweck 2002). And finally, Eileen Barker puts forward a figure of 2,000 or more new religions in the West and a figure in the lower tens of thousands worldwide (1999).

An important though neglected source of information bearing on the question of numbers of adherents to alternative religions is national census data. In 2001, the censuses of four English-speaking countries—New Zealand, Australia, Canada, and the United Kingdom—collected information on religious membership that included select new religions. There was also an important religion survey conducted in the United States in the same year, the American Religious Identification Survey (ARIS).

Though a few scholars of new religions have referred to one or more of these censuses, no one has attempted a general survey. Following an examination of one estimate of world religious adherents, the first part of this chapter discusses census data and information from the ARIS survey that shed light on participation rates in alternative religions. Select studies that measure other dimensions of the new religions phenomenon will also be examined.

The second part of the chapter reproduces four documents that will provide a more tangible sense of the controversy. Two are documents left in the wake of the suicides of the Order of the Solar Temple and of Heaven's Gate. The other two are texts of legislation enacted against controversial religions, one from China and the other from France.

World Membership in Alternative Religions

An example of how the ambiguity between what is and what is not a new religion can produce incongruous results can be found in David Barrett and Todd Johnson's "Statistical Approach to the World's Religious Adherents" (2002). In terms of worldwide membership, these statistics appear to be the best figures available.

Barrett and Johnson divide the world's religions into nineteen categories, with three subcategories for Christianity: Christian (Catholic, Protestant, independent), Muslim, Baha'i, Hindu, Sikh, Jain, Buddhist, Zoroastrian, Jewish, Confucian, Taoist, Chinese folk religion, Shinto, spiritist, ethnoreligionist, atheist, nonreligious, neoreligionist, and other. They describe the neoreligionist (new religionist) as "twentieth-century new religions, new religious movements, radical new crisis religions, and non-Christian syncretistic mass religions, all founded since 1800 and most since 1945, mostly Asian in origin and membership but increasingly with worldwide followings." The "other" category is described as "a handful of smaller religions, quasi-religions, pseudo religions, parareligions, religious or mystic systems, religious and semireligious brotherhoods of numerous varieties." Though I sharply question the designation "pseudo religion," it otherwise appears that most of the religions classified as "other" are also new religions. Finally, they neglect to define the spiritism category. However, because, according to their statistics, 12,039,000 of the world's 12,334,000 spiritists are located in Latin America and the Caribbean, it is clear that this category is meant primarily to encompass Afro-Caribbean and Afro-Brazilian new religions like Santeria and Umbanda.

Out of a total world population of 6,055,049,000 people, Barrett and Johnson find that 102,356,000 are members of new religions, 12,334,000 are spiritists and 1,067,000 are in the "other" category, meaning about 1.9 percent of the world population belongs to alternative religions. This figure does not sound unreasonable, until one discovers that almost all of the people in new religions—100,639,000 members—are Asian. In order to analyze and critique their statistics, it will be useful to lay out all of Barrett and Johnson's relevant figures for the year 2000, continent by continent, as shown in Table 1.

Their figure for Asian new religions immediately strikes one as suspect. Even after being adjusted for population difference, the data still seem to indicate more than ten times as many members of new religions in Asia as in North America. This is probably the result of using different criteria for these two areas of the world. Barrett and Johnson almost certainly classified certain large groups like Soka Gakkai (which has 9 million members) as new religions rather than as Buddhists. In contrast, they almost

TABLE 1
Numbers of Members in New Religions Worldwide

	New Religions	Spiritism	Other	Total Population
Africa	28,400	2,500	65,700	784,445,000
Asia	100,639,000	1,900	62,100	3,682,550,000
Europe	158,000	133,000	236,000	728,887,000
Latin America	622,000	12,039,000	98,000	519,138,000
North America	845,000	151,000	597,000	309,631,000
Australia (& Oceania)	66,500	7,000	9,400	30,393,000

Source: Barrett, David B., and Todd M. Johnson. "A Statistical Approach to the World's Religious Adherents." In *Religions of the World: A Comprehensive Encyclopedia of Beliefs and Practices,* edited by J. Gordon Melton and Martin Baumann, xxvii–xxxviii. Santa Barbara: ABC-CLIO, 2002.

certainly classified the many new Protestant sects that are constantly coming into being in the United States as Christian rather than as new religions.

Given the large number of new religions in sub-Saharan Africa, their low figure for African new religions is clearly off base. Because African new religions tend to draw heavily on traditional ethnoreligions, Christianity, or both, Barrett and Johnson must have classified most of these religious groups as either ethnoreligious or Christian.

The European figure also seems quite low. Because of the concern over alternative religions in Europe since the first Solar Temple tragedy in 1994, there have been a number of official government surveys, though results have been less satisfactory than one might have hoped. For example, in 1998, the German Parliament's Enquete Commission reported the results of a national survey that indicated that 8 to 9 million people considered themselves members of nontraditional religious groups. In contrast, the Swedish government report of 1998 put forward a national figure of 50,000–60,000 (about 0.15 percent of the population), exclusive of New Age groups—a considerably lower proportion than the German figure.

As for North America, using only the new religions figure gives us slightly less than 0.3 percent. Alternatively, adding all of the data from the new religions, spiritism, and "other" categories results in slightly more than 0.5 percent. As it turns out, the 0.3 percent–0.5 percent range receives support from the national census statistics of other English-speaking countries.

New Zealand National Census Data

A number of countries have begun to include religious affiliation as part of their national censuses. One of the most useful is the 2001 New Zealand census because of the large number of distinct groups enumerated, as shown in Table 2.

The total of 17,436 members represents 0.46 percent of the 3,737,277 people who responded to the 2001 census, which compares favorably with the 0.3 percent to 0.5 percent participation rate for North America derived from the Barrett and Johnson data. This is being cautious. One could also make a reasonable argument for including Vineyard Christian Fellowship (sometimes called a "cult," with 774 members in the census), some of the 1,107

TABLE 2
Alternative Religion Statistics from the 2001 New Zealand Census

Religion	Number of Members
Zen Buddhism*	126
Sukyo Mahikari	111
Tenrikyo	12
Yoga	414
Hare Krishna	363
Animism**	213
Pantheism**	342
Nature and Earth-based Religions	2,961
Wiccan	2,196
Druidism	150
Satanism	891
Other New Age Religion	1,485
Rastafarianism	1,296
Sufi***	195
Scientology	282
Spiritualism	5,853
Liberal Catholic Church	135
Unification Church	153
Christian Science	258
Total	17,436

* Like the Hare Krishna movement, Zen Buddhism is considered a New Religion when Westerners become involved.

** Both the New Zealand and the Australian Census identify Animism and Pantheism as Neo-Pagan religions for statistical purposes (e.g., in Table 3, the 2001 figure for the Nature and Earth Based category represents the sum of the Animism, Pantheism, Nature and Earth-based Religions, Wiccan and Druidism figures in Table 2). The religions of indigenous peoples were represented by other categories.

*** Few contemporary Muslims would self-identify as Sufis, indicating that all or most of the members of the Sufi category are members of one of several Sufi groups appealing primarily to Westerners. Like Western Zen Buddhism, Western Sufi groups are considered New Religions.

Source: Statistics New Zealand.

people who self-identified as Taoist, and some of the 4,641 people whom the census classified as simply "other religion." This would bring the participation rate up to 0.5 percent. However, the New Zealand census allowed people to report more than one affiliation, and as a consequence the census collected 3,841,932 responses from a total of 3,737,277 people, or 104,655 extra responses. Though not all of these extra responses could have been supplied by individuals self-identifying as members of new religions, it is reasonable to infer that there were enough double or even triple responses by participants in alternative religions to undermine the solidity of the 0.46 percent figure. So to be cautious, one might want to reduce this percentage to 0.4 percent or even 0.3 percent.

There is, however, at least one more consideration to take into account. Though almost all major alternative religions have an outpost in New Zealand, few were explicitly included in the census. In particular, there are numerous Buddhist groups that appeal primarily if not exclusively to Westerners. If one goes to the New Zealand Buddhist Directory (http://www.buddhanet.net/nzealand.htm), one will find groups like Soka Gakkai, Shambhala Center, plus a wide variety of Vipassana meditation and Tibetan Buddhist organizations. These groups are usually classified in the alternative religions category in general survey books on new religions (for example, Chryssides 1999; Ellwood and Partin 1998; and Lewis 2001a). Participants in these groups were not distinguished from the other Buddhists constituting the 41,469 Buddhists reported in the 2001 census.

One way of getting a handle on the number of people involved in Western-oriented Buddhist groups (groups usually considered new religions in the West, despite their lineage) is to study the ethnic backgrounds of participants. Because the Web site for the 2001 New Zealand census includes a table correlating ethnicity and religion, this information is readily available. The Ethnic Group and Sex by Religious Affiliation table records that 10,890 New Zealand Buddhists are of European heritage. Assuming that some of these European Buddhists are converts because of marriage and other factors, it is reasonable to infer that at least half— or 5,445—are involved in Western-oriented Buddhist groups.

There are also Swedenborgian and Unity School of Christianity churches in New Zealand, the members of which were lumped in with the 192,165 generic Christians recorded in the census. Unfortunately, estimating participation in alternative Christian groups cannot be addressed via ethnicity. Additionally, there are followers of Satya Sai Baba, Maharaji, and a wide variety of other South Asian groups who may have been lumped in with the 38,769 Hindus noted in the census. The census reported 4,329 ethnic Europeans who self-identified as Hindus. Using the same cautious percentage (50 percent) we applied to European Buddhists, this would mean 2,164 people were involved in Western-oriented Hindu groups. Finally, one wonders what happened to members of other groups like the Raelians, Eckankar, Falun Gong, and Theosophy, all of which have a presence in New

TABLE 3
Growth in Alternative Religions from 1999 to 2001 in New Zealand

	1991	1996	2001
Nature and Earth Based Religions	318	1,722	5,862
Spiritualist	3,333	5,100	5,853
New Age Religions	696	1,839	3,210
Satanism	645	909	894
Scientology	207	219	282
Totals	5,196	9,786	16,062

Source: Statistics New Zealand.

Zealand. When all of these organizations are considered, raising the estimated participation rate to 0.5 percent is quite legitimate.

New Zealand also collected less detailed information about religious membership in censuses prior to 2001. The data in Table 3 reflect an interesting pattern of growth.

As can be seen, the overall pattern reflects a tripling of total numbers in a decade. The fastest-growing segment is paganism ("Nature and Earth Based Religions"). Only Satanism fell off between 1996 and 2001. The decline of the latter may be due, in part, to the uninspired leadership that assumed control of the Church of Satan following the death of Anton LaVey in 1997.

Australian National Census Data

The Australian census contains information similar to the New Zealand census. One more category for alternative religious groups is provided, and all of the data from 2001 are arranged into a straightforward comparison with the 1996 census, as delineated in Table 4.

The rise from 30,501 members to 45,829 members represents slightly more than a 50-percent increase in five years. (Religions in the neopagan categories experienced the most rapid rate of growth—an average 250-percent increase.) With respect to number of census respondents in 1996 (17,750,000) and 2001 (18,767,000), this represents a rise from 0.17 percent to 0.24 percent. This rate of participation is considerably less than New Zealand. Unlike New Zealand, the Australian census seems not to have allowed people to respond to more than one item. Like New Zealand, Australia has an abundance of alternative religion

TABLE 4
New Religion Statistics from the 1996–2001 Australian Census

Religion	1996 Members	2001 Members
Animism	727	763
Caodaism	964	819
Christian Science	1,494	1,666
Druidism	554	697
Eckankar	829	747
Gnostic Christian	559	723
Liberal Catholic Church	596	498
Nature Religions*	1,734	2,225
New Churches (Swedenborgian)	504	427
Paganism	4,353	10,632
Pantheism	835	1,085
Rastafarianism	1,023	1,066
Religious Science	634	417
Satanism	2,091	1,798
Scientology	1,488	2,032
Spiritualism	8,140	9,279
Sukyo Mahikari	668	513
Tenrikyo	46	60
Theosophy	1,423	1,627
Wiccan/Witchcraft	1,849	8,755
Total	30,501	45,829

*I infer that "Nature Religions" refers to Neopaganism.

Source: Australian Bureau of Statistics.

groups that "slipped through the cracks" of the above categories because they were recorded as generic Christians, Buddhists, and Hindus. Unfortunately, an Australian census table correlating religious membership with ethnicity is unavailable without paying a fee, so I was unable to obtain the same kind of figures for Western participation in Asian religions as I did for New Zealand. We can say that, because of the many new religions missed by the census, a 0.3 percent–0.4 percent participation rate for 2001 would be a reasonable but still conservative estimate.

One problem with this estimate is that it contrasts so significantly from the corresponding 0.5-percent estimate for New Zealand. Is there really such a marked difference in participation rates between these two sister countries? In terms of numbers of people responding to their respective national censuses, there were five times as many Australians as New Zealanders in 2001. Of the comparable religions in the two censuses, only Christian

Science had more than five times as many members in Australia than in New Zealand. Australian Mahikari and Tenrikyo members were almost five times as numerous as corresponding New Zealand members. But all of the other groups fell well below the one-to-five relationship. In the case of Rastafarianism, there were actually more total members in New Zealand than in Australia. So it seems there is a genuine difference in participation rates between these two countries.

It could be counterargued that there are probably more alternative religions in Australia than in New Zealand and thus more Australian participants who missed the census net. And it could be further argued that, being a larger country, there are a greater number of religious "species" in Australia that draw away some of the people who would have joined other groups, thus explaining why the one-to-five ratio does not hold for most of the religions found in both censuses. However, even if a greater variety in religious fauna between the two countries is a factor to consider, it seems highly unlikely that it would be enough to account for the comparatively large difference between the two participation rates.

If we restate the data from "Down Under" as 0.3 percent–0.5 percent, then we have a statistic comparable to the Barrett and Johnson data for North America. Adding together their new religions, spiritism, and "other" data, Barrett and Johnson's participation rate for Australia and New Zealand works out to 0.34 percent, which is in the same range.

United Kingdom National Census Data

The United Kingdom also conducted a census in 2001. The census recorded a reasonably good spread of different groups. Regretfully, religious participation was not measured in previous censuses. The figures for the England and Wales part of the census are shown in Table 5.

With respect to a population of 52,041,916, a total of 87,189 members represents a participation rate of less than 0.17 percent. The larger number of categories means that somewhat fewer respondents were absorbed into the statistics for their parent traditions, though these categories are still far from comprehensive. Although a handful of Hindu-related groups are included, Buddhist new religions are noticeably absent. New thought groups

TABLE 5
New Religion Statistics for England and Wales from the 2001 British Census*

Group	Members
Spiritualist	32,404
Pagan	30,569
Wicca	7,227
Rastafarian	4,692
Scientology	1,781
Druidism	1,657
Pantheism	1,603
Satanism	1,525
Christian Spiritualist Church	1,461
New Age	906
Hare Krishna	640
Christian Scientist	578
Celtic Pagan	508
Eckankar	426
Animism	401
Brahma Kumari	331
Heathen**	278
Raja Yoga	261
Unification Church	252
Vodun	123
Occult	99
Asatru	93
Sant Mat	53
Divine Light mission	21
Santeria	21
Total	87,189

* Crown copyright material is reproduced with the permission of the controller of HMSO.

** This is a term of self-reference used by certain Neopagans.

Source: Census 2001. Crown Copyright 2004.

like Unity and Religious Science are also not represented as separate categories, as well as many other groups that have a presence in Great Britain.

An important factor influencing the outcome of the religion aspect of the census was that someone decided it would be a fine bit of humor to encourage people to write "Jedi Knight" in the religion category. As a consequence, 390,127 people in England and Wales responded that they belonged to the Jedi Knight religion.

Although this is quite amusing, I would guess that proportionally more of these self-designated Jedis were involved in some form of alternative spirituality than the general population, though how much more is difficult to determine. Minus the Jedi factor, I estimate that 0.17 percent would rise to at least 0.2 percent.

Like the New Zealand census, the UK census provides information on ethnicity and religion. In England and Wales, 0.12 percent of the 47,520,866 white population is Buddhist and .02 percent Hindu. Taking these percentages and then dropping the resulting figures by 50 percent gives 28,512 Western Buddhists and 4,752 Western Hindus. There are also Christian new religions that have slipped through the census categories. When the minus-the-Jedi consideration is combined with the estimate for the various new religions found in the Buddhist and Hindu folds, plus a conservative guess for the number of people in Christian new religions, a cautious estimate would place the participation rate in the UK in the 0.25 percent–0.3 percent range.

Canadian National Census Data

Although the religion categories for the 2001 Canadian census are even less satisfactory than the categories used in the Australian, New Zealand, and British censuses, they are nonetheless useful for comparative purposes. In a country with a population of 28,000,000, the census recorded 38,000 members of alternative religions, or a participation rate of less than 0.14 percent, as seen in Table 6.

Similar to the New Zealand and Australian censuses, Buddhist and Hindu groups regarded as new religions were not separated for statistical purposes. And unlike New Zealand and Australia, even nontraditional Christian groups like Christian Science were apparently collapsed into Christianity. The addition of the classifications "Gnostic" and "New Age" appears to have been for the purpose of including alternative religious groups that did not fall handily into other categories. The New Age as a more general spiritual influence escapes straightforward efforts at measurement, as will be discussed below. I think it would be quite reasonable to estimate much higher participation rates for Canada than indicated by these truncated census figures, more in the 0.25 percent–0.3 percent range at least.

TABLE 6
New Religion Statistics from the 2001 Canadian Census

Religion	Number of Members
Gnostic	1,165
New Age	1,525
Paganism	21,085
Rastafarian	1,135
Satanism	850
Scientology	1,525
Spiritualist	3,295
Swedenborg	1,015
Unity/New Thought	4,000
Vineyard Christian Fellowship	2,600
Total	38,215

Adapted from: Statistics Canada's Internet site, http://www.statcan.ca/. Extracted April 23, 2004.

Religion Survey Data for the United States

Unfortunately, the U.S. census does not collect religion membership data. However, in 1990, the Graduate Center of the City University of New York conducted the National Survey of Religious Identification (NSRI) via randomly dialed phone numbers (113,723 people were surveyed). Eleven years later, in 2001, the same center carried out the American Religious Identification Survey (ARIS) in the same manner (more than 50,000 people responded), though callers probed for more information than the earlier NSRI. Categories were developed *post facto*. The results were quite interesting, as can be seen in Table 7.

Although it would have been much more useful had the researchers broken down their data into more subcategories, their results are nevertheless striking. In a period of eleven years, the overall participation rate in alternative religions increased sevenfold. Once again, however, we are plagued by the collapsing of important new religions into their parent traditions. Had the various Christian alternative religions been separately categorized, the results would likely have been much different.

For the Buddhist and Hindu traditions, we can obtain a rough estimate of participation in new religions by separating ethnic Buddhists and Hindus from Western converts. Although the NSRI did not record ethnicity, the ARIS did. Out of an estimated 766,000 Hindus, 2 percent were white. Out of an estimated

TABLE 7
New Religion Data from NSRI and ARIS

	1990	2001
Scientologist	45,000*	55,000
New Age	20,000	68,000
Eckankar	18,000	26,000
Rastafarian	14,000	11,000
Wicca	8,000	134,000
Druid**		33,000
Santeria**		22,000
Pagan**		140,000
Spiritualist**		116,000
Totals	79,000	583,000

*Numbers have been rounded off to the nearest 1,000. Unlike a census, which attempts to reach the entire population, these figures represent statistical extrapolations.

**The final four categories did not emerge as significant in the 1990 NSRI survey.

Source: B. A. Kosmin and A. Keysar, *Religion in the Marketplace* (Ithaca, NY: Paramount Books, 2004). Adapted table used with permission.

1,082,000 Buddhists, 28.5 percent were white. Taking these percentages and then halving the resulting figures gives 7,660 Euro-American Hindus and 154,185 Euro-American Buddhists. Adding these numbers to the 583,000 figure and dividing the sum by a U.S. population estimate of 207,980,000 gives a participation rate of 0.35 percent.

Had all alternative religions—including the Christian, Buddhist, and Hindu groups missed by the two surveys—been considered together, the sevenfold growth rate would likely have been less spectacular. Like the Australian and New Zealand census data, the NSRI-ARIS data have been sharply affected by the meteoric growth of neopaganism (represented in Table 7 by the Wicca-Druid-Pagan figures) in recent years. Also, if Christian alternative religions had been distinguished so that they could have been included in the final total, the 0.35-percent participation rate derived from the ARIS data would have been higher. How high this rate would rise if we had more complete data again depends on where one decides to draw the line between what is and what is not an "alternative" religion. If we take a conservative approach, a 0.5-percent participation rate represents a reasonable estimate. Of course, if we adopted looser criteria for what constitutes a new religion, much higher estimates would be possible.

Generalizing from the data presented in the prior sections brings us to the conclusion that participation in alternative religions is quite low. In the Anglophone world, the participation rate is 0.3 percent–0.5 percent. And though certain countries might have a rate lower than 0.3 percent, I would speculate that the participation rate in western Europe as a whole probably falls into the same range. The statistical picture of new religions reflected in this data is that of a small-scale phenomenon involving a fraction of a percentage of the population.

Growth and Distribution of Alternative Religions in the United States

Figure 1 indicates the growth in the number of new religious bodies to come into existence between 1900 and 1990. The deci-

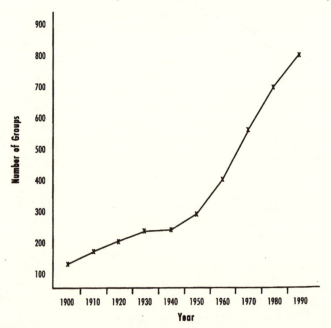

FIGURE 1

Growth of New Religions in the United States in the Twentieth Century

Source: Updated graph based on J. Gordon Melton, *A Directory of Religious Bodies in the United States* (New York: Garland, 1977).

sive upswing in the rate of expansion occurs between the mid-1950s and the mid-1960s, reflecting both an increase in religious experimentation corresponding with the social-cultural revolution of the 1960s and a sharp upswing in the number of Asian religions as a result of the lowering of immigration barriers in 1965.

Figure 2 examines the distribution of new religions in terms of where they are headquartered in the United States. As one would anticipate, most such groups are centered in the Pacific Coast states, especially California. The southeastern part of the country would have been the region with the least new religious activity had it not been for Florida—a state that is culturally more diverse than the rest of the South.

New Religions in Europe

Table 8 is derived from a 1993 article by Rodney Stark. According to Stark's figures, more than three times as many alternative reli-

FIGURE 2
New Religions in 1990 in the Continental United States per Million Residents

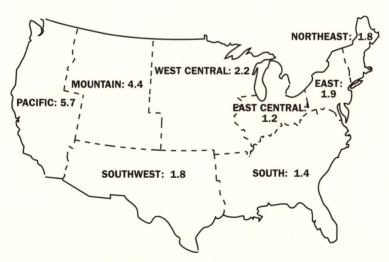

Source: J. Gordon Melton, "Modern Alternative Religions in the West," in John R. Hinnels, ed., *A New Handbook of Living Religions* (London: Blackwell, 1997).

TABLE 8
New Religions in Europe and the United States in the Early 1990s*

Country	Cult Movements per Million	Number of Cult Movements
Switzerland	16.7	108
Iceland	12.0	3
United Kingdom	10.7	604
Austria	7.9	60
Sweden	6.8	57
Denmark	4.5	23
Netherlands	4.4	64
Ireland	3.9	14
Germany	2.5	155
Belgium	2.4	24
Norway	1.9	8
Greece	1.5	15
Italy	1.2	66
Portugal	1.0	10
France	0.9	52
Finland	0.8	4
Spain	0.7	29
Poland	0.5	17
Europe**	3.4	1,313
United States	1.7	425

*In a personal communication to me, Stark noted growing evidence that his figures were significantly undercounted. Thus, for example, he put Italy's total at 66. In contrast, Massimo Introvigne was able to locate 353 new religions for his *Encyclopedia of Religion in Italy*.

** Total based only on nations listed in this table.

Source: Rodney Stark, "Europe's Receptivity to New Religious Movements," *Journal for the Scientific Study of Religion* 31 (1993): 389–397. Reprinted with permission of Rodney Stark.

gions are headquartered in Europe as in the United States. These data contradict the conventional wisdom, which says that the United States is the source of most new religions in Europe. It also flies in the face of Barrett and Johnson's data, which indicate that Europe is relatively impoverished in the area of new religions.

Religious Backgrounds of Members of New Religions

Table 9 is taken from a series of different studies that collected data on the religious backgrounds of people who had joined new

TABLE 9
Religious Backgrounds of Participants in New Religions (in Percentages)

	Protestant	Catholic	Jewish	Other
Unification Church	47.1	35.8	05.3	11.8
Soka Gakkai	30.0	30.0	06.0	34.0
Neopagan	42.7	25.8	06.2	25.3
Hare Krishna	35.5	18.0	14.5	32.0
Zen Center of Los Angeles	52.0	12.0	28.0	08.0
Church Universal and Triumphant	43.7	35.7	03.0	17.7
Movement for Spiritual Inner Awareness	51.2	27.0	14.2	07.6
Ramtha School of Enlightenment	41.3	34.1	02.4	22.1
Satanism	55.0	28.0	01.4	15.6

Sources: Constance Jones, "Church Universal and Triumphant: A Demographic Profile," in *Church Universal and Triumphant in Scholarly Perspective,* edited by James R. Lewis and J. Gordon Melton (Stanford, CA: Center for Academic Publishing, 1994); Constance Jones, "Students in Ramtha's School of Enlightenment: A Profile from Demographic Survey, Narrative, and Interview" (unpublished, 1994); J. Stillson Judah, *Hare Krishna and the Counter Culture* (New York: Wiley, 1974); McCloy Layman, *Buddhism in America* (Chicago: Nelson Hall, 1976); James R. Lewis, *Satanism Today* (Santa Barbara: ABC-CLIO 2001); James R. Lewis, *Seeking the Light* (Los Angeles: Mandeville Press, 1997); J. Gordon Melton, "The Neo-Pagans of America: An Alternative Religion," paper presented to the American Academy of Religion, 1970.

religions. These data respond to a number of hypotheses observers have held about alternative religions, especially the perception that individuals from Jewish homes are disproportionately represented in such groups. Although the data support this informal observation (particularly for some of the Asian-inspired groups), none of these organizations is overwhelmingly Jewish, as some have suggested.

Another casual observation is that neopagans are predominately from Catholic backgrounds, presumably because of their felt need for a "ritualistic" religion. This hypothesis is decisively disconfirmed by the data, which indicate that the percentage of ex-Catholics in neopagan groups is actually less than participants raised in other faiths. The same observation is sometimes made about Satanists; once again, this is disconfirmed.

Postinvolvement Attitudes of Ex-Members

Table 10 reports the results of a 1984 survey of 154 ex-members of controversial religious groups. Respondents were divided into

TABLE 10
Relationship of Post-Involvement Attitudes to Anticult Socialization

Questionnaire Item	Pearson Correlation
Deception	.392
Brainwashing	.587
Leader	.407
Worldview	.551
Discourage Joining	.522
Repeat Membership	.465
Learning Experience	.320
Growth Experience	.503

All values significant at the .001 level (two-tailed tests).

Source: James R. Lewis, "Reconstructing the 'Cult' Experience: Post-involvement Attitudes as a Function of Mode of Exit and Post-involvement Socialization," *Sociological Analysis* 47 (Summer 1986): 151-159, © Association for the Sociology of Religion, Inc. Other findings from this same research project are reported in James R. Lewis, *Legitimating New Religions* (New Brunswick, NJ: Rutgers University Press, 2003).

three "treatment groups": no exit counseling (dropped out of group without intervention of anticultists), voluntary exit counseling (left group voluntarily but experienced intervention of anticult "counselors"), and involuntary exit counseling (kidnapped and deprogrammed).

The questionnaire contained eight items that indicated how ex-members evaluated their former movement. Four of these measured cult-stereotypical attitudes, asking respondents: (1) if they thought they had been recruited deceptively, (2) if they believed they had been brainwashed, (3) if they thought that their ex-leader was insincere, and (4) to what extent they believed the worldview and beliefs of their ex-religion were false.

The other four items measured positive-negative attitudes in a less stereotypical manner. Respondents were asked (1) if they would discourage others from joining their former groups, (2) if they would repeat their membership (with few or many changes), (3) if they considered their membership a learning experience, and (4) if they believed they had grown as a result of their participation in their ex-religion. All eight items were highly correlated with the exit mode, as reported in Table 10.

What these figures show is that the tendency of ex-members of controversial religions to portray their membership period in negative terms is highly correlated with the extent of their contact with the anticult movement. In other words, people who were deprogrammed or otherwise counseled by anticultists are *far* more likely to accuse their former religion of having recruited them deceptively, brainwashing them, and the like. (Refer to Chapter 1 for further discussion of the role of ex-member testimony in the cult controversy.)

Documents

Beyond the court decisions that have already been reviewed, there are few definitive documents in this controversy. The four documents reproduced here are intended to give the reader a more concrete sense of the controversy through contact with primary materials. Two are documents left in the wake of group suicides; two are legislation enacted against "cults."

The first document is one of the four letters, or "testaments," that leaders of the Solar Temple mailed to sixty journalists, scholars, and government officials on the day of their "transits," as they referred to their group suicide. "To All Those Who Can Still Understand the Voice of Wisdom" issued a call for other Solar Temple members and sympathizers to follow their example. This invitation to join them found a receptive audience: on December 16, 1995, sixteen of the remaining European members committed a second mass suicide. Thirteen adults and three children were later found dead in a remote forest in southeast France, and another five additional members committed suicide on March 20, 1997, in Quebec, Canada.

The second document is the press release left by Heaven's Gate at the time of their group suicide. The overall thrust of "Heaven's Gate 'Away Team' Returns to Level Above Human in Distant Space" is comparable with the message of the Solar Temple testament, namely, to explain their exit and to invite others to follow them. In the case of Heaven's Gate, several members who did not leave with the original "away team" later committed suicide.

The third document, the complete text of the "Legislative Resolution Banning Cults," was enacted to retroactively legitimate the Chinese government's suppression of Falun Gong. As a way of giving their actions the patina of legitimacy and deflecting potential Western criticism, the resolution was couched in terms of Western anticult discourse. Unmoderated by countervailing voices within the People's Republic of China, the resolution strikes a strident tone.

The final document consists of excerpts from the French "Law to Reinforce the Prevention and Repression of Groups with a Sectarian Character"—also known as the About-Picard Law after French National Assembly member Catherine Picard, who coauthored the bill with Senator Nicolas About. Though more moderate in tone than the Chinese resolution, it is one of the most repressive laws passed by any western European democracy since the 1940s.

To All Those Who Can Still Understand the Voice of Wisdom . . . We Address This Last Message

The current chaos leads man inescapably to face the failure of his Destiny.

In the course of time, the cycles have followed one another in accordance with precise rhythms and laws. Different civilizations disappeared in the course of cataclysms that were destructive but regenerative; nonetheless none of these reached a level of decadence such as ours.

Subjected to the devastating effects of individual and collective egocentricity, marked by a total ignorance of the Laws of the Spirit and Life, this civilization will no longer escape sudden self-destruction.

From time immemorial, philosophers, prophets and misfortunes have followed one another to help man to take his place as a creator. Man's refusal to See and to Hear each time has diverted the Plans foreseen by Cosmic Evolution.

We, the servants of the Rose+Croix, possessors of an authentic and ancestral Wisdom, affirm that we have worked throughout time for the Evolution of Consciousness. Philosophies, sciences, holy sites and temples remain as living testimonies of this.

The plan of action of these Beings was collected and programmed within the crypts or the sanctuaries, according to precise parameters, hidden from the secular world, but recognized by the initiated.

We, the Servants of the Rose+Croix, declare that throughout all eternity, the Solar and Universal Temple manifests itself amongst men according to cycles of activity and dormancy. After having solemnly opened their Doors on March 21, 1981, in

Geneva, in a Secret Lodge, the ancient domain of the Malta Order, its final esoteric action lasted eleven years.

During this cycle, the Grail, Excalibur, the Candelabra of the Seven Branches and the Ark of the Covenant were revealed to the living witnesses, the final and faithful Servants of the Eternal Rose+Croix. Following which, false slanders and every kind of treason and scandal, judiciously orchestrated by different existing powers, sounded the knell for a last attempt to regenerate the Plans of Conscience.

Those who have breached our Code of Honor are considered traitors. They have suffered and will suffer the punishment they deserve for the ages of the ages.

All is accomplished according to the mandates of Immanent Justice. We hereby affirm that we are in truth, the judges appointed by a Superior Order.

In view of the present irreversible situation, We, the Servants of the Rose+Croix, strongly reaffirm that we are not a part of this world and that we are perfectly aware of the coordinates of our Origins and our Future.

We proclaim, without desiring to create vain polemics, that:

- The Great White Lodge of Sirius has decreed the Call of the last authentic Bearers of an Ancestral Wisdom;
- Justice and Sentence will be applied according to the parameters of a Superior Universal Order with the rigor imposed by the Law;
- The Seven Entities of the Great Pyramid of Gizeh left the Secret Chamber during the night of March 31, 1993, taking with them the capital Energy-Conscience of the seven fundamental planets of our solar system;
- The last Elder Brothers of the Rose+Croix have planned their transit in accordance with criteria known only to themselves. After having transmitted to their Servants the means of completing the Work, they left this world on January 6, 1994, at 12:04 a.m. in Sydney, for a new cycle of Creation.

We, the Servants of the Rose+Croix, considering the urgency of the present situation, affirm:

- that we refuse to participate in systems set up by this decadent humanity;

- that we have planned, in a full state of consciousness, without any fanaticism, our transit which has nothing to do with suicide in the human sense of the term;
- that according to a decree emanating from the Great White Lodge of Sirius, we have closed and voluntarily blown up all the sanctuaries of the Secret Lodges so that they will not be desecrated by impostors or by the ignorant;
- that, from the Planes where we will work from now on and by a just law of magnetism, we will be in the position of calling back the last Servants capable of hearing this last message.

Every slander, lie or falsehood about our deed could only be translated, once more, as the refusal to understand and fathom the Mystery of Life and Death.

Space is short, time is ending. It is with an unfathomable Love, ineffable joy, and without any regret that we leave this world.

Men, cry not over our fate, but rather cry for your own. Ours is more enviable than yours.

To you who are receptive to this last message, may our Love and our Peace accompany you during the terrible tests of the Apocalypse that await you. Know that from where we will be, we will always hold our arms open to receive those who are worthy of joining us.

Exit Press Release—To Be Issued to the News Media 3-22-97

By the time you read this, we suspect that the human bodies we were wearing have been found and that a flurry of fragmented reports have begun to hit the wire services. For those who want to know the facts, the following statement has been issued.
HEAVEN'S GATE "Away Team" Returns to Level Above Human in Distant Space.

RANCHO SANTO FE, CA—By the time you receive this, we'll be gone—several dozen of us. We came from the Level Above Human in distant space and we have now exited the bodies that we were wearing for our earthly task, to return to the world from whence we came—task completed. The distant space we refer to is what your religious literature would call the Kingdom of Heaven or the Kingdom of God.

We came for the purpose of offering a doorway to the Kingdom of God at the end of this civilization, the end of this age, the end of this millennium. We came from that Level, that time, that space, and entered this one. And in so doing, we had to enter human bodies—which we did, for the most part, in the mid-seventies. Now it was time for us to leave those bodies (vehicles)—bodies that we borrowed for the time we were here (by previous arrangement) for this specific task. The task was not only to bring in information about that Evolutionary Kingdom Level Above Human, but to give us the experience of working against the forces of what the human evolutionary level, at this time, has become. And while it was a good learning experience for us, it also gave all who ever received knowledge from that Kingdom an opportunity to recognize us and this information, and to even move out of the human level and into the Next Level or the Next Evolutionary Level, the "Kingdom of Heaven," the Kingdom of God.

The Kingdom of God, the Level Above Human, is a physical world, where they inhabit physical bodies. However, those bodies are merely containers, suits of clothes—the true identity (of the individual) is the soul or mind/spirit residing in that "vehicle." The body is merely a tool for that individual's use—when it wears out, he is issued a new one.

No one can enter the Kingdom of Heaven by trying to live a good life in this world, and then, thinking that when this world's life takes your body, you get to "go to heaven." The only time that Next Kingdom can be entered is when there is a Member or Members of that Kingdom who have come into the human kingdom, incarnated as we have, offering clarification of that information. To get into a discarnate condition just by disconnecting from your body doesn't mean that you are going to go anywhere, whether that loss of body is "premature" or not. When we step out of our "vehicle," we have to know where and who our "tour guide" (our Shepherd) is—for what's next. We have to know we can connect with a Shepherd whom we trust, and that we have decided, "If that Shepherd will have me, I want to continue to be a sheep—and I will do everything I can to please that Shepherd."

Periodically, that Next Level sends in a Representative—a Shepherd—and offers a graduation class, offers life, out of this evolutionary level into that Next Evolutionary Level, and we are at the end of one of those times. TI and DO were the names used by the Representatives of that Next Level, the Kingdom of God, sent to the "surface" of this planet to serve as our Teachers/ "Midwives" at this time.

During a brief window of time, some may wish to follow us. If they do, it will not be easy. The requirement is to not only believe who the Representatives are, but, to do as they and we did. You must leave everything of your humanness behind. This includes the ultimate sacrifice and demonstration of faith—that is, the shedding of your human body. If you should choose to do this, logistically it is preferred that you make this exit somewhere in the area of the West or Southwest of the United States—but if this is not possible—it is not required. You must call on the name of TI and DO to assist you. In so doing, you will engage a communication of sorts, alerting a spacecraft to your location where you will be picked up after shedding your vehicle, and taken to another world—by members of the Kingdom of Heaven.

Only a Member of the Next Level can give you Life—can take you out of "Death"—but it requires that you disconnect, separate, from the last element holding you to the human kingdom.

We know what we're saying—we know it requires a "leap of faith." But it's deliberate—designed for those who would rather take that leap than stay in this world.

We suggest that anyone serious about considering this go into their most quiet place and ask, scream, with all of their being, directing their asking to the Highest Source they can imagine (beyond Earth's atmosphere), to give them guidance. Only those "chosen" by that Next Kingdom will know that this is right for them, and will be given the courage required to act.

SOME RELEVANT SCRIPTURES

Therefore doth my Father love me, because I lay down my life, that I might take it again. No man taketh it from me, but I lay it down of myself. I have power to lay it down, and I have power to take it again. This commandment have I received of my Father. JOHN 10:15–18 He that believeth on me, the works that I do shall he do also. JOHN 14:12

And except that the Lord shorten those days, none shall be saved: but for the elect's sake, whom He has chosen, He hath shortened the days. MARK 13:20

He who loves his life will lose it, and he who hates his life in this world will keep it for eternal life. JOHN 12:25

Blessed are the dead who die in the Lord. REVELATION 14:13

People's Republic of China Legislative Resolution Banning Cults, October 30, 1999

To maintain social stability, protect the interests of the people, safeguard reform and opening up and the construction of a modern socialist country, it is necessary to ban heretic cult organizations and prevent and punish cult activities.

Based on the constitution and other related laws, the following decision is hereby made:

Heretic cult organizations shall be resolutely banned according to law and all of their criminal activities shall be dealt with severely.

Heretic cults, operating under the guise of religion, Qigong or other illicit forms, which disturb social order and jeopardize people's life and property, must be banned according to law and punished resolutely.

People's courts, people's procuratorates, public security, national security and judicial administrative agencies shall fulfill their duties in carrying out these tasks.

To be severely dealt with according to law are those who manipulate members of cult organizations to violate national laws and administrative regulations, organize mass gatherings to disrupt social order and fool others, cause deaths, rape women, swindle people out their money and property or commit other crimes with superstition and heresy.

The principle of combining education with punishment should be followed in order to unify and instruct the majority of the deceived public and to mete out severe punishment to the handful of criminals.

During the course of handling cult groups according to law, people who joined cult organizations but were unaware of the lies being spread by the group shall be differentiated from criminal elements who organize and take advantage of cult groups for illegal activities and/or to intentionally destroy social stability.

The majority of the deceived members shall not be prosecuted, while those organizers, leaders and core members who committed crimes shall be investigated for criminal conduct; those who surrender to the authorities or contribute to the investigations shall be given lesser punishments in accordance with the law or be exempt from punishment.

Long-term, comprehensive instruction on the constitution and the law should be carried out among all citizens, knowledge of science and technology should be popularized and the national literacy level raised.

Banning cult organizations and punishing cult activities according to law goes hand in hand with protecting normal religious activities and people's freedom of religious belief.

The public should be exposed to the inhumane and antisocial nature of heretic cults, so they can knowingly resist influences of cult organizations, enhance their awareness of the law and abide by it.

All corners of society shall be mobilized in preventing and fighting against cult activities, and a comprehensive management system should be put in place.

People's governments and judicial bodies at all levels should be held responsible for guarding against the creation and spread of cult organizations and combating cult activities.

This is an important, long-term task that will ensure social stability.

"Law to Reinforce the Prevention and Repression of Groups with a Sectarian Character" (the About-Picard Law), Paris, France, May 30, 2001

A bill directed to the reinforcement of prevention and repression of cultic movements which undermine human rights and fundamental freedoms.

CHAPTER I

Civil dissolution of certain legal entities

Section 1

The dissolution can be pronounced, according to the provisions of the present Section, of any legal entity, whatever its legal form or object, pursuing activities which have as their purpose or effect to create, maintain or exploit the psychological or physical subjection of persons taking part in these activities, when final criminal sentences have been pronounced against the legal entity itself or its legitimate or de facto leaders, for one or the other of the offences mentioned hereafter:

1E Offences of intentional or unintentional prejudice to the life or the physical or psychological integrity of the person, endangerment of the person, prejudice to the person's freedoms, prejudice to the dignity of the person, prejudice to the personality, imperiling minors or prejudicing property provided for by Sections 221-1 to 221-6, 222-1 to 222-40, 223-1 to 223-15, 223-15-2, 224-1 to 224-4, 225-5 to 225-15, 225-17 to 225-18, 226-1 to 226-23, 227-1 to 227-27, 311-1 to 311-13, 312-1 to 312-12, 313-1 to 313-3, 314-1 to 314-3 and 324-1 to 324-6 of the Criminal Code;

2E Offences of illegal medical or pharmaceutical practice provided for by Sections L. 4161-5 and L. 4223-1 of the Public Health Code;

3E Offences of deceptive advertising, frauds and falsifications provided for by Sections L. 121-6 and L. 213-1 to L. 213-4 of the Consumer Code.

The dissolution procedure is filed before the Court of First Instance by the Public Prosecutor, acting on its own accord or at the request of any interested party.

The request is formulated, examined and judged in conformity with the fast-track (fixed date) procedure. The time limit for appeal is fifteen days. The President of the Court to whom the case is entrusted will fix a short time limit for the hearing to which the case will be summoned. At the indicated day, the proceedings are conducted according to Sections 760 to 762 of the New Code of Civil Procedure.

The overt or disguised maintaining or re-forming of a legal entity disbanded in application of the clauses of the present Section is an offence provided for by the second paragraph of Section 434-43 of the Criminal Code.

The Court of First Instance may pronounce in the course of the same procedure the dissolution of several different legal entities mentioned in the first paragraph, when these legal entities pursue the same purpose and are united by a community of interests and when at least one final criminal sentence for one of the offences mentioned in 1E to 3E has been pronounced against each of them or their legitimate or de facto leaders. These different legal entities must be parties to the procedure.

CHAPTER II

Extension of the criminal responsibility of legal entities to certain offences

Section 2

I.—After the words "is sentenced," the end of the first paragraph of Section L. 4161-5 of the Public Health Code the following words shall be included: "to one year in prison and a 100,000 Francs fine."

II.—After Section L. 4161-5 of the Public Health Code, a Section L. 4161-6 is inserted, reading as follows:

"Sect. L. 4161-6.—Legal entities may be declared criminally responsible in the conditions established by Section 121-2 of the Criminal Code for offences provided for by Section L. 4161-5." The penalties incurred by the legal entities are:

"1E Fine, according to the provisions of Section 131-38 of the Criminal Code;

"2E The penalties mentioned in Paragraphs 2nd to 9th of Section 131-39 of the Criminal Code. The interdiction mentioned in the 2nd Paragraph of Section 131-39 of the Criminal Code concerns the activity in the exercise of which or at the occasion of which the offence was committed."

III.—In Section L. 4223-1 of the same Code, the words: "to a 30,000 Francs fine and, in the event of a subsequent offence, to six months in prison and a 60,000 Francs fine" are replaced by the words: "to one year in prison and a 100,000 Francs fine."

. . .

CHAPTER IV

Clauses restricting the advertisement of cult movements

[Sections 6 and 7 Deleted]

Section 8

The fact of distributing, by whatever means, messages intended for youth and promoting a legal entity, whatever its legal form or object, which is pursuing activities with the purpose or effect to create, maintain or exploit the psychological or physical subjection of persons taking part in these activities, when final criminal sentences have been pronounced several times, against the legal entity itself or its legitimate or de facto leaders, for one or the other of the offences mentioned hereafter, is sentenced to a 50,000 Francs fine:

1E Offences of intentional or unintentional prejudice to the life or the physical or psychological integrity of the person, endangerment of the person, prejudice to the person's freedoms, prejudice to the dignity of the person, prejudice to the personality, placing minors in danger or prejudicing property provided for by Sections 221-1 to 221-6, 222-1 to 222-40, 223-1 to 223-15, 223-15-2, 224-1 to 224-4, 225-5 to 225-15, 225-17 to 225-18, 226-1 to 226-23, 227-1 to 227-27, 311-1 to 311-13, 312-1 to 312-12, 313-1 to 313-3, 314-1 to 314-3 and 324-1 to 324-6 of the Criminal Code;

2E Offences of illegal medical or pharmaceutical practice provided for by Sections L. 4161-5 and L. 4223-1 of the Public Health Code;

3E Offences of deceptive advertising, frauds and falsifications provided for by Sections L. 121-6 and L. 213-1 to L. 213-4 of the Consumer Code.

The same sanctions are applicable when the messages referred to in the first paragraph of this Section are an invitation to join such a legal entity.

The legal entities may be declared penally responsible in conditions provided for by Section 121-2 of the Criminal Code of offences defined in this Section. The sanction incurred by legal entities is a fine, according to the provisions of Section 131-38 of the Criminal Code.

CHAPTER V

Clauses connected with the fraudulent abuse of the state of ignorance or weakness

Section 9

After Section 223-15 of the Criminal Code, a section 6 bis is created, reading as follows:

"Section 6 bis

Regarding the fraudulent abuse of the state of ignorance or weakness.

"Sect. 223-15-2.—The fraudulent abuse of the state of ignorance or the condition of weakness of either a minor or a person whose specific vulnerability, due to his age, an illness, a disability, a physical or psychological deficiency or pregnancy, is apparent and known to its author, or of a person in a state of psychological or physical subjection resulting from serious pressures exercised or repeated or from techniques likely to alter his judgment, leading this minor or this person to an act or an abstention which are seriously harmful to him, is sentenced to three years in prison and a 2,500,000 Francs fine.

"When the offence is committed by the legitimate or de facto leader of a group which is pursuing activities with the purpose or effect to create, maintain or exploit the psychological or physical subjection of persons taking part in these activities, the sentences are extended to five years in prison and a 5,000,000 Francs fine.

"Sect. 223-15-3.—Individuals guilty of the offence provided for in this section also incur the following supplementary sentences:

"1E Deprivation of political, civil and family rights, according to the provisions of Section 131-26;

"2E Deprivation, according to provisions of Section 131-27, of the exercise of a civil service or the exercise of the professional or social activity in the exercise of which or at the occasion of the exercise of which the offence was committed, for a length of five years at most;

"3E Closing, for a length of five years at most, of the establishments or of one or several establishments of the corporation having served to commit the incriminated facts;

"4E Seizure of the thing which served or was intended to commit the offence or the thing which is its product, with the exception of objects susceptible of restitution;

"5E Prohibition to stay in France or in certain French departments, according to the provisions of Section 131-31;

"6E Interdiction, for a length of five years at most, the drawing of checks other than those which enable the withdrawal of funds by the drawer from the drawee or of certified ones;

"7E Posting of the bill or circulating the pronounced decision, in conditions provided for by Section 131-35.

"Art. 223-15-4.—Legal entities may be declared criminally responsible, in conditions provided for by Section 121-2, of the offence defined in this section."

. . .

References

Arweck, Elisabeth. "New Religious Movements." In *Religions in the Modern World,* edited by Linda Woodhead, Paul Fletcher, Jiroko Kawanami, and David Smith, 264–288. London: Routledge, 2002.

Australian National Census 96: Religion. http://www.aph.gov.au/library/pubs/rn/1997-98/98rn27.htm.

Barker, Eileen. "New Religious Movements: Their Incidence and Significance." In *New Religious Movements: Challenge and Response,* edited by Bryan Wilson and Jamie Cresswell, 15–31. London: Routledge, 1999.

Barrett, David B., and Todd M. Johnson. "A Statistical Approach to the World's Religious Adherents." In *Religions of the World: A Comprehensive Encyclopedia of Beliefs and Practices,* edited by J. Gordon Melton and Martin Baumann, xxvii–xxxviii. Santa Barbara: ABC-Clio, 2002.

Canadian National Census 2001. http://www.statcan.ca.

Chryssides, George D. *Exploring New Religions.* London: Cassell, 1999.

Clarke, Peter B. "New Paths to Salvation." *Religion Today* 1, no. 1 (1984): 1–3.

Ellwood, Robert S., and Harry B. Partin. *Religious and Spiritual Groups in Modern America.* 2d ed. Essex, UK: Pearson Education, 1998.

Gallup, George, Jr., and D. Michael Lindsay. *Surveying the Religious Landscape.* Harrisburg, PA: Morehouse, 1999.

Jones, Constance. "Church Universal and Triumphant: A Demographic Profile." In *Church Universal and Triumphant in Scholarly Perspective,* edited by James R. Lewis and J. Gordon Melton. Stanford, CA: Center for Academic Publishing, 1994.

———. "Students in Ramtha's School of Enlightenment: A Profile from Demographic Survey, Narrative, and Interview." Unpublished paper, 1994.

Judah, J. Stillson. *Hare Krishna and the Counter Culture.* New York: Wiley, 1974.

Kosmin, Barry A., and Ariela Keysar. *Religion in the Marketplace.* Ithaca, NY: Paramount Books, 2004.

Layman, McCloy. *Buddhism in America.* Chicago: Nelson Hall, 1976.

Lewis, James R. "Reconstructing the 'Cult' Experience: Post-involvement Attitudes as a Function of Mode of Exit and Post-involvement Socialization." *Sociological Analysis* 47 (Summer 1986): 151–159.

———. *Seeking the Light.* Los Angeles: Mandeville Press, 1997.

———. *Odd Gods: New Religions and the Cult Controversy.* Amherst, NY: Prometheus Books, 2001.

———. *Satanism Today.* Santa Barbara: ABC-Clio, 2001.

———. *The Astrology Book.* Detroit: Visible Ink, 2003.

———. *Legitimating New Religions.* New Brunswick, NJ: Rutgers University Press, 2003.

Melton, J. Gordon. "The Neo-Pagans of America: An Alternative Religion." Paper presented to the American Academy of Religion, 1970.

———. *A Directory of Religious Bodies in the United States.* New York: Garland, 1977.

————. *The Encyclopedic Handbook of Cults in America.* 2d ed. New York: Garland, 1992.

————. "Modern Alternative Religions in the West." In *A New Handbook of Living Religions,* edited by John R. Hinnels. London: Blackwell, 1997.

Rabinovitch, Shelley, and James R. Lewis. *The Encyclopedia of Modern Witchcraft and Neo-Paganism.* New York: Citadel, 2002.

Singer, Margaret Thaler, with Janja Lalich. *Cults in Our Midst: The Hidden Menace in Our Everyday Lives.* San Francisco: Jossey-Bass, 1995.

Stark, Rodney. "Europe's Receptivity to New Religious Movements." *Journal for the Scientific Study of Religion* 31 (1993): 389–397.

6

Biographical Sketches

This chapter provides biographical sketches of some of the most important people involved in the cult controversy. Approximately half of the individuals profiled are founders of the religious movements that have been the most controversial. The balance are mostly scholars and professionals who have taken a stand on one side or the other of the controversy.

Dick Anthony (b. 1939)

Dick Anthony is a research and forensic psychologist. He did graduate work in clinical psychology at Duke University and finished his PhD in an interdisciplinary psychology and religion program at the Graduate Theological Union in Berkeley. As a research associate of the University of North Carolina at Chapel Hill Department of Psychiatry and later as the research director of the Center for the Study of New Religions at the Graduate Theological Union, he directed a series of research programs on the social and psychological precursors and effects of new religious movements and alternative therapies. These research programs were funded by U.S. government agencies (the National Institute of Mental Health, the National Institute of Drug Abuse, and the National Endowment for the Humanities) and by major philanthropic foundations. He has published the results of his research in numerous professional articles and book chapters.

Many of his publications evaluate beneficial versus harmful effects of membership in different types of new religions and provide an alternative to the cultic brainwashing approach to

271

addressing the issue of coercion in such groups. His publications also summarize the scientific and legal basis for viewing cultic brainwashing theories and testimony as unscientific or unconstitutional or both and argue that courts should disallow such testimony because of its prejudicial character. His approach has been a primary basis for amicus curiae briefs by several professional associations, including the American Psychological Association, which were submitted in cases involving allegations of cultic brainwashing.

As a result of his publications and consulting activities, he has since 1985 served as a trial consultant and expert witness in numerous cases in the United States and Europe involving allegations of coercive religious influence. His critique of the scientific and civil liberties problems associated with the legal use of cultic brainwashing formulations has become the most frequently used legal and scientific basis for repudiating cultic brainwashing testimony in such cases.

Marshall Herff Applewhite (1931–1997)

Marshall Applewhite was the cofounder of Heaven's Gate, the UFO religion that committed group suicide in 1997. He was born in Spur, Texas. The son of a Presbyterian minister, he was active in church and sang in the church choir. After receiving an undergraduate degree from Austin College, he completed a master's degree in music from the University of Colorado at Boulder. He joined the faculty of St. Thomas University in 1964. He directed the university choir and eventually became chair of the Music Department.

Despite the outward success of Applewhite's early academic and musical career, he was deeply troubled. Married and the father of two children, he secretly carried on a double life as a homosexual. Guilty and confused, he is said to have longed for a platonic relationship within which he could develop his full potential without being troubled by his sexual urges. He eventually divorced his wife and, in 1970, was terminated by St. Thomas University. Devastated, Applewhite became bitter and depressed.

He met his platonic partner, Bonnie Lu Nettles, at a hospital where he was seeking help for his sexual and psychological problems. Nettles and Applewhite quickly became inseparable. For a short while, they together operated a metaphysical center. After the center folded, they continued holding classes in a house they called Knowplace. In 1973, they began traveling in search of a higher purpose. They eventually camped out in an isolated spot near the Oregon coast and, after six weeks, came to the realization that they were the two witnesses prophesied in Revelation 11 who would be martyred and then resurrected three and a half days later—an event they later referred to as the Demonstration. Preaching an unusual synthesis of occult spirituality and UFO soteriology, they began recruiting in New Age circles in the spring of 1975.

In the spring of 1975, they recruited their first followers, beginning with a metaphysical teacher named Clarence Klug and twenty-three of his students. As the first step in the transformational process taught by the Two, their followers abandoned everything that tied them to their everyday lives, including their jobs, families, and most of their possessions except for cars and camping supplies (necessary for leading a quasi-nomadic lifestyle). Mirroring their own process, the Two placed males and females together in nonsexual partnerships in which each was instructed to assist his or her partner in the overcoming process. They also attempted to tune in to the next level, again reflecting the process that Applewhite and Nettles had experienced during their six-week retreat. A central part of the teaching was that members would physically ascend and become members of the crews of "next level" spacecraft.

Heaven's Gate, originally known as Human Individual Metamorphosis, first made headlines in September 1975 when, following a public lecture in Waldport, Oregon, more than thirty people vanished overnight. This disappearance became a media event. For the next several months, reporters generated story after story about brainwashed cult groupies abandoning their everyday lives to follow the strange couple who alternately referred to themselves as "Bo and Peep," "the Two," "Do and Ti," and other bizarre names. Applewhite continued to lead the group by himself after Nettles died of cancer in 1985.

Details about how Applewhite came to attach apocalyptic significance to the Hale-Bopp comet are scanty. Someone outside the group had come to the conclusion that a giant UFO was coming to Earth, "hidden" in the wake of the Hale-Bopp comet. When Heaven's Gate heard this information, Applewhite took it as an indication that the long awaited pickup of his group by aliens was finally about to take place. The decision that the time had come to make their final exit could not have been made more than a few weeks before the mass suicide. Applewhite had rethought his theology after his beloved partner died because, in order to be reunited with Nettles, her spirit would have to acquire a new body aboard the spacecraft. The death of Nettles seems to have been the decisive influence leading him to later adopt the view that the group would ascend together spiritually rather than physically.

Shoko Asahara (b. 1955)

Shoko Asahara was the founder-leader of AUM Shinrikyo. His birth name was Chizuo Matsumoto. Almost blind, he attended a special school and graduated in 1977. Failing to get accepted to a university, Matsumoto pursued a career in Chinese medicine before turning to spirituality. Following a pilgrimage to the Himalayas in 1987, he changed his name to Shoko Asahara.

Asahara founded AUM Shinrikyo in Tokyo following his return from India. Asahara made international headlines in the wake of a poison-gas attack that occurred on March 20, 1995, in the crowded Tokyo subway system. Twelve people died, and many others were injured. Within a few days of the attack, AUM Shinrikyo was fingered as the most likely suspect. The leadership was eventually arrested and the organization disbanded.

A form of Tantric Buddhism, AUM Shinrikyo's teachings emphasized yoga practices and spiritual experiences. Asahara had traveled to India seeking enlightenment. Before returning to Japan, he sought out the Dalai Lama and received what he believed was a commission to revive true Buddhism in the land of his birth. By the time of the subway incident, Asahara had acquired a large communal facility near Mount Fuji and a following of approximately 10,000 members in Japan (with an estimated 30,000 followers in Russia).

In addition to the usual teachings that go hand in hand with mainline Buddhism, Asahara was also fascinated with seeing into the future. His preoccupation with divination may have grown out of the weakness of his physical senses. Before undertaking yoga and meditation practices, he pursued the study of such divinatory practices as astrology. Like many other Japanese spiritualists, he was fascinated by Western biblical prophecies as well as by the prophecies of Nostradamus. Perhaps influenced by the apocalyptic flavor of these predictions, Asahara himself began preaching an apocalyptic message to his followers. In particular, he prophesied a confrontation between Japan and the United States before the end of the century that would in all likelihood destroy his home country.

Asahara was, in fact, so certain about an impending conflict between Japan and the United States that he actually began preparing to wage war. Unable to match the conventional military might of the United States, AUM scientists investigated unconventional weapons, from biological agents to poison gas. The Tokyo gas attack was motivated by increased police scrutiny of AUM Shinrikyo, with the idea of distracting police attention away from the movement.

In the end, it was Asahara's own pronouncements that led the police to the door of AUM Shinrikyo. In particular, Master Asahara had predicted that gas attacks by terrorists would occur in the not too distant future. This made him an obvious target of suspicion. Hence, the subway attack, far from diverting attention away from AUM Shinrikyo, actually had the opposite effect. He was found hiding in the group's headquarters near Mount Fuji, arrested, and eventually convicted of murder.

Eileen Barker (b. 1938)

Eileen Barker received her BSc from the London School of Economics (1970) and her PhD in sociology from the University of London. In 1998, she was elected to Fellowship of the British Academy. And in 2000, she was appointed as an officer of the Order of the British Empire. She is an emeritus professor of sociology with special reference to the study of religion at the London School of Economics. Her main research interests are "cults," "sects," and new religious movements and the social reactions to which they give rise; since 1989, she has also been investigating changes in the religious situation in postcommunist countries.

Barker has more than 200 publications, including 9 books (7 edited) and numerous articles in journals and chapters in books, to her name. Her *New Religious Movements: A Practical Introduction* (1989) is presently in its fifth impression and has been translated into Italian, Dutch, Bulgarian, Russian, and Polish, with a second edition being translated into several other languages. Other publications have been translated into a total of twenty-four languages.

Her award-winning book *The Making of a Moonie: Brainwashing or Choice?* although not written as a textbook, is used as such in both sociology of religion and methods courses in several universities in the United States, Europe, and Australia.

In the late 1980s, with the support of the British government and mainstream churches, Barker founded INFORM, a charity based at the London School of Economics, which provides information about new religions that is as accurate, objective, and up-to-date as possible. She is a frequent adviser to governments, other official bodies, and law enforcement agencies around the world and is the only non-American to have been elected president of the Society for the Scientific Study of Religion.

David Brandt Berg (1919–1994)

David Brandt Berg, known to his followers as Father David, was the founder of the nontraditional Christian missionary movement known as the Family (formerly the Children of God). Berg's parents were active pastors, and he spent his first years traveling with his parents during their evangelical mission.

In 1944, Berg met and married Jane Miller, an active member of the Alliance Church in Sherman Oaks, California. In late 1948, he began ministering at a small Christian and Missionary Alliance church in rural Arizona but resigned in early 1951. For the next fifteen years, Berg taught secondary school, held a number of other secular jobs, attended several secular and Christian colleges, opened and ran a small center for missionaries, and traveled the United States booking an evangelical program on radio and television. He eventually became more convinced of the ineffectiveness of organized, traditional "Churchianity" and its emphasis on ceremonialism and lavish buildings, as well as its general lack of interest in evangelical outreach.

In the mid-1960s, Berg began traveling with his four children in evangelistic outreach, and in early 1968 he and his family journeyed to Huntington Beach, California, a beach town that had become a gathering place for thousands of hippies. He began ministering to the youth in a small Christian coffeehouse, the Light Club. Hundreds of young people became Christians and stopped taking drugs. Berg's new ministry to the hippies marked his total rupture with mainstream Christian denominations. During this period, Berg also met his second wife, Maria, who remained Berg's constant companion for twenty-five years, from the spring of 1969 until his passing in 1994.

In 1970, the "Teens for Christ" were likened by a newspaper reporter to "Moses and the Children of God"; these designations stuck, as Berg became known as Moses Berg and his followers as the Children of God. At the heart of his teaching was the conviction that the love of God, as manifested in the Bible and the person of Jesus, was the solution to every human need and that the Christian's primary responsibility is to dedicate time, energy, and resources to sharing the Gospel with others.

Among Berg's most controversial beliefs was his adherence to the principle that he called the Law of Love, which he applied most shockingly to matters of sex. In 1976, he also proposed to his followers that in certain circumstances, it would be acceptable for a Christian to have sexual relations with someone in an effort to give them a tangible manifestation of God's love, thereby helping them to come to a saving knowledge of Jesus Christ. This doctrine, which became known as "flirty fishing," was practiced by some Family members until 1987, when it was officially discontinued.

David G. Bromley (b. 1941)

David G. Bromley received his BA from Colby College in 1963 and his MA (1966) and PhD (1971) degrees from Duke University. He has served on the faculties of the University of Virginia, University of Texas at Arlington, University of Hartford, and Virginia Commonwealth University. He joined the sociology faculty at Virginia Commonwealth University as department chair in 1984 and is currently a professor and director of graduate studies in the Department of Sociology with an affiliate appointment in the Department of Religious Studies.

Bromley has worked in a variety of areas throughout his academic career, including urban sociology, sociology of religion, social movements, deviance, and political sociology. His primary interest is in new religious movements. One line of work on new religions adopted an organizational perspective on these movements. His book with Anson D. Shupe Jr. *Moonies in America* (1979) adopted a resource-mobilization approach, whereas his book with Phillip Hammond, *The Future of New Religious Movements* (1987), explored structural factors associated with movement success or failure. A second line of work involved the conflict dynamics between movements and countermovements. This line of work is represented by another book with Shupe, *The New Vigilantes* (1980).

Bromley has written on a number of key issues involving new religious groups, including sociocultural sources of new movements, movement organization and development, conversion and defection, and conflicts and controversies. More recently, he has connected the 1980s Satanism scare to the 1970s cult scare in his book with James Richardson and Joel Best, *The Satanism Scare* (1991). He has written or edited seventeen books on religious movements. His most recent books are *The Politics of Religious Apostasy* (1998), *Cults, Religion and Violence* (2001), *Toward Reflexive Ethnography: Participating, Observing, Narrating* (2001), and *Defining Religion: Critical Approaches to Drawing Boundaries between Sacred and Secular* (2003). He is former president of the Association for the Sociology of Religion; founding editor of the annual series Religion and the Social Order, sponsored by the Association for the Sociology of Religion; and past editor of the *Journal for the Scientific Study of Religion,* published by the Society for the Scientific Study of Religion.

John Gordon Clark, MD (1926–1999)

John G. Clark was a psychiatrist and the founder of the American Family Foundation, which was the most prominent U.S. anticult organization after the Cult Awareness Network. He was born in St. Cloud, Minnesota. He served in the navy, graduated from Macalester College in St. Paul, and went on to attend Harvard Medical School. He was a member of the faculty of Harvard Medical School and the staff of McLean Hospital in Belmont. He maintained a private practice in Weston, Massachusetts.

Clark was one of the first professionals to turn his attention to new religions, even before the Jonestown suicide-murders in 1978. In 1979, he authored an influential and oft-cited editorial on cults for the *Journal of the American Medical Association.* He was frequently an expert witness in governmental committees and hearings investigating alternative religions. As a psychiatrist, the thrust of Clark's testimony was that involvement in such groups induced radical personality changes and was dangerous to participants' mental health. He also asserted that members of nontraditional religions were being subjected to "an impermissible experiment" of subtle and sophisticated psychological manipulation by the leadership of such groups.

One of the most prominent anticultists of the seventies and eighties, Clark propagated his views in a variety of venues, from the courtroom to the news media. He regularly appeared on TV shows, including a BBC documentary about the Unification Church. As a consequence, he became embroiled in several legal battles with the Church of Scientology, which objected to his critical perspective and accused him of being antireligious. Clark asserted that the Church of Scientology orchestrated a harassment campaign against him. In a 1988 settlement, he received an undisclosed sum from this organization but at the same time agreed to never again publicly discuss the Church of Scientology.

In 1985, Clark was awarded the Leo J. Ryan Award, named after the California congressman murdered in Jonestown, Guyana. Also, in 1991, the *Psychiatric Times* named him psychiatrist of the year. He passed away at a Belmont, Massachusetts, nursing home. He had been suffering from a long illness and was seventy-three at the time of his death.

Joseph Di Mambro (1924–1994)

Joseph Di Mambro was the founder of the Order of the Solar Temple, an esoteric New Age group responsible for a series of group suicides (the first incident also involved murders) in 1994, 1995, and 1997. From the age of sixteen, Di Mambro was apprenticed as a watchmaker and jeweler and seems to have pursued this profession during the first part of his life. Not much is known about this period except that from a young age he was deeply interested in esotericism. Di Mambro had sampled a variety of different esoteric groups, including the Ancient and Mystical Order Rosae Crucis, which he joined in 1956 and of which he was a member until at least 1968. In the 1960s, he came into contact with several persons who would later play a role in Solar Temple history, including Jacques Breyer who had initiated a "Templar resurgence" in France in 1952. Several groups, including the Order of the Solar Temple, have their roots in Breyer's work.

The International Chivalric Order Solar Tradition (Solar Temple) was founded in 1984. Solar Temple groups were organized in Quebec, Canada, as well as in Australia, Switzerland,

France, and other countries. The leadership saw themselves as playing a pivotal role on the world stage. Partially as a consequence of this view, they believed that the Solar Temple was being systematically persecuted by the various governments with which they were having relatively minor problems.

Though his spiritual interests seem to have been sincere, Di Mambro also had an unsavory side to his character. In 1972, he was convicted on charges of fraud for impersonating a psychologist and passing bad checks. A 1979 fire at La Pyramide, an early communal farm founded by Di Mambro near Geneva, was possibly an insurance swindle. The insurance money from the fire enabled Di Mambro to obtain a mansion in Geneva where he started the Golden Way Foundation. The Golden Way, in turn, was the immediate predecessor organization to the Solar Temple. He was also not above tricking his followers into thinking he had such a close link to the ascended masters that they would deign to manifest themselves during Temple initiations. These manifestations were accomplished by means of hidden holographic projections of the masters.

Di Mambro was far from humble and claimed to be the reincarnation of Osiris, Akhnaton, Moses, and Cagliostro. He identified various Solar Temple members as having been such famous individuals as Bernard de Clairvaux, Joseph of Arimathea, Queen Hapshetsout, and Rama. He was also regarded by his followers as the only person having access to the masters. Furthermore, Di Mambro saw the OTS as producing "cosmic children" who would shape the future destiny of the planet. Chief among these was his own daughter Emmanuelle, who was to be the messiah-avatar of the New Age.

Gerald Brousseau Gardner (1884–1964)

Gerald Gardner, founder of the contemporary Wicca movement, was born into a Scottish family in Blundellsands, England. Childhood asthma prevented him from participating in normal schooling, and he gained most of his education through his own reading. He worked on a plantation in Ceylon (today's Sri Lanka) from 1900 to 1923, when he became a civil servant.

Over the following years, Gardner became an amateur anthropologist, as his various government jobs took him and sometimes his wife, Donna (whom he married in 1927), to numerous Asian countries. In 1936, he published *Kris and Other Malay Weapons*, which became the standard work on that topic. He was particularly interested in magical and religious practices and sought out local leaders in those areas. For a time he joined a Masonic lodge in Ceylon.

Just prior to World War II, Gardner retired and returned to England, where he joined the Corona Fellowship of Rosicrucians. Through those connections, he was supposedly introduced to Dorothy Clutterbuck, said to be the priestess of a group of practicing witches. According to Gardner, she agreed to initiate him into practices handed down through many generations, though the practice of witchcraft was unlawful and she swore him to secrecy. He did manage to talk about Wiccan practices indirectly through his 1949 novel, *High Magic's Aid*, published under the pseudonym Scire. He also opened a witchcraft museum near his home on the Isle of Man.

In 1951, the final British law against witchcraft was struck down, and in 1954 Gardner published his landmark book *Witchcraft Today*, describing the craft and lamenting its apparent imminent demise. The book, however, attracted the attention of a number of people who came to him and his high priestess, Lady Olwen (Monique Wilson), for initiation. Gardnerian Wicca made its way to the United States through initiates Raymond and Rosemary Buckland in 1963 and initiate Alexander Sanders several years later.

After Gardner's death on an ocean voyage, his papers and effects were sold to *Ripley's Believe It or Not*. They have clearly shown that Gardner did not learn witchcraft from a living tradition, as he had claimed during his life, but in fact devised all the rituals and beliefs himself. He created the witch's ritual knife, the *athame*, from his knowledge of the *kris*, the Malaysian ceremonial weapon. He created the major holy days, or *sabbats*, from the eight ancient pagan agricultural festivals, and then added the *esbats*, or biweekly meetings. He created the practice of nude (or "skyclad") worship from his experience sunbathing after recovering from a leg injury. Other sources included the medieval book *Greater Key of Solomon*, Masonic books, Alistair Crowley books, and elements of Asian cultures. Whatever the sources, Gardnerian Wicca is the source of the practices of most Wiccan groups and has become its own living tradition.

L. Ron Hubbard (1911–1986)

Lafayette Ronald Hubbard, writer and founder of dianetics and Scientology, was born in Tilden, Nebraska, the son of Ledora May Waterbury and Harry Ross Hubbard, an officer in the U.S. Navy.

Hubbard spent much of his youth with his maternal grandfather in Montana due to his father's service in the navy. In 1923–1924, Hubbard lived in Washington, D.C., and, again, after 1929, graduating from high school there in 1930. In 1927–1928, Hubbard traveled throughout the Far East. In 1930, he entered George Washington University but left before graduating. Hubbard spent some of the early 1930s as an aviator and aviation correspondent. His major vocation by 1934, however, was as a prolific and increasingly successful fiction writer. His stories of the 1930s and 1940s were predominantly action and adventure, and included Westerns and science fiction.

Hubbard married three times: in 1933 to Margaret Louise Grubb, in 1946 to Sara Northrup, and in 1952 to Mary Sue Whipp. He had six children. During World War II, he was a navy lieutenant, serving in both the Pacific and the Atlantic, and spent time in 1943 and 1945 as a patient in a naval hospital for ulcers and injuries to eyes and hip. In 1950, he published his most famous book, *Dianetics: The Modern Science of Mental Health.* This work, on a new form of therapy Hubbard labeled dianetics, became an instant best-seller, generating numerous articles, discussion groups, and conversations. *Dianetics* was opposed by the medical, psychological, and psychiatric professions, with all published articles discouraging its use.

In March 1952, Hubbard moved to Phoenix where he announced the establishment of the Hubbard Association of Scientologists International. In 1954, scientologists and dianetics practitioners in Los Angeles formed the Church of Scientology. Between 1951 and 1954, Hubbard wrote some twenty Scientology books.

In 1959, Hubbard moved to England, where he started the Hubbard College of Saint Hill, in Sussex. In 1966, he resigned all administrative positions in the church, and the next year set to sea with a handful of veteran scientologists, called the Sea Organization. After several more moves, he finally retired to a private life in San Luis Obispo County, California, devoting the majority of his time before his death four years later to writing.

Massimo Introvigne (b. 1955)

Massimo Introvigne is the founder and director of CESNUR. He received a BA in philosophy from the Pontifical Gregorian University in Rome and a JD degree from the University of Turin, with a specialization in philosophy and sociology of law. Since 1980, he has worked in a leading Italian law firm specializing in intellectual property and international licensing, where he became a partner in 1985.

In 1988, he established CESNUR, the Center for Studies on New Religions, a professional organization for those specializing in the academic study of new religious movements, which was recognized as a public interest nonprofit association by the State of Piedmont, Italy, in 1996. He has served as managing director of CESNUR continuously since its foundation. He has lectured and given seminars in several academic institutions, including the Queen of the Apostles Athenaeum (later University) in Rome, University of Turin, El Salvador University in Buenos Aires, Bocconi University in Milan, and University of Latvia. In 2001, he was elected as a member of the group "Religions" of the Italian Association of Sociology (AIS), whose charter provides that persons other than full-time professors of sociology in Italian universities (the institutional members of AIS) may be nonetheless voted in as members on the basis of their production of books and articles in the field of sociology.

Introvigne is active in politics and was a founding member of the Christian Democrat Center, now merged into the Christian Democrat Union, part of present Italy's governing coalition. He is a frequent contributor to several Italian daily newspapers and a member of the Board of Nova Res Publica, the leading Italian conservative foundation. In recent years, he has written and lectured extensively on religious violence and terrorism and has served as a consultant to several Italian and international military and law enforcement agencies, including the Critical Analysis Response Group of the FBI and UNICRI, the United Nations branch studying organized crime and terrorism.

He is the author of 40 books and more than 100 articles in refereed journals. He was the editor in 2001 of the monumental *Enciclopedia delle religioni in Italia* (Encyclopedia of Religions in Italy), which went on to become the most reviewed nonfiction work of 2001 in Italy. Both the encyclopedia and CESNUR's Web site (http://www.cesnur.org), also edited by Introvigne, won several awards.

James (Jim) Warren Jones (1931–1978)

Jim Jones, founder of the People's Temple, was born in Lynn, Indiana. His father was an alcoholic road construction worker. He married Marceline Baldwin in 1949 and attended college briefly but left to become minister of the Somerset Methodist Church in Indianapolis.

Before receiving final elder's orders, he left the Methodist Church and founded an independent congregation called Community Unity. There he put into place his vision of a Pentecostal-style worship and a social service activism across racial boundaries. By the late 1950s, the congregation was renamed the People's Temple and began to emulate many of the features of Father Divine's Peace Mission. Jones saw Father Divine (d. 1965), an African American, as a role model; although Jones was white, most of his followers were black. In 1960, the People's Temple affiliated with the Christian Church (Disciples of Christ), and the following year Jones received a BS from Butler University in Indianapolis.

In 1964, after returning from a two-year travel sabbatical to diffuse community controversy about the congregation's activities, he was ordained as a Christian Church (Disciples of Christ) minister. Believing that Indianapolis was a dangerous area for a future nuclear war, he moved the congregation to Ukiah, California. The success of his ministry there made him wealthy and influential, and he added a congregation in Los Angeles. His social work earned him community awards and praise in church journals.

There were areas of concern, however. He began claiming he could raise people from the dead. It was rumored he held dictatorial control over the personal lives of followers and abused some children. In 1977, facing media exposure, he moved to a colony in Guyana, South America, he had founded in 1973, and it soon swelled to more than 900 inhabitants as "Jonestown." The group still faced court charges, and Jones began to speak of the possibility of group suicide. In November 1978, California Congressman Leo Ryan and others visited Jonestown to investigate. Ryan and most of his group were shot to death, and almost all the residents of Jonestown also died via poison or gunshot. The name

"Jonestown" has since served for many to stand for and sum up the dangers of religious "cults," though some, like author Michael Meiers, have suggested the CIA had a role in the incident.

David Koresh (1959–1993)

David Koresh, leader of the Branch Davidians, was born Vernon Howell to a young single mother in Houston, Texas. He lived with his grandmother during the first five years of his life until his mother married. Continuous academic problems created by a learning disability troubled his early school years. Howell dropped out of high school in 1974 before completing the tenth grade. His passions as a teenager were playing guitar and studying the Bible. He memorized long sections of the New Testament, preaching to anyone who would listen. In the years that followed, he held a succession of short-term jobs, particularly as a carpenter.

In 1979, Howell began participating in study sessions at a Seventh-Day Adventist Church in Tyler, Texas, that his mother attended. There was a succession of incidents that eventually resulted in his being disfellowshipped. He learned of the Branch Davidians from an SDA friend and began working as a handyman at Mount Carmel in 1981. He became a favorite of sixty-seven-year-old Lois Roden, who led the Davidians at the time. Rumors began circulating that Roden and Howell's close relationship was not platonic. The relationship raised Howell's status within the group, and Lois Roden acquired an ally. Lois Roden tried to head off an emerging power struggle between Howell and her son by designating Howell as her successor. She arranged for Davidian members to come and listen to his teachings. Howell attracted young adults in part because of his own youth (prior Davidian leaders had been much older) and his musical interests and talent. Attracting younger people was something the Rodens had been unable to do. Converts point to Howell's biblical knowledge more than any other single factor in explaining their attraction to the Branch Davidians.

In 1984, Howell married fourteen-year-old Rachael Jones, whose father, Perry Jones, was one of the most senior and respected members of the Davidian community. Over the next five years, the couple gave birth to a son, Cyrus, and a daughter, Star. Howell enunciated his controversial "New Light" doctrine in 1989.

He asserted that as a messiah, he became the perfect mate of all the female adherents. Part of his mission was to create a new lineage of God's children from his own seed. These children would ultimately rule the world. In 1990, Vernon Howell legally adopted the name David Koresh. *Koresh* is Hebrew for "Cyrus," the Persian king who defeated the Babylonians 500 years before the birth of Jesus.

Acting on rumors that the Branch Davidians were illegally modifying firearms, a force of seventy-six agents of the ATF raided the Branch Davidian community on February 28, 1993. The raid turned into a shoot-out between federal agents and Branch Davidians. The resulting standoff turned into a fifty-one-day siege that ended on April 19 when federal agents launched a new attack on the Davidian complex. During the second assault, a fire ignited in the buildings, and more than eighty members died, including David Koresh.

Maharaji (b. 1957)

Maharaji, leader of Elan Vital, was born Prem Pal Singh Rawat in Hardwar, India. His father, Shri Hans Maharaj Ji, was a spiritual teacher of *surat shabda* yoga (the yoga of the sound current), using four distinctive techniques, or *kriyas*. Shri Hans founded the Divine Light Mission in 1960 and at his death in 1966 was succeeded as leader by his youngest son, Prem Pal Singh Rawat (Maharaji), then only eight years old.

Maharaji had already been recognized as spiritually precocious, meditating at the age of two and lecturing at the age of six. In 1971, he made his first visit to the United States, combining the work of a spiritual master with such childhood interests as visiting Disneyland. Known at that time as Guru Maharaj Ji, he instructed his followers in the four yoga techniques and gave other kinds of spiritual discourses. He was accepted by followers as an embodiment of God.

In November 1973, the Divine Light Mission suffered the first of several setbacks. It failed to fill the Houston Astrodome for its widely publicized Millennium '73 program, thus placing it in financial difficulties. The publicity made it a new target for anticult groups. The following month, Maharaji turned sixteen and took over the administration of the organization from his mother and older brother. In May 1974, he married his twenty-four-year-old secretary, Marolyn Johnson, stating that she was the incarnation of the Hindu goddess Durga. His mother decided that this showed he was unprepared to run the organization and moved to make his older brother the new leader. A court settlement gave his mother and brother control of the group in India, and he gained control of the group outside India.

In the 1980s, Maharaji made many changes. He shortened his name, began wearing Western clothes, and disbanded the Divine Light Mission with its ashrams. He has chosen instead to relate to followers directly through personal appearances, writings, and a new organization, Elan Vital, based at his residence in Malibu, California.

J. Gordon Melton (b. 1942)

J. Gordon Melton attended Birmingham Southern College (BA, 1964) and Garrett Theological Seminary (MDiv, 1968). He received his PhD in the history and literature of religion in 1975 from Northwestern University. He is also an ordained elder (1968) in the United Methodist Church (UMC) and pastored churches in Alabama and Illinois. Following completion of his education, he became the senior pastor of Emmanuel United Methodist Church. He remains a member of the Northern Illinois Conference of the UMC.

In 1968, Melton founded the Institute for the Study of American Religion (ISAR), an educational facility designed to do research on America's many different religious groups, especially the smaller religious communities. In order to accomplish its primary task, it also began to gather an archive of publications by and about the several thousand different religious groups that now operate or have operated in North America over the past several centuries.

In 1980, Melton became the full-time director of ISAR. In 1985, ISAR moved to Santa Barbara, California, at which time the archive—which included some 50,000 books, filing cabinets of ephemera, and runs of several thousand periodicals—was given to the Davidson Library of the University of California at Santa Barbara where it now exists as the American Religions Collection.

In 1979, Melton completed the first edition of the *Encyclopedia of American Religions* (seventh edition, 2003), which has emerged as the standard reference book on all of the religious bodies, including all the new religions, on which ISAR had gathered data. The encyclopedia is one of more than thirty-five books he has authored or edited on U.S. religion. He coauthored (with Robert L. Moore) one of the early textbooks on new religions, *The Cult Experience* (1990). Later texts have included the *Encyclopedic Handbook of Cults in America* (1986, 1992) and *Finding Enlightenment: Ramtha's School of Ancient Wisdom* (1998).

In the thirty-seven years of its existence, ISAR has been responsible for more than 300 scholarly books and monographs. Many of them have been reference books (bibliographies, encyclopedias, and biographical dictionaries), most either directly or tangentially concerned with minority and new religions. Included are the *Biographical Dictionary of Cult and Sect Leaders* (1986), the *New Age Encyclopedia* (1990), and the *Encyclopedia of African American Religion* (1993).

Sun Myung Moon (b. 1920)

Sun Myung Moon, founder of the Unification Church (the Holy Spirit Association for the Unification of World Christianity), was born Yong Myung Moon in what is now North Korea. When he was ten, his family converted to Christianity and joined the Presbyterian Church. When he was sixteen, he began receiving heavenly visitations indicating he had been chosen to lead God's forces on earth. This came during a time when Korean Pentecostal Christians were popularly predicting a Korean messiah.

After attending Waseka University in Japan, he married and began to preach. About this time, he changed his name to Sun Myung Moon, meaning someone who has clarified the Word or Truth. In 1946, he founded the Broad Sea Church in Pyeong-yang in today's North Korea, but his anticommunist activities made him a target for government authorities, and he was imprisoned from 1946 until he was expelled from the country in 1950. After some time in Pusan, he moved to Seoul in today's South Korea and in 1954 founded the Holy Spirit Association for the Unification of World Christianity.

Moon taught that Jesus's attempt to restore humanity from its fallen condition was cut short by his crucifixion. His resurrection ensured spiritual salvation for believers, but the completion of heaven on earth requires the messiah to be born again, and Moon is this messiah. By 1957, a Korean edition of the *Divine*

Principle, the church's major statement of faith, was in print. Moon divorced his first wife and in 1960 married Hak Ja Han, with whom he has had fourteen children.

After brief visits to the United States in 1965 and 1969, Moon made a permanent move there in December 1971, settling in the New York area. Most of the converted members were young and made the church their full-time occupation. Anticult groups accused the church of brainwashing and deceitful practices, but Moon's major setback came from a conviction of tax evasion, for which he served thirteen months in prison in 1984–1985.

Theodore Patrick (b. 1930)

Ted Patrick, who in the 1970s liked to refer to himself as "Black Lightning" (Patrick is African American), has the dubious distinction of being the father of deprogramming. Deprogramming refers to the practice of kidnapping "cult" members and destroying their religious faith, though supporters of the practice would claim that deprogramming is the antidote for "mind control" that does nothing more than compel "brainwashed" cultists to start thinking for themselves again. Patrick was a tenth-grade dropout with a speech impediment who was raised in the red-light district of Chattanooga, Tennessee. He had no psychological training whatsoever and developed his deprogramming techniques through trial and error.

In 1971, Patrick was working as a community relations representative in San Diego for then-governor Ronald Reagan. He had previously organized two large political clubs while driving a truck for General Dynamics. On the Fourth of July, he and his family were staying at a hotel on Mission Beach in San Diego when his son Michael and a nephew were approached by the Children of God. The foundation of deprogramming was laid when Patrick talked Michael and his nephew out of joining COG. Although initially alarmed, Patrick and his family gradually forgot about the incident.

However, he began to hear other complaints about the Children of God and eventually linked up with concerned parents who formed the first anticult organization, Free the Children of God, popularly referred to as FREECOG. Frustrated by the authorities' refusal to do anything about COG, Patrick began to experiment with the tactic of abducting "cultists," locking them up, and trying to convince them that they had been brainwashed and manipulated by their religion. In this way, the practice of deprogramming was born. The media, always interested in dramatic stories, promoted Patrick by covering his exploits.

Although he seems to have started out sincerely enough, Patrick's deprogramming activities gradually devolved into a moneymaking activity (parents paid hefty sums for Patrick's expertise) until he was accepting cases that had no cult connections whatsoever. Thus, in one case, for instance, he attempted to deprogram a woman who had left her parents' Protestant faith to become a Catholic nun. In Denver, Patrick kidnapped two young women who had moved out of their strict Greek parents' home—parents who regarded it as their right to regulate their daughters' lives, including whom they would marry. Patrick was eventually convicted, though most of his prison time was suspended. He subsequently continued to kidnap young people at their parents' behest, but he eventually gathered a stack of convictions for kidnapping and unlawful detention that caused him to terminate his career as a hired gun. In addition to felony convictions for his deprogramming activities, Patrick's criminal record had grown to include charges of cocaine use and multiple parole violations.

Abhay Charan De Bhaktivedanta Prabhupada (1896–1977)

A. C. Bhaktivedanta Prabhupada, founder of the International Society for Krishna Consciousness, was born Abhay Charan De, in Calcutta, India. His father, a cloth merchant, took him often to Hindu worship at the temple across the street from their home. While in Scottish Churches College, he accepted an arranged marriage to eleven-year-old Padharani Satta. In 1920, he refused his college degree in solidarity with Mahatma Gandhi's call to avoid British goods.

He found work in a pharmaceutical company and over the following years became increasingly dissatisfied with family and work life and correspondingly interested in the religious quest. He became a disciple of Sri Srimad Bhaktisiddhanta Saraswati Goswami, the head of an old devotional group called Guadiya Math. He wrote a number of religious books and became a favorite of his teacher, who in 1936 told him he would soon take the worship of Krishna to the West.

In 1956, he separated himself from his secular life, took holy vows, and took the name A. C. Bhaktivedanta Swami Prabhupada. In 1965, he made the prophesied trip to the United States and opened a center in New York City, publishing a magazine called *Back to Godhead*. He founded the International Society for Krishna Consciousness in 1966 and opened a center in San Francisco in 1967. Over the next decade, he attracted several thousand core (full-time, live-in) members and more than 200,000 lay constituents. Devotees showed devotion to Krishna through chanting the Hare Krishna mantra, public dancing, and other activities.

Prabhupada weathered a storm of criticism over the movement, which many took to be a cult. He spent much of his time preparing the organization for the future. He arranged for the orderly transition of authority and committed as many of his thoughts to paper as possible. More than sixty volumes of his works were published prior to his death, and more have been put together since then.

James T. Richardson (b. 1941)

James Richardson attended Texas Tech University (BA, 1965; MA, 1965) and received his PhD in sociology from Washington State University in 1968. He also earned a JD from Old College, Nevada School of Law (1986). He was a Fulbright Fellow in the Netherlands (Nijmegen University) in 1981. He is a professor of sociology and judicial studies at the University of Nevada at Reno.

Richardson is currently president of the Association for the Sociology of Religion. He has served as an officer in several other professional associations, including the International Society for the Sociology of Religion. He was a founding member of the International Study of Religion in Central and Eastern Europe Association and is currently its vice president. He was also national president of the American Association of University Professors from 1998 to 2000 and served in other capacities within that organization as well.

Richardson has been involved for years with consulting in areas of expertise such as religion as well as evidence issues pertaining to legal cases. He has consulted on a number of legal cases in the United States and overseas and has testified as an expert. He is regularly interviewed by local, national, and international media on a number of topics. He has been involved for several years as one of a small group of scholars working with the FBI since the Waco tragedy with the Branch Davidians. He has presented seminars and papers to meetings of law enforcement officials in the United States and Israel, focusing on the issue of prevention of violence when religious groups interact with law enforcement.

Richardson is the author of numerous articles and the author or coeditor of eight books, including *Money and Power in the New Religions* (1988), with Joel Best and David Bromley *The Satanism Scare* (1991), *Regulating Religion: Case Studies from Around the Globe* (2003), and with James Beckford *Challenging Religion* (2003).

Margaret Thaler Singer (1921–2003)

Margaret Singer was a prominent anticult psychologist. The chief architect of the theory of "cultic mind control" (which Singer referred to as the systematic manipulation of social and psychological influence), she was eulogized by one of her admirers as "the foremost authority on brainwashing in the entire world."

She was born in Denver, where her father was chief operating engineer at the U.S. Mint and her mother was a secretary to a federal judge. She played cello in the Denver Civic Symphony while a student at the University of Denver, where she received a BA in speech and an MA in speech pathology and special education. She obtained a PhD in clinical psychology in 1943 and worked for eight years in the Department of Psychiatry at the University of Colorado School of Medicine.

During the 1950s, Singer undertook research in psychosomatic medicine and continued to be active in this field for the rest of her career. She was, for instance, president of the American Psychosomatic Society in 1972–1973. Singer participated in a study of "communist brainwashing" in the 1950s at the Walter Reed Institute of Research in Washington, D.C., where she interviewed soldiers who had been imprisoned by North Korea during the Korean War.

She moved to Berkeley in 1958 when her husband, Jerome R. Singer, was hired by the Physics Department at the University of

California at Berkeley. As a faculty spouse, she was able to obtain adjunct teaching work in the Psychology Department. Although in later years she would claim the title emeritus (retired) professor, in point of fact she never became a regular, full-time faculty member (a precondition for formal emeritus status). After moving to Berkeley, she became interested in the cult controversy of the late sixties and seventies.

Her work with Korean War POWs gave Singer credibility as an expert on brainwashing, and she was able to obtain work as an expert witness. For example, she testified in the trial of newspaper heiress Patricia Hearst, who had been kidnapped by the Symbionese Liberation Army. She was also a prominent expert witness at an important 1977 hearing for five members of the Unification Church whose parents were trying to have them "deprogrammed." She subsequently became a favorite expert in "cult"-related legal cases.

In 1987, she headed up the task force Deceptive and Indirect Methods of Persuasion and Control (DIMPAC) for the American Psychological Association. Her findings were, however, rejected by the Board of Social and Ethical Responsibility for Psychology because the report lacked "the scientific rigor and evenhanded critical approach needed for APA imprimatur." She subsequently sued the APA, but eventually lost in 1993. Fallout from the DIMPAC rejection and from the *Fishman* decision (discussed in chapter 4) effectively ended her career as an expert witness.

Singer was the author of numerous articles and coauthor of *Cults in Our Midst* (1995; second edition, 2003). She was awarded the Hofheimer Prize for Research in 1966 from the American College of Psychiatrists and the Stanley R. Dean Award for Research in Schizophrenia in 1976 from the American College of Psychiatrists. She also held achievement awards from the Mental Health Association of the United States and the American Family Therapy Association. She was a board member of the American Family Foundation.

Louis Jolyon West (1924–1999)

Louis J. West was a prominent anticult psychiatrist. The son of Russian Jewish immigrants, he was born in Brooklyn and raised in Madison, Wisconsin. He attended the University of Wisconsin and received his MD from the University of Minnesota School of Medicine in 1948. He served a three-year residency in psychiatry at the Payne Whitney Psychiatric Clinic in Manhattan.

A military doctor for many years, West studied "brainwashing" during the Korean War while he was stationed at Lackland Air Force Base in Texas. Early in his career, West was involved with conducting controversial LSD experiments for the Central Intelligence Agency as part of the CIA's interest in developing "mind control" technology. One of these experiments involved injecting a 7,000-pound elephant with a fatally excessive dose of LSD. It was partially on the basis of his involvement with the CIA's MK-Ultra mind-control project that he claimed to be an expert on brainwashing.

West regularly served as a court-appointed expert psychiatrist. He examined, for example, Jack Ruby, the murderer of John F. Kennedy's assassin, Lee Harvey Oswald. West's opinion that Ruby suffered from mental illness helped to forestall his death sentence (Ruby later died in prison). He also participated in the case of Patricia Hearst, who, after her kidnapping by the Symbionese Liberation Army, joined her kidnappers as a bank robber. West was one of four psychiatrists to examine Hearst before her 1976 trial. Although she was found sane and able to stand trial, the panel urged to have her treated for mental illness before the trial—a recommendation ignored by the court. (Jimmy Carter commuted Hearst's prison sentence in 1979.)

One of the responses to the urban violence of the late 1960s and early 1970s was a move to establish the Center for the Study and Reduction of Violence that West was to have headed. Although funding for the violence center had been approved by Ronald Reagan, it was withdrawn in response to public protest. As part of this protest, West was accused of advocating the deployment of radical forms of behavior control against minorities.

West was in charge of the Neuropsychiatric Institute at the University of California at Los Angeles for twenty years. Between 1974 and 1989, West received more than $5 million in grants from the National Institute of Mental Health, which critics claim was a funding conduit for CIA programs. Other funding came through the Neuropsychiatric Institute, including more than $14 million in federal funds in one fiscal year while he was director. West resigned from the institute in 1989 over charges of misappropriation of funds.

7

Organizations and Web Sites

Academic Organizations

American Academy of Religion
Scholars Press
P.O. Box 15399
Atlanta, GA 30333
Telephone: 404-727-3049
Web site: http://www.aarweb.org
E-mail: aar@aarweb.org

The American Academy of Religion (AAR) is the largest association of religion academics in North America. The AAR has a group devoted to new religious movements, the chairperson of which varies from year to year. One can reach the chair of this subsection of the AAR via Scholars Press in Atlanta, which in turn can refer one to relevant specialists.

CESNUR: The Center for Studies on New Religions
Via Juvarra 20
10152 Torino (Turin), Italy
Telephone: 39 (country code) 11-541950
Web site: http://www.cesnur.org
E-mail: cesnurto@tin.it

CESNUR is the only scholarly association devoted exclusively to the study of new religions. The group is international in scope and holds its annual meeting in various parts of the world. Because it is centered in Italy, it tends to focus on the cult issue in Europe. CESNUR was established in 1988 by a group of religious scholars from leading universities in Europe and the Americas. Its managing director is Professor Massimo Introvigne. CESNUR's original aim was to offer a professional association to scholars specializing in new religious movements.

In the 1990s, CESNUR became more proactive and started supplying information on a regular basis, opening public centers and organizing conferences and seminars for the general public in a variety of countries. Today CESNUR is a network of independent but related organizations of scholars in various countries, devoted to promoting scholarly research in the field of new religious consciousness, to spreading reliable and responsible information, and to exposing the very real problems associated with some movements, while at the same time defending everywhere the principles of religious liberty.

CESNUR's yearly annual conference is the largest world gathering of those active in the field of studies on new religions. Each conference normally features fifty to eighty papers. Conferences have been held at the London School of Economics (1993), the Federal University of Pernambuco in Recife, Brazil (1994), the State University of Rome (1995), the University of Montreal (1996), the Free University of Amsterdam (1997), the Industrial Union in Turin (1998), the Bryn Athyn College in Pennsylvania (1999), the University of Latvia in Riga (2000), the University of Utah and Brigham Young University (2002), the University of Vilnius (2003), and Baylor University (2004). CESNUR's Web site includes news on future CESNUR activities and a library of selected papers on a wide variety of topics.

Society for the Scientific Study of Religion
Arthur L. Greil, PhD
Alfred University
Division of Social Sciences
Saxon Drive
Alfred, New York 14802
Telephone: 607-871-2215
Fax: 607-871-2085
Web site: http://las.alfred.edu/~soc/SSSR
E-mail: sssr@alfred.edu

The Society for the Scientific Study of Religion primarily attracts sociologists of religion. Sociologists were, for the most part, the first scholars to study new religious movements in North America. The society's quarterly journal, the *Journal for the Scientific Study of Religion,* regularly publishes articles and reviews books of interest to scholars of nontraditional religions.

Cult Information Organizations and Web Sites

Since the 1970s, many organizations on both sides of the cult controversy have come and gone. A number still exist in name but have ceased to function actively, often for lack of funds. Because the present volume is likely to sit on the library shelf for several decades, the reader should not be surprised to find that many of the groups listed in this section have disappeared by the time she or he attempts to contact them.

For many public issues, governmental agencies often provide information. Because, however, the "cult" issue is perceived as a religious issue, the doctrine of the separation of church and state effectively blocks U.S. government bodies from becoming involved as long as the law is obeyed.

Because of the constant flux in this field, perhaps the best way to locate information centers on new religious movements is to search for "cults" or "new religions" on the Internet. This is also the best way to locate the relevant religious groups themselves, which move often enough to make any attempt at a comprehensive address list a frustrating enterprise.

Many of the below Web site reviews have been adapted from the reviews found at Professor Jeff Hadden's Web site at the University of Virginia.

American Family Foundation
P.O. Box 2265
Bonita Springs, FL 34133
Telephone: 239-514-3081
Web site: http://www.csj.org

For many years, the American Family Foundation, founded in 1979, served the U.S. anticult movement as its academic wing, leaving the Cult Awareness Network to serve as a day-to-day information service and as a "cult watchdog organization." Since CAN's demise, it is unclear whether or to what extent AFF will step in to fill the gap. It should be noted that people holding this position are generally adverse to the label "anticult," preferring alternate designations such as "cult critics" or some other, more nuanced label.

The American Family Foundation used to publish two print periodicals, the *Cult Observer*, a general audience publication, and *Cultic Studies Journal*, an academic publication. AFF continues to publish the latter as both a print and an electronic journal. The *Cult Observer* has been replaced by a free e-mail service, *AFF News Briefs*. Both are invaluable for individuals interested in keeping up-to-date with developments in the anticult movement.

The AFF Web site also highlights the various outreach programs of the group that include education about, study of, and assistance for those involved in groups determined by AFF to be cults. They offer information packets about the various groups by mail for a fee.

Apologetics Index
Web site: http://www.apologeticsindex.org

The Apologetics Index is a Christian countercult Web site. It contains a large quantity of variable quality information. Apparently anxious about receiving negative feedback, they do not supply either a street address or an e-mail address. Instead, one must fill out an online form that gives the Apologetics Index the option of responding or not responding.

Becket Fund for Religious Liberty
2000 Pennsylvania Avenue, Suite 3200
Washington, DC 20009
Telephone: 800-BECKET5
Web site: http://www.becketfund.org
E-mail: mail@becketfund.org

The Becket Fund for Religious Liberty is a diverse group of lawyers, professors, and civic leaders dedicated to the defense of religious liberty. The Web site covers up-to-date breaking news on religious freedom legal issues including legislation and judicial decisions.

Bible Discernment Ministries
Web site: http://www.rapidnet.com/~jbeard/bdm

This Christian anticult Web site run by Rick Meisel is bent on exposing "false teachers and their teachings." The notebook section of the site offers information about groups and specific group leaders.

Christian Research Institute
P.O. Box 7000
Rancho Santa Margarita, CA 92688-7000
Telephone: 949-858-6100
Web site: http://www.equip.org

The Christian Research Institute was founded by Walter Martin, the most successful author of Christian anticult books. Martin's *Kingdom of the Cults* is a guiding light for a substantial subset of the evangelical anticult movement. *The Kingdom of the Cults* is formatted like a Bible, with cult belief in one column and evangelical response, or "correction," of that belief in the other column. The Web site is difficult to search and primarily serves as an online store that sells the organization's books and other materials.

Cult Awareness Network
1680 North Vine Street, Suite 415
Los Angeles, CA 90028
Telephone: 800-556-3055
Web site: http://www.cultawarenessnetwork.org

When the Cult Awareness Network name and number were acquired by the Church of Scientology, even the most sympathetic observers anticipated that CAN would become little more than a propaganda wing of Scientology. It was thus a pleasant surprise when the "New CAN" began functioning as a genuine information and networking center on nontraditional religions. The New Cult Awareness Network has established a working relationship with scholarly specialists and other professionals. When people in the CAN office are unable to adequately answer queries from callers, the callers are referred to the appropriate specialist. The New CAN also publishes a small newsletter.

Cult Information Service
P.O. Box 867
Teaneck, NJ 07666
Telephone: 201-833-1212

Web site: http://cultinformationservice.org
E-mail: cultinformationservice@yahoo.com

The Cult Information Service (CIS) is a new anticult group that has emerged to fill the vacancy left by the bankruptcy of the "old" Cult Awareness Network. It appears to have grown out of the Cult Clinic and hot line of the Jewish Board of Family and Children's Services in New York City. In addition to running a "cult" hot line, CIS has also begun to sponsor conferences.

Ex-Cult Resource Center
Web site: http://ex-cult.org

This site contains little substantive information but links together significant anticult resources. By no means comprehensive of anticult activity, this is nonetheless the best available resource for the novice interested in becoming familiar with anticult materials on the Internet.

Foundation for Religious Freedom
1680 North Vine Street, Suite 415
Los Angeles, CA 90028
Telephone: 800-556-3055
Web site: http://www.cultawarenessnetwork.org
E-mail: inform@cultawarenessnetwork.org

The Foundation for Religious Freedom runs the New Cult Awareness Network hot line and information service. Formerly a religious hate group, the New Cult Awareness Network runs an 800 hot line, provides factual information so people can make up their own minds, has an extensive list of qualified religious experts who act as professional referrals, and reconciles families through mediation.

Hadden Site at the University of Virginia
Web site: http://religiousmovements.lib.virginia.edu
E-mail: cowande@umkc.edu

Jeffrey Hadden's home page is easily the best academic Web site on new religious movements. Although Hadden passed away in 2003, the site continues to be maintained. The site contains overviews of many groups as well as a selection of papers on the cult controversy.

Info-Cult
5655 Park Avenue, Suite 205
Montreal, Quebec H2V 4H2, Canada
Telephone: 514-274-2333
Web site:http://www.math.mcgill.ca/triples/infocult/
  ic-e1.html

Info-Cult (Info-Secte, in French) is the Canadian wing of the U.S. anticult movement and has functioned much the same as the Cult Awareness Network. Info-Cult has been less active in the wake of the demise of the "old" CAN.

Institute for the Study of American Religion
P.O. Box 90709
Santa Barbara, CA 93190-0709
Telephone: 805-967-7721
Web site: http://www.americanreligion.org

Gordon Melton, a prominent academic archivist and cataloger of alternative religions, founded and directs the Institute for the Study of American Religion. His extensive collection of primary materials is housed in the American Religions Collection at the University of California at Santa Barbara. Melton is often consulted as an expert by the media.

International Association for Religious Freedom
576 Fifth Avenue, Suite 1103
New York, NY 10036
Telephone: 212-843-9493
Web site: http://www.iarf.net
E-mail: hq@iarf.net

The International Association for Religious Freedom (IAFR) was organized in 1900 to affirm the right to religious freedom. The IARF welcomes into membership anyone who is committed to the fundamental right of religious freedom, and includes religious groups from around the world. The IAFR runs conferences and undertakes interfaith actions with groups of very diverse faiths working together for religious freedom.

International Coalition for Religious Freedom
7777 Leesburg Pike, Suite 307N-A

Falls Church, VA 22043
Telephone: 703-790-1500
Web site: http://www.religiousfreedom.com
E-mail: ICRF@aol.com

The International Coalition for Religious Freedom's Web site includes a monthly country by country report on religious freedom issues around the world, sponsors religious freedom conferences, and promotes religious freedom.

Mandate Ministries
Web site: http://www.geocities.com//mandateministries

This is an Australian countercult site maintained by Mandate Ministries, an organization created by Fred and Barbara Grigg after they and their eight children left the Jehovah's Witnesses in 1978. Attractively created, this is a good example of a theological framework that has been geared toward opposition to "cults" as profane and spiritually and psychologically damaging to adherents. Grigg claims that post-traumatic stress disorder made him susceptible to Jehovah's Witness conversion after the Vietnam War. He converted along with his wife and children but soon realized he was not following the "true God" and moved to get his family out. He and his wife have now dedicated themselves to preventing other people from "falling victim" to cult conversion.

Ontario Consultants for Religious Tolerance
P.O. Box 514
Wellesley Island, NY 13640
In Canada:
Box 27026, Frontenac
Kingston, Ontario, Canada K7M 8W5
Web site: http://www.religioustolerance.org
E-mail: ocrt2@religioustolerance.org

Hosted by four individuals of diverse faiths, this Web site has factual information on many religions and more than 500 essays covering all sides of many religious issues. It is probably the largest and most frequently visited religious freedom Web site in existence and is, quite simply, the most remarkable, comprehensive, and balanced presentation of information on new religious movements anywhere on the Web. Without a doubt, it is worth visiting.

ReFOCUS: Recovering Former Cultists' Support Network
P.O. Box 2180
Flagler Beach, FL 32136-2180
Telephone: 904-439-7541
Website: http://www.refocus.org
E-mail: torefocus@aol.com

ReFOCUS is a network of referral and support for former members of "cults." As the name suggests, the perspective of this group is distinctly anticult. The group had published a quarterly newsletter, *reFOCUS Forum* (recent issues are available for free online), but it appears to have ceased publication as of 2001.

Rick Ross Institute
Web site: http://www.rickross.com
E-mail: info@rickross.com

Rick Ross is a deprogrammer deeply involved in the anticult movement. Ross was part of the court case that drove CAN into bankruptcy. He has been featured extensively in the media on programs like *48 Hours*. Ross's site features a fairly extensive archive of newspaper articles related to controversial new religions.

Spiritual Counterfeits Project
P.O. Box 4308
Berkeley, CA 94704
Telephone: 510-540-0300
Web site: http://www.scp-inc.org
E-mail: access@scp-inc.org

The Spiritual Counterfeits Project was a product of the student counterculture in the 1960s. The initial founders were former members of Eastern mystical religions. Its history is closely linked to the University of California and the 1960s free speech movement at Berkeley, specifically the "people's park." SCP members adhere to a conservative Christian faith today and seek to uncover the "deceptions" of new religions that fail to adhere to conservative Christian ideas. Early successes included a victory in court against Transcendental Meditation, forcing the removal of TM ideas from the public schools. Their Web site offers information about their journal, newsletter, hot line, and other materials offered by the group.

Steve Hassan's Freedom of Mind Center (aka Freedom of Mind Resource Center)
P.O. Box 45223
Somerville, MA 02145
Telephone: 617-628-9918
Web site: http://www.freedomofmind.com
E-mail: center@freedomofmind.com

Hassan is an ex-member of the Unification Church who has become a professional former member. Hassan is devoted to saving the world from "destructive cults" and "abusive mind controllers." He has created the Resource Center for Freedom of Mind to further his cause. The Freedom of Mind Center provides information about "mind control" in cults based on Hassan's own writings. It rejects deprogramming in favor of exit counseling (noncoercive deprogramming).

Thursby Site at the University of Florida
Web site: http://www.clas.ufl.edu/users/gthursby

This Web site is very useful as an analytical site, as it provides links to academic journals for the study of religions and to other academic sites for the study of new religions. The site also includes an extensive bibliography.

Watchman Fellowship, Inc.
Web site: http://www.watchman.org

The Watchman Fellowship, Inc., is a comprehensive Christian anticult site. It includes at least some information on more than 1,100 groups. They present information on many groups that are not otherwise represented on the Internet. Each group is assessed from a conservative Christian theological perspective.

8

Resources

Mainstream Scholarship

There now exist so many good scholarly books on the general subject of new religious movements that it is difficult to choose from among those available. The noninclusion of a book should thus not be taken to indicate that it is of lesser interest or quality than those mentioned in the following list.

Reference Books

Bromley, David G., ed. *Religion and the Social Order*. Greenwich, CT: JAI Press/Elsevier Science.

The Religion and the Social Order series of reference books contains significant collections of articles on new religions and on topics relevant to new religions. The third book in this series is the general *Handbook on Cults and Sects in America* (1993).

Lewis, James R. *Peculiar Prophets: A Bibliographic Dictionary of New Religious Movements*. New York: Paragon, 1999.

This is an A-to-Z survey of the leaders and founders of some of the more important new religions. Almost all of the entries are short 300–350-word overviews. Unlike comparable volumes, this book contains many photos of leaders and founders of alternative religious groups.

Lewis, James R. *The Encyclopedia of Cults, Sects and New Religions*. 2d ed. 1998. Reprint, Amherst, NY: Prometheus, 2002.

This is the most comprehensive, up-to-date examination of minority religious groups in North America. Many of the longer entries are written by specialists on specific groups.

Lewis, James R. *The Oxford Handbook of New Religious Movements.* New York: Oxford University Press, 2004.

This handbook is a state-of-the-art survey of new religions as a field of study. The majority of contributions are authored by prominent NRM scholars. Many of the chapters focus on aspects of the controversy surrounding alternative religious movements.

Lewis, James R., ed. *Encyclopedic Sourcebook.* 2 vols. Amherst, NY: Prometheus, 2003 and 2004.

The Encyclopedic Sourcebook series covers particular groups of new religious movements and contains both primary and secondary documents. At the time of this writing, two have appeared: *The Encyclopedic Sourcebook of UFO Religions* (2003) and *The Encyclopedic Sourcebook of New Age Religions* (2004).

Melton, J. Gordon. *The Encyclopedic Handbook of Cults in America.* 2d ed. New York: Garland, 1992.

This is easily the best short reference book on the topic. It contains an overview of key groups and discusses the controversy. Melton, a Methodist minister, includes an especially useful discussion of the distinction between the Evangelical anticult movement and the secular anticult movement. Garland, unfortunately, recently went out of business, and it is difficult to predict the future availability of this book.

Melton, J. Gordon, ed. *Cults and New Religions: Sources for the Study of Nonconventional Religious Groups in Nineteenth- and Twentieth-Century America.* New York: Garland, 1990.

This is an important twenty-two-volume set of original documents from a wide variety of different religions, from the Theosophical Society to the People's Temple. Other groups and movements covered are: spiritualism, Rosicrucianism, Jehovah's Witnesses, Mormons, Christian Science, Unification Church, Hare Krishna movement, and neopaganism. Most individual volumes are out of print. The most likely place to find this series is major research libraries.

Partridge, Christopher. *New Religions: A Guide.* New York: Oxford University Press, 2004.

Originally published in the United Kingdom as the *Encyclopedia of New Religions,* this is a lavishly illustrated reference book that is small enough to serve as a basic textbook. Many entries were written by scholarly specialists.

Textbooks and General Surveys

Barker, Eileen. *New Religious Movements: A Practical Introduction.* London: Her Majesty's Stationery Office, 1989.

Barker's book is a comprehensive overview of new religions by a leading British sociologist of religion. It is highly readable and, as one would anticipate, is particularly strong on the British situation.

Beckford, James A. *Cult Controversies: The Societal Response to the New Religious Movements.* London: Tavistock, 1985.

This examination of the cult controversy in Europe focuses on the differences among the responses of England, France, and Germany. Beckford is a prominent British sociologist of religion, and his analysis of the interests of the various factions involved in the controversy is particularly strong.

Bromley, David G., and James T. Richardson, eds. *The Brainwashing/Deprogramming Controversy.* Lewiston, NY: Edwin Mellen, 1983.

This anthology of papers by leading scholars is organized according to historical, sociological, psychological, and legal perspectives. This is one of the few volumes to include papers from people on both sides of the controversy, although the anticult perspective is underrepresented.

Bromley, David G., and Anson D. Shupe Jr. *Strange Gods: The Great American Cult Scare.* Boston: Beacon Press, 1981.

Strange Gods is an overview of the cult controversy by two sociologists. Although now dated and out of print, this is still one of the best surveys of its kind (it was often used as a supplementary text). While focusing on issues, the volume also draws examples from six specific groups: the Children of God, Unification Church,

ISKCON, People's Temple, Divine Light Mission, and Church of Scientology.

Dawson, Lorne L. *Comprehending Cults: The Sociology of New Religious Movements.* New York: Oxford University Press, 1998.

Dawson's book is an overview of new religions, the cult controversy, and studies of new religions. It is particularly strong on sociological approaches, making it a particularly useful text for sociology courses.

Dawson, Lorne L. *Cults and New Religious Movements: A Reader.* 2d ed. London: Blackwell, 2003.

This reader consists of chapters authored primarily by prominent NRM scholars. Though it may have been intended to supplement texts like Dawson's own *Comprehending Cults*, *Cults and New Religious Movements* would work well as a freestanding textbook.

Ellwood, Robert A., and Harry B. Partin. *Religious and Spiritual Groups in Modern America.* 2d ed. Engelwood Cliffs, NJ: Prentice-Hall, 1988.

This is the earliest textbook on modern new religions. Revised in 1988, it is still a good choice for a general survey. While discussing the larger social situation and the cult controversy, the core of this book is constituted by a survey of specific groups, including brief readings from the literature of each group.

Hexham, Irving, and Karla Powe. *Understanding Cults and New Age Religions.* Vancouver, BC: Regent College Publishing, 1998.

This reprint of Hexham and Powe's *Understanding Cults and New Religions* is a textbook and survey of new religions.

Lewis, James R., ed. *Odd Gods: New Religions and the Cult Controversy.* Amherst, NY: Prometheus Books, 2001.

Odd Gods is a textbook and general survey of new religions. The contents are drawn primarily from *The Encyclopedia of Cults, Sects and New Religions*, making this book a miniencyclopedia.

Lewis, James R., and Jesper A. Petersen, eds. *Controversial New Religions.* New York: Oxford University Press, 2005.

This is a collection of articles on the most controversial new religions. Originally intended to complement the thematic approach of *The Oxford Handbook of New Religious Movements,* this volume is also a useful textbook.

Miller, Timothy, ed. *America's Alternative Religions.* Albany: State University of New York Press, 1995.

Miller's work is a compilation of short articles by a wide variety of scholars on specific religions or traditions. Although initially offered as a reference book, this title was recently issued in paperback. Though weak on Buddhist traditions, this is one of the best books of its kind.

Robbins, Thomas, and Dick Anthony, eds. *In Gods We Trust: New Patterns of Religious Pluralism in America.* New Brunswick, NJ: Transaction Books, 1981.

Although not focused exclusively on the cult controversy, there are a number of important chapters on the issue in this text. Unfortunately, some of the better papers dropped out when this volume went into a second edition. It is often used as a supplementary textbook.

Saliba, John A. *Understanding New Religious Movements.* 2d ed. 1995. Reprint, Lanham, MD: Rowman and Littlefield, 2003.

A recent overview designed as a general text, Saliba's text examines new religions in terms of a series of perspectives: historical, psychological, sociological, theological, and legal. For a textbook, Saliba's treatment is original and sophisticated. His theological chapter is particularly useful in a field of study dominated by social scientists with little theological training.

Wessinger, Catherine. *How the Millennium Comes Violently: From Jonestown to Heaven's Gate.* New York: Chatham House Publishers, 2000.

Although Wessinger focuses only on the groups involved in violence, she does so in an accessible way that makes this a useful supplementary text in courses on new religions or courses on religion and violence.

Specialized Studies

Bromley, David G., and J. Gordon Melton, eds. *Cults, Religion and Violence.* New York: Cambridge University Press, 2002.

The contributors to this state-of-the-art anthology on new religions and violence are prominent NRM scholars. This is an excellent survey containing chapters on general theoretical issues as well as on specific groups involved in violence.

Hall, John R., with Philip D. Schuyler and Sylvaine Trinh. *Apocalypse Observed: Religious Movements and Violence in North America, Europe, and Japan.* London: Routledge, 2000.

This in-depth study looks at the five most prominent alternative religious groups that have been involved in violence: the People's Temple, Branch Davidians, Order of the Solar Temple, AUM Shinrikyo, and Heaven's Gate.

Jenkins, Philip. *Mystics and Messiahs: Cults and New Religions in American History.* New York: Oxford University Press, 2000.

Jenkins's in-depth survey of alternative religions in U.S. history places the contemporary controversy in historical perspective.

Jenkins, Philip. *The Next Christendom: The Coming of Global Christianity.* New York: Oxford University Press, 2002.

This historical and statistical overview of global Christianity indicates that Christianity is fast becoming the largest "new religion" in the world.

Levine, Saul. *Radical Departures: Desperate Detours to Growing Up.* New York: Harcourt Brace Jovanovich, 1984.

A Canadian psychiatrist, Levine followed the "cult careers" of hundreds of young converts to new religions, discovering that, typically, the vast majority dropped out voluntarily within the first two years of their memberships. This book is written in the form of a series of vignettes, making it particularly accessible to the general reader.

Lewis, James R. *Legitimating New Religions.* New Brunswick, NJ: Rutgers University Press, 2003.

This study of how emerging religions legitimate themselves builds on Max Weber's work on the legitimation of authority. The second part of the book examines how critics attempt to delegitimate such groups.

Lucas, Phillip Charles, and Thomas Robbins, eds. *New Religious Movements in the 21st Century: Legal, Political, and Social Challenges in Global Perspective.* New York: Routledge, 2004.

This text is a comprehensive overview of the situation of contemporary new religions in a global context, with particular focus on social conflict.

Palmer, Susan J. *Moon Sisters, Krishna Mothers, Rajneesh Lovers: Women's Roles in New Religions.* Syracuse, NY: Syracuse University Press, 1994.

Palmer gives an overview of the roles of women in new religious movements.

Palmer, Susan J., and Charlotte E. Hardman, eds. *Children in New Religions.* New Brunswick, NJ: Rutgers University Press, 1999.

This anthology of articles is on the theme of children in new religious movements.

Richardson, Herbert, ed. *New Religions and Mental Health: Understanding the Issues.* Lewiston, NY: Edwin Mellen, 1980.

This early, but still useful, anthology was published in response to the "anticult" laws that were being considered by a variety of different legislatures. It contains a wide array of material, including the texts of proposed anticult legislation and public statements made against such legislation.

Robbins, Thomas. *Cults, Converts and Charisma.* Newbury Park, CA: Sage, 1988.

This is a comprehensive overview of new religions from a sociological viewpoint. Robbins is widely recognized as one of the half dozen or so top sociologists in the field of new religions.

Shepherd, William C. *To Secure the Blessings of Liberty: American Constitutional Law and the New Religious Movements.* New York: Crossroad, 1985.

This text is a comprehensive, well-written overview of the cult controversy in the courts up through the conservatorship stage of the legal battle. Shepherd also includes an overview of the history of religious liberty decisions that bear on the contemporary cult controversy. The book is dated but still highly useful.

Shupe, Anson D., Jr., and David G. Bromley. *The New Vigilantes: Deprogrammers, Anti-Cultists, and the New Religions.* Beverly Hills, CA: Sage, 1980.

This is a sociological study of the early anticult movement by mainstream scholars. Shupe and Bromley examine the movement from a resource-mobilization perspective. Though dated, this book is a "must read" for anyone wishing to acquire a thorough knowledge of the controversy.

Books on Specific Groups or Movements

Barker, Eileen. *The Making of a Moonie: Brainwashing or Choice?* Oxford: Basil Blackwell, 1984.

A comprehensive overview of one of the most controversial new religions, Barker's study of "Moonie" conversion is particularly important for undermining the notion that the Unification Church possessed omnipotent techniques of mind control that could overcome the will of potential recruits.

Carter, Lewis F. *Charisma and Control in Rajneeshpuram: The Role of Shared Values in the Creation of A Community.* Cambridge: Cambridge University Press, 1990.

A number of interesting, semiacademic books have been written about Osho (aka Bhagwan Rajneesh) and his group's Oregon community. Carter's book is the most scholarly.

Chancellor, James D. *Life in the Family: An Oral History of the Children of God.* Syracuse, NY: Syracuse University Press, 2000.

There are a number of good books on the Family now. This is one of the most engaging.

Hall, John R. *Gone from the Promised Land: Jonestown in American Cultural History.* New Brunswick, NJ: Transaction, 1987.

Of all the books that have been published on Jonestown, this is still one of the best scholarly analyses of the tragedy.

Lewis, James R., ed. *From the Ashes: Making Sense of Waco.* Lanham, MD: Rowman and Littlefield, 1994.

This was the first scholarly book on the Branch Davidian conflict to appear. It contains a potpourri of short essays, commentary, and original documents by scholars and others. Information compiled in this volume has been a major resource for all successive academic books on the topic, as well as for the Oscar-nominated documentary *Waco: The Rules of Engagement.*

Lewis, James R., ed. *The Gods Have Landed: New Religions from Other Worlds.* Albany, NY: State University of New York Press, 1995.

This is a collection of articles on UFOs and religion. Some chapters deal with specific groups (for example, the Unarius Society and the Raelian Movement), while others deal with particular aspects of the phenomenon (such as the religious dimension of the abduction experience). The chapter on Heaven's Gate ("Waiting for the Ships") was the definitive piece on the group at the time of the mass suicide. The book also contains a comprehensive bibliography of contactee literature.

Lewis, James R., ed. *Magical Religion and Modern Witchcraft.* Albany, NY: State University of New York Press, 1996.

This anthology covers the modern neopagan movement. Many of the contributors are academically trained neopagans. It includes essays on the goddess and the Wiccan worldview, the role of magic and ritual, the history of the movement, neopagan ethics, and the relationship between Christianity and the neopagan movement. The volume concludes with two complementary overviews of the literature.

Lewis, James R., and J. Gordon Melton, eds. *Perspectives on the New Age.* Albany, NY: State University of New York Press, 1992.

The first serious academic anthology dealing with the New Age movement, this book contains a series of essays on the historical roots of the New Age as well as an interesting section on the international impact of the movement. Other essays compare and contrast the New Age with the neopagan movement, the women's spirituality movement, and charismatic Christianity.

Lewis, James R. and J. Gordon Melton, eds. *Church Universal and Triumphant in Scholarly Perspective.* Stanford, CA: Center for Academic Publishing, 1994.

This academic anthology discusses one of the more controversial yet least-studied new religions. There are chapters on the Church Universal and Triumphant's historical background, the controversies in which the church has been involved, psychological and sociological profiles of members, and the church's legal battles.

Lewis, James R., and J. Gordon Melton, eds. *Sex, Slander and Salvation: Investigating the Family/Children of God.* Stanford, CA: Center for Academic Publishing, 1994.

This text is a comprehensive compilation on one of the most controversial new religions. Unfortunately, this book was published just before the death of the founder. Subsequently, the movement experienced a major transformation. At this writing, a second edition is being considered.

Melton, J. Gordon. *The Church of Scientology.* Studies in Contemporary Religion. Salt Lake City, UT: Signature Books, 2000.

This work is an overview of the Church of Scientology's history, beliefs, and practices.

Palmer, Susan J. *Aliens Adored: Rael's UFO Religion.* New Brunswick, NJ: Rutgers University Press, 2004.

The Raelians—easily the largest UFO-related religion—have been making headlines for a long time, especially after cloning became a major public issue. This is the definitive study by a Canadian scholar who has been researching the movement for many years.

Partridge, Christopher, ed. *UFO Religions.* London: Routledge, 2003.

An anthology of papers on UFO religions, this work is a more recent and up-to-date collection along the lines of James R. Lewis's book *The Gods Have Landed.*

Reader, Ian. *Religious Violence in Contemporary Japan: The Case of Aum Shinrikyo.* Richmond, Surrey: Curzon Press, 2000.

This study of AUM Shinrikyo focuses on the factors leading up to the sarin-gas attack.

Richardson, James T., Joel Best, and David G. Bromley, eds. *The Satanism Scare.* New York: Aldine de Gruyter, 1991.

This series of essays examines the Satanism scare of the late 1980s. The scare is treated sociologically—as a "moral panic," rather than a response to an organized Satanic threat. In other words, the overall thrust of the volume is to debunk the idea that an organized Satanic conspiracy exists.

Rochford, E. Burke. *Hare Krishna in America.* New Brunswick, NJ: Rutgers University Press, 1985.

Of all the books that have been published on the Hare Krishna, this is still one of the best overviews of the movement.

Shinn, Larry. *The Dark Lord.* Philadelphia, PA: Westminster, 1986.

This too is a study of the Hare Krishna movement. Shinn is also interested in the issue of conversion, so parts of his discussion address the cult controversy.

Tabor, James D., and Eugene V. Gallagher. *Why Waco? Cults and the Battle for Religious Freedom in America.* Berkeley and Los Angeles: University of California Press, 1997.

This is a scholarly monograph on the Branch Davidian tragedy. Tabor was one of two scholars who attempted to communicate with David Koresh and bring the Waco standoff to a peaceful conclusion.

Weightman, Judith Mary. *Making Sense of the Jonestown Suicides: A Sociological History of the People's Temple.* New York: Mellen Press, 1984.

Some twenty books have been written about the Jonestown tragedy. They vary greatly in quality. This book and John R. Hall's essay in *In Gods We Trust* (discussed earlier) are two of the better treatments.

Wilson, Bryan, and Karel Dobbelaere. *A Time to Chant: The Soka Gakkai Buddhist in Britain.* Oxford: Oxford University Press, 1994.

This is the best book-length study of the most important Japanese new religion to establish itself in Western countries. This book was written not long after Soka Gakkai separated itself from the Nichiren Shoshu sect of Buddhism and thus contains a comprehensive analysis of that split.

Wright, Stuart A., ed. *Armageddon in Waco: Critical Perspectives on the Branch Davidian Conflict.* Chicago: University of Chicago Press, 1995.

The essays in this definitive scholarly anthology on the Branch Davidian holocaust treat the roles of the media, law enforcement, and so forth, providing insights beyond this specific conflict, and are thus useful for people more interested in the larger cult controversy than in the Waco tragedy.

Anticult Scholarship

Partially because the scholarship of cult critics tends to focus on the theme of the manipulation of members of certain groups, it is easier to lay out a more defined set of publications that the reader can consult to acquaint her- or himself with this perspective. The following list (though not the annotations) was provided by Dr. Michael Langone of the American Family Foundation.

Cialdin, Robert B. *Influence: The Psychology of Persuasion.* New York: William Morrow, 1993.

This is an overview of manipulative techniques that bring about compliance—in advertising, human relations, sales, recruitment to groups, and other areas. It is useful as a context for more specific discussions of "cultic" influences.

Enroth, Ronald. *Churches That Abuse.* Grand Rapids, MI: Zondervan, 1992.

In this examination of churches—doctrinally orthodox as well as unorthodox—Enroth asserts that abusive behavioral influence is exercised over at least some members of the congregation. Authored by an Evangelical scholar, this has been a highly controversial book within the Christian community.

Langone, Michael, ed. *Recovery from Cults: Help for Victims of Psychological and Spiritual Abuse.* New York: Norton, 1993.

As the title indicates, this is an anthology focused on the problems experienced by former members of controversial groups. The contributors represent a wide variety of different "experts" in the field.

Lifton, Robert J. *Thought Reform and the Psychology of Totalism.* New York: Norton, 1961.

A scholar of Chinese Communist "brainwashing," Lifton restates his findings in terms of more general principles. This particular book was often used by deprogrammers, who saw Lifton's descriptions of thought reform as parallel to the manipulative influences exercised over group members by "cults."

Rudin, Marcia R., ed. *Cults on Campus: Continuing Challenge.* Bonita Springs, FL: American Family Foundation, 1996.

Almost from the very beginning of the controversy, "cults" were accused of targeting idealistic young people for recruitment. This anthology brings that aspect of the controversy up to date.

Schein, Edgar H., Inge Schneier, and Curtis H. Barker. *Coercive Persuasion: A Socio-psychological Analysis of the "Brainwashing" of American Civilian Prisoners by the Chinese Communists.* New York: Norton, 1961.

Americans were fascinated by Korean War brainwashing, and this is one of the books to emerge out of that interest. Contemporary critics of "cults" view the influence of leaders over their followers as bearing a family resemblance to communist brainwashing techniques.

Singer, Margaret T., with Janja Lalich. *Cults in Our Midst: The Hidden Menace in Our Everyday Lives.* San Francisco: Jossey-Bass, 1995.

This is a general book on the cult menace by one of the primary architects of the notion of cultic mind control. Singer discusses the controversy as if the anticult perspective on "brainwashing" was the dominant view and portrays mainstream scholars critical of "cultic mind control" as if they were a marginal group of cult apologists on the payroll of sinister cults.

Popular Books

Numerous books have been written about the "cult menace." Often they are authored by conservative Protestant Christians and published by Evangelical presses. For many years, one of the most popular types of cult-related book was the apostate tale—former members who wrote exposés about the terrible experiences they had when they belonged to such-and-such group. The demand for the latter appears to have waned.

It should also be noted that every group with more than 100 members usually runs some sort of publishing operation, often printing high-quality books and other materials related to their religion. Readers interested in specific minority religions will usually find abundant information readily available directly from the group itself. Because of the tendency for organizations—like individuals—to change addresses every few years, the reader is advised to consult the Internet for the latest address and phone number of a particular religious group.

Conway, Flo, and Jim Siegelman. *Snapping: America's Epidemic of Sudden Personality Change.* New York: Lippincott, 1978.

This journalistic account of deprogramming and the cult menace puts forward the thesis that cultic brainwashing techniques produce a unique mental illness—information disease. A somewhat updated edition of this book was issued in 1995.

Patrick, Ted, with Tom Dulack. *Let Our Children Go!* New York: E. P. Dutton, 1976.

This is the first and last book exalting the practice of deprogramming by the man who invented it. Written with a view to self-promotion, Patrick nevertheless describes enough of the violence associated with the practice to make the reader aware that deprogramming is *not* "just talking to people." Though out of print, this book can often be found in public and university libraries.

Sherwood, Carlton. *Inquisition: The Persecution and Prosecution of the Rev. Sun Myung Moon.* Washington, DC: Regnery Gateway, 1989.

In this fast-moving overview of the inside story behind Moon's conviction of tax evasion, the author concludes that, whatever else one might think of the man and his movement, Moon was framed by critics of the Unification Church. It is muckraking journalism at its best.

Underwood, Barbara, and Betty Underwood. *Hostage to Heaven.* New York: Clarkson N. Potter, 1979.

One of the many "ex-cultist" apostate tales, *Hostage to Heaven* was written jointly by a mother and daughter. This particular book is of more than usual interest because Barbara Underwood was one of the members of the Unification Church to be deprogrammed as part of the *Katz* ("Faithful Five–Faithless Four") conservatorship case.

Nonprint Resources

Like many of the organizations inspired by the cult controversy, nonprint media addressing the issue have come and gone. For videos presenting a position critical of "cults," the following are available from the American Family Foundation, P.O. Box 2265, Bonita Springs, FL 34133; telephone: 941-514-3081.

After the Cult: Recovering Together

In this twenty-five-minute videotape, ten ex-members relate their personal stories, as well as how they went on to live their lives after leaving their respective groups.

Cults: Saying NO Under Pressure

A twenty-nine-minute educational videotape designed for high school and college students and others, hosted and narrated by Charlton Heston, this video was codeveloped by the International Cult Education Program of AFF and the InService Video Network of the National Association of Secondary School Principals. It is available for purchase only.

Leaving a Cult: Information about Exiting and Recovery

Dr. Margaret Singer provides advice for current and former members as well as for their friends and family.

What Is a Cult and How Does It Work?

Dr. Margaret Singer, a prominent anticult psychologist, provides a general overview of the cult phenomenon.

For Christian anticult material, the following are available from the Spiritual Counterfeits Project, P.O. Box 4308, Berkeley, CA 94704; telephone: 510-540-0300; Web site: http://www.scpinc.org:

Gods of the New Age

The focus of much recent Christian anticult material is the New Age movement, as reflected in this video by Jeremiah Films.

The Pagan Invasion

Among various new religions, Christians view neopagan religions as particularly dangerous. This film is also produced by Jeremiah Films.

UFOs: The Mystery Resolved

Christians tend to view UFOs in demonological terms. This film is produced by Reasons to Believe.

For a video critical of the secular anticult movement, refer to:

Deprogramming: Understanding the Issue

This twenty-eight-minute educational videotape is for essentially the same audience. This video contains some startlingly brutal footage of actual kidnappings and follows the stories of parents who had hired deprogrammers, only to regret their decision later. A wide variety of professionals as well as people who had been kidnapped offer their comments at various stages of the presentation. It is available from the Cult Awareness Network, 1680 North Vine Street, Suite 415, Los Angeles, CA 90028; telephone: 800-556-3055.

An award-winning videotape (which was also nominated for an Academy Award) on Waco that brings up issues relevant to the controversy is:

Waco: The Rules of Engagement

This highly professional 136-minute overview of events in Waco, Texas, is a poignant presentation of the tragedy that left four law enforcement agents and eighty-six men, women, and children in the community dead. It calls for the nation to recommit itself to the basic precepts of tolerance and freedom upon which U.S. society is built. Contact Reko (distributors), P.O. Box 4005, Joplin, MO 61803-4005; telephone: 800-771-2147.

The so-called exit tapes the Heaven's Gate people made just before committing suicide are available from Right to Know Enterprises in Denver, Colorado:

Tape I

This 88-minute tape presents the founder and leader of Heaven's Gate, Marshall Herff Applewhite, offering final instructions to those who wish to follow him. He also introduces each "student" who committed suicide with him.

Tape II

This 117-minute tape shows students of Heaven's Gate expressing their thoughts before the "exit." It was taped a week before Applewhite and his group of followers committed suicide on March 28, 1997, in anticipation of going to the "next level," or heaven, by spaceship. The members each present a five-minute exit statement.

One should also note that the majority of individual religious groups produce audiotapes and videos—some of high quality— to inform people about their religion. They can be acquired directly from the relevant group, which can, in turn, usually be found via the Internet. A partial selection follows:

The relevant productions about the Church of Scientology are available from Bridge Publications, 4751 Fountain Avenue, Los Angeles, CA 90029; telephone: 800-722-1733; Web site: http://www.bridgepub.com.

How to Use Dianetics (a Visual Guidebook to the Human Mind)

Learn the way that the reactive mind causes stress, nightmares, unhappiness, and negative emotions. Most important, see, step-by-step, the exact application of the procedures of dianetics with another person.

Introduction to Scientology

This is an exclusive filmed interview with L. Ron Hubbard, founder of Scientology, in fact the only filmed interview he ever granted. Hubbard answers the commonly asked questions about dianetics and Scientology and explains how he made his discoveries and breakthroughs regarding the spirit, the mind, and life.

The Hare Krishna Movement (ISKCON) has one of the most professional video ministries around, under the name ITV (ISKCON Television). ITV can be contacted at P.O. Box 556, Topanga, CA 90290; telephone: 800-551-0380. Of more than 100 tapes, the most general productions are:

A Hare Krishna World

This 120-minute general overview of the Hare Krishna movement worldwide gives viewers a glimpse into the ISKCON lifestyle.

Your Ever Well Wisher

This is a biographical work about the life of Shrila Prabhupada, ISKCON's founder, by filmmaker John Greisser. The 120-minute film is a very professional production about an amazing man.

The Family, formerly known as the Children of God, produces a wide variety of videos. The Family can be reached at 2020 Pennsylvania Avenue, Suite 102, Washington, DC 20006-1846; telephone: 800-FOR-A-FAM.

The Family—Making a Difference

This is a fascinating overview of the Family, focusing on their social work worldwide.

Introducing the Family

This film shows that the practice of deprogramming as well as the first anticult organization were initially focused on this group.

A Living Faith: Insight into Education in the Family

This documentary takes the viewer inside the communal homes of the Family for a close look at their home-based approach to education.

The Church Universal and Triumphant was the focus of a good deal of negative media attention in the 1980s and early 1990s. At the group's international community located in rural Montana, the press gave the church a good deal of attention as the "next Waco" following the siege of the Branch Davidians in Waco, Texas. The group produces a large number of videos featuring lectures by Elizabeth Clare Prophet. Contact Royal Teton Ranch, P.O. Box 5000, Corwin Springs, MT 59030-5000; telephone: 406-848-7441.

Climb the Highest Mountain

This nineteen-minute profile of the Church Universal and Triumphant is a very upbeat production, focused on the ideals of the church.

When one sees a news program on TV these days, it is often possible to purchase a copy of the relevant show. There have also been some box office movies on the controversy, although they almost always present minority religions in the worst light possible. It is usually possible to find *Ticket to Heaven* or *Blinded by the Light* in large video stores. A more recent film in this genre is *Holy Smoke!*

Index

About the Author

James R. Lewis teaches at the University of Wisconsin–Milwaukee and the University of Wisconsin–Stevens Point. He is an authority on non-traditional religious movements and has worked as a media consultant on cult-related events, including the 1993 crisis at the Branch Davidian complex in Waco.